MW00996912

cabinology

cabinology

A HANDBOOK TO YOUR PRIVATE HIDEAWAY

DALE MULFINGER

The Taunton Press

The Taunton Press, Inc.
63 South Main Street
Newtown, CT 06470-2344
e-mail: tp@taunton.com

Editor: Steve Culpepper
Copy editor: Diane Sinitsky
Indexer: Jay Kreider
Jacket/Cover design: Naomi Mizusaki and Teresa Fernandes
Interior design and layout: Naomi Mizusaki, Supermarket
Title page illustration: Christopher Silas Neal

Library of Congress Cataloging-in-Publication Data
Mulfinger, Dale, 1943-
Cabinology : a handbook to your private hideaway / Dale Mulfinger.
p. cm.
Includes bibliographical references and index.
ISBN 978-1-56158-948-7 (alk. paper)
1. Vacation homes--United States--Design and construction.
TH4835.M85 2008
690'.873--dc22
2008013630

Printed in China
10 9 8 7 6 5 4 3

DEDICATION

To my new grandson, Cleo, whose young, bright eyes bridge continents.

ACKNOWLEDGMENTS

The text of *Cabinology* rolls off my pen and then through three key players before seeing the light of your eyes. My wife Jan makes it digital and peels away some rough edges; writer Bill Swanson turns text into sweet prose; and editor Steve Culpepper and his staff at Taunton Books who shape the whole into the construct of a viable book. I am deeply indebted to this team. I am particularly grateful to the writers of cabin stories who have brought this book alive with their personal reflections.

I also extend my thanks to the many cabin owners who have welcomed my curiosity, to my many clients who have challenged me with their unique cabin projects, and to the staff at SALA Architects who helped realize my clients' dreams. Radio personality Joe Soucheray anointed me "cabinologist" and I thank him sincerely for my instantaneous Ph.D.

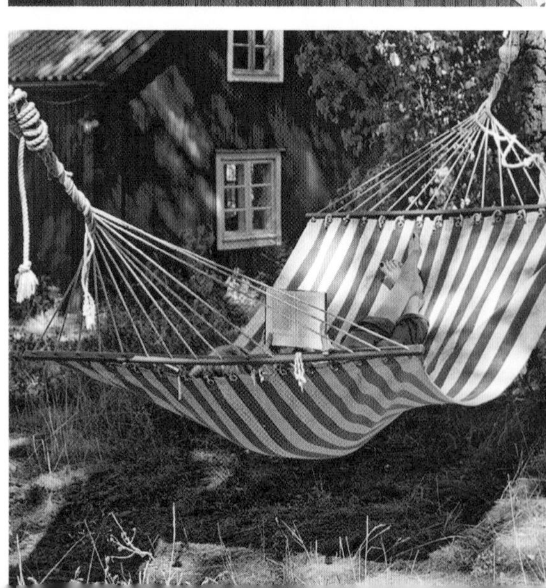

CONTENTS

INTRODUCTION

CABINS CAN EXIST FOR US IN TWO WAYS. They're places we visit in person every time we get the chance. And for some of us, they're places we visit only in spirit, where we mentally take ourselves during a boring business meeting or whenever the modern world seems too encroaching.

Transcending the cabin in your mind to the reality of your own, very real cabin plopped down on your own little slice of heaven is what *Cabinology* is all about. This book of all things "cabin" will help you mold your dreams into the reality of that glowing fireplace, that predawn aroma of freshly brewed coffee, and to the pitter-patter of your loved one just rousing overhead in the loft.

It's not that you simply want a cabin. You *need* a cabin to bring some balance into your life, to recharge those rundown batteries, to cleanse the soul, to reconnect to nature. Your cabin is a realm of tranquility where sleeping in is not just reserved for Sunday morning, and where a good book and an Adirondack chair are an afternoon's marriage.

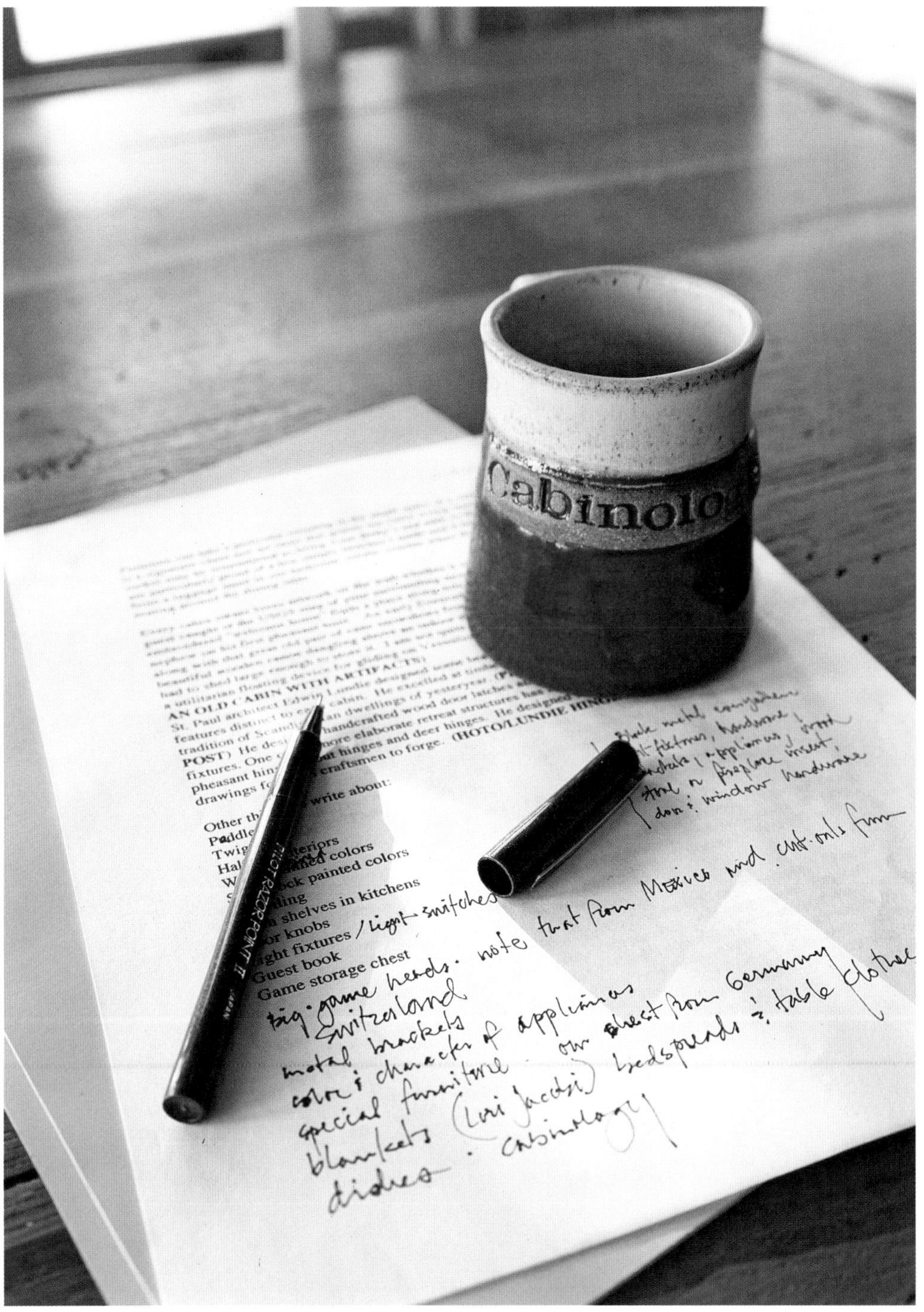
Cabinolo
AN OLD CABIN WITH ARTIFACTS
craftsmen to forge. (HOTO/LUNDIE HING
write about:
painted colors
shelves in kitchens
Guest book
Game storage chest
PILOT RAZOR POINT II

Cabins contrast the vast world outside with the intimate world within. Unlike in our suburban world, the world of the cabin is a place where modesty and charm outweigh size and grandeur, while simplicity and flexibility outshine the sophisticated and complicated.

We go to the cabin to get away from phones, television, computers, and other symbols of our interconnected world. At the cabin we will have time to complete a jigsaw puzzle with Aunt Betty or spend a slow yet memorable afternoon fishing with Uncle Bob.

Privacy will go out the same window that a fresh summer breeze comes in. The larder will have to store the essential ingredients for s'mores. And you can leave that recipe for Chateaubriand back in the city.

THE BROWN BAT
507 NORTH SHORE
DRIVE

Sports
FSU-Miami will be state, sibling rivalry

THE CABIN IN YOUR MIND

CHAPTER ONE

EVER SINCE AMERICANS BEGAN WRITING histories of themselves, the simple cabin in the wilderness has been an abiding symbol of who we are and how we see ourselves. No sooner had we built cities and created neighborhoods than we began longing to return to the simple life of the cabin in the woods—longing to get away.

It's almost as if getting away were a genetic predisposition, as if something is spun into our DNA, beyond our control.

Besides, whose life wouldn't be a whole lot better if somewhere out in that wild distance we all had a quiet, isolated little hideaway where the noise and clutter fade away and we can hear ourselves think? At least until we get back to the city.

If you suspect that you have the cabin gene, you've got company. I know a lot of people with the same genetic disposition. It's my business to know them. I am a cabinologist.

The fact that you're reading this means you already understand this need. It means that somewhere in that dusty attic of your brain where

Since Europeans first settled in North America, the rustic cabin has symbolized our connection to the continent's original wilderness.

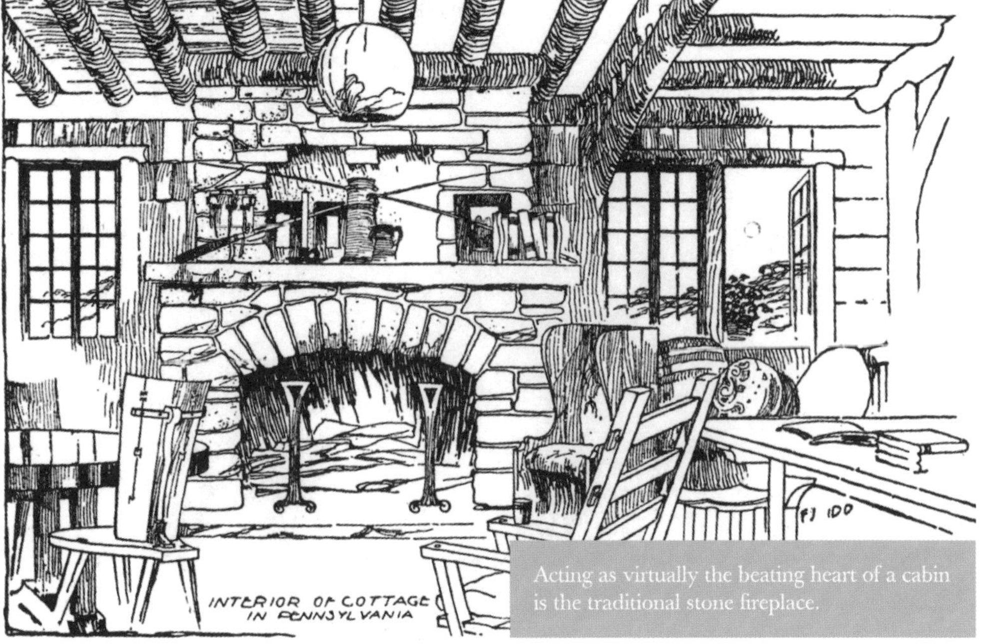

Acting as virtually the beating heart of a cabin is the traditional stone fireplace.

your inner hunter-gatherer bides his time, you nourish a hunger for some form of wilderness place. You may even have built it—figuratively, in your head. Or you may already own a cabin that somehow doesn't quite measure up to your vision, one that needs some thought and some work. Whether you're ready for the real thing or just content with being an armchair *cabinist,* this book is for you.

CABINS ON MY MIND

In the early 1960s, I went with a college pal to his parents' cabin in northern Minnesota. I didn't know it at the time, but that's when I became a cabinologist. I was a prairie farm boy who knew something about nature, weather, and the seasons, but when I visited that cabin on Lake Vermilion, my eyes were opened to some of nature's finer points.

You know what I mean: the way the night sky out there is ridiculously bright with stars. The deep quiet of the woods before anybody else is up. The smell of wood smoke. The startling tug of a fish on the line. For me, that trip revealed a new world. All the images, feelings, experience of cabin life sank in deep and never left me. I was hooked and I wanted a cabin of my own.

GET STARTED

I'm an architect in Minnesota, where, if you're nuts for cabins, there are worse jobs to have and less advantageous places to live. Years ago, not long out of school, I designed and built a cabin for my young family just an hour from our Minneapolis home. It was simple and practical and not much more than a screened-in sleeping porch in the woods without a house attached. But it let us get away from the traffic and television for a weekend or for a week and live simply (or simply live).

It wasn't the tiny cabin but nature, weather, the seasons (at least spring, summer, and fall—when we used it) that drew us out there. Covered from the rain, we read to each other and played checkers under the rattling roof. When the sun came out, we hunted mushrooms and scanned the poplars for chickadees and waxwings. We went to bed early and got up early. It was a treat.

At about that same time, I designed my first cabin for a client. It was larger, more complicated, and better equipped than mine, but it taught me that, unlike a lot of city houses, it is rare for any two cabins to be quite the same. Since then, I've designed more than 50 cabins, cottages, lodges, and camps (that's something else I learned: what you call a cabin depends on where in this country you live), and, as I write this, I have several more on the drawing board. Safe to say, I'm as hooked on cabins as I was 40 years ago.

One of the unique characteristics of cabin life is that it gives you the power to not worry, to be happy, and even to be a bit goofy.

A contemporary cabin in Texas opens up to the woods around it yet contains sheltered and intimate spaces within.

I'LL SHOW YOU HOW

You don't have to be an architect to design, build, renovate, or much less buy the cabin you want. Nearly every cabin owner I know is like you (which means you're probably not an architect), and most of the cabins I've visited and written about were designed by somebody other than an architect (and frequently built by somebody other than a builder). If you're starting from scratch, or if your fantasy involves either a heavy-duty update or an addition to an existing cabin, you'd find the services of an architect to be helpful. But essential? No, usually not.

As far as that goes, you don't have to live an hour from a lake in the Land of Sky Blue Waters or some other state's equivalent. A cabin can go almost anywhere–mountain, woods, coastal dunes. People tend to want their cabin close to something they love or love to do. Skiers and snowboarders are drawn to mountains; sailors, swimmers, and anglers to water; and birdwatchers to woods.

A reasonable proximity to home is nice, especially with the price of gas, but nearness to home is no more of an essential than an architect is. For most cabin folk, the basic idea of a getaway is to get away. If that means a commute across three states, so be it.

The point is, either by design or happenstance, your cabin will be or should be pretty much what you want it to be and where you want it to be. Few of the things we own better reflect our true selves than our cabins. That's because, whatever else we use it for–family reunions, the guys' fishing weekend–that cabin is where we unwind, kick back, decompress, and get back to being ourselves, all under the happy fiction that we're light years away from *civilized society*.

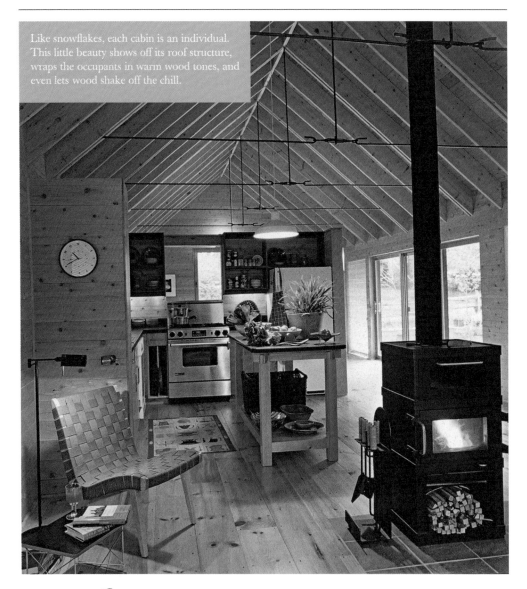

Like snowflakes, each cabin is an individual. This little beauty shows off its roof structure, wraps the occupants in warm wood tones, and even lets wood shake off the chill.

WHERE CABINOLOGY COMES IN

Here's the rub: It's not all quite so simple. As casual, relaxed, and even haphazard as cabin life is at its best, the cabin of your dreams requires thought, planning, and care in its design and construction.

There's no one "right way" to build a cabin, but some ways are definitely better than others. Your cabin may be as simple as four walls and a roof, but a lot of other, depressingly practical factors, from sanitation issues to zoning laws, require your attention. As do plenty of other, much cooler considerations, such as the building materials you'll want to use, the color you'll want to paint the loft, and the location of your site relative to, say, the North Star or the rising sun.

Which is where this book comes in. My objective is to get you from here, your dream, to there, an actual cabin. I'll share the lessons I've learned while designing, building, and hanging out in cabins all over. When you're finished with this book, you can get started on the real thing. Or maybe the dream will have to remain a dream for a while–until your kids finish college or you win the lottery. That's okay, too. I'm ready when you are.

WHAT LIES AHEAD

If you're like me, you open a book like this somewhere in the middle and flip through the pages until you find where you want to start reading. Here, I've taken a straightforward where-what-how approach to the chapters, which are laid out in such a way that you can jump in just about anywhere and find something interesting and, I hope, helpful.

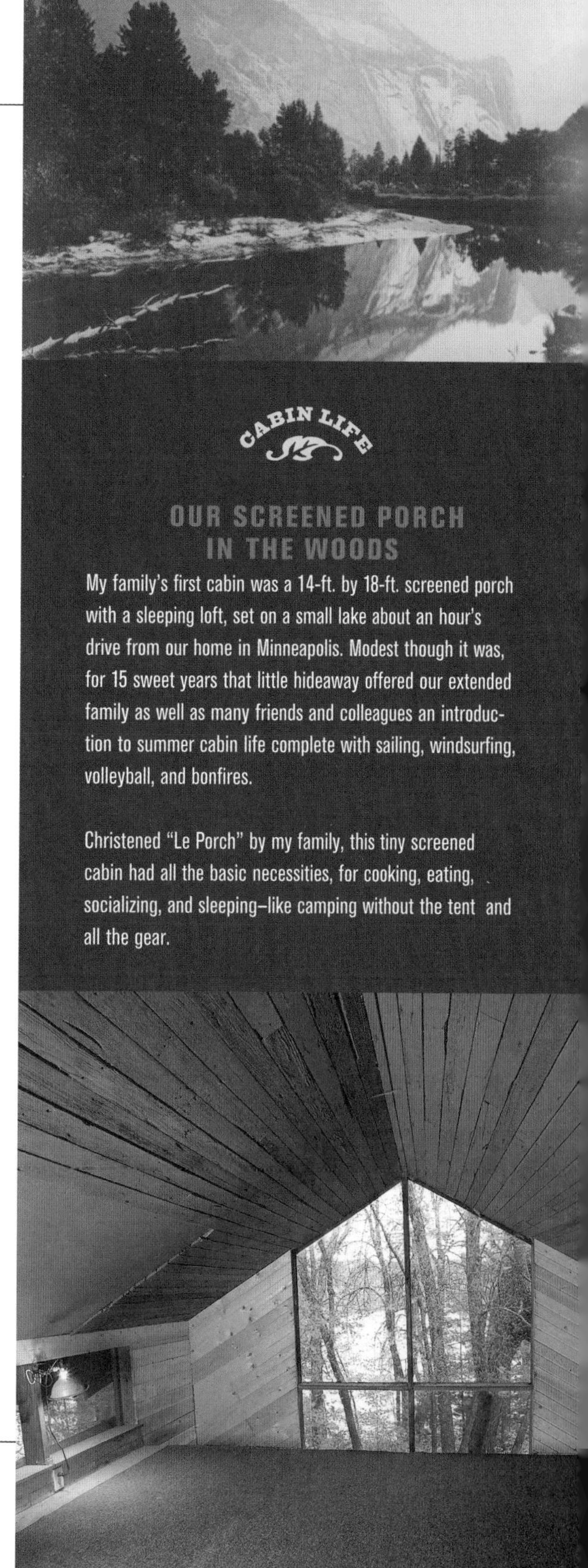

CABIN LIFE

OUR SCREENED PORCH IN THE WOODS

My family's first cabin was a 14-ft. by 18-ft. screened porch with a sleeping loft, set on a small lake about an hour's drive from our home in Minneapolis. Modest though it was, for 15 sweet years that little hideaway offered our extended family as well as many friends and colleagues an introduction to summer cabin life complete with sailing, windsurfing, volleyball, and bonfires.

Christened "Le Porch" by my family, this tiny screened cabin had all the basic necessities, for cooking, eating, socializing, and sleeping–like camping without the tent and all the gear.

LUDLOW'S ISLAND

This enclave of 15 cabins dotting a lovely little island in Lake Vermilion has inspired many of the cabins I've written about over the years and many of the designs I've applied to other cabins.

The island is, in fact (albeit unintentionally), a kind of cabin laboratory, with old cabins and new cabins, cabins built with local timber and out of discarded doors, one-story cabins and two-story cabins, and even a four-story tower cabin that the students in one of my architecture classes conceived and designed.

What Ludlow's cabins have in common is their setting in the Land of Sky Blue Waters–a little slice of paradise on the lake. And even the magic of the final boat ride to the island solidifies our escape from that "other" world into the bucolic realm of sunfish, sunsets, and s'mores.

There are plenty of photos, sketches, and sidebars throughout. So even if you ramble aimlessly through the text, I'm sure you'll find useful information and insights wherever you drop in.

I've also added something else, something from you. Throughout *Cabinology* I've added little stories, with snapshots submitted by folks like you, from all over the country, who have a special cabin story to share. Some are funny and some are very personal. You probably have a similar story of your own to share.

So if you're one of those folks who take things in chronological order–not a bad way to read a book, most people would agree–you'll find the chapters laid out as follows:

Chapter One: The Cabin in Your Mind (the chapter you're reading) provides a breezy overview of the subject and gives me the opportunity to craft some context around the subject of cabinology. I tell you a little about me and where I'm coming from on the subject and give you a broad sense of what to expect throughout the book.

Chapter Two: Cabinology 101 begins with the fundamental first question you need to consider when thinking about a cabin: Where are you going to put it? You should read this chapter with your maps and real estate brochures and chamber of commerce glossies spread out on the table in front of you.

The "where" question requires you to answer other basic questions as well, such as what do you want to do at your cabin–fish, ski, hike, watch the sunset, vegetate, eat, drink beer, all of the above?

And then there are the practical issues, such as working with architects, bankers, and suppliers–and, importantly, playing by the local rules, including codes and customs. You may be looking for solitude, but you need to think about how much community you'll need to sustain it.

Chapter Three: Making the Cabin Your Own provides a deliberate, documented approach to essential planning issues such as: Who will use the cabin? When will they use it? How exactly? The information you review at this stage will help you determine how big, how many bedrooms, what size kitchen you'll want, and how much you need to remodel if remodeling is your plan. You may, for instance, be able to make do with a smaller cabin than you originally thought and, thus, enjoy quality over quantity.

Chapter Four: The Master Plan is about turning your dream into the real thing. This includes, among other tactical approaches,

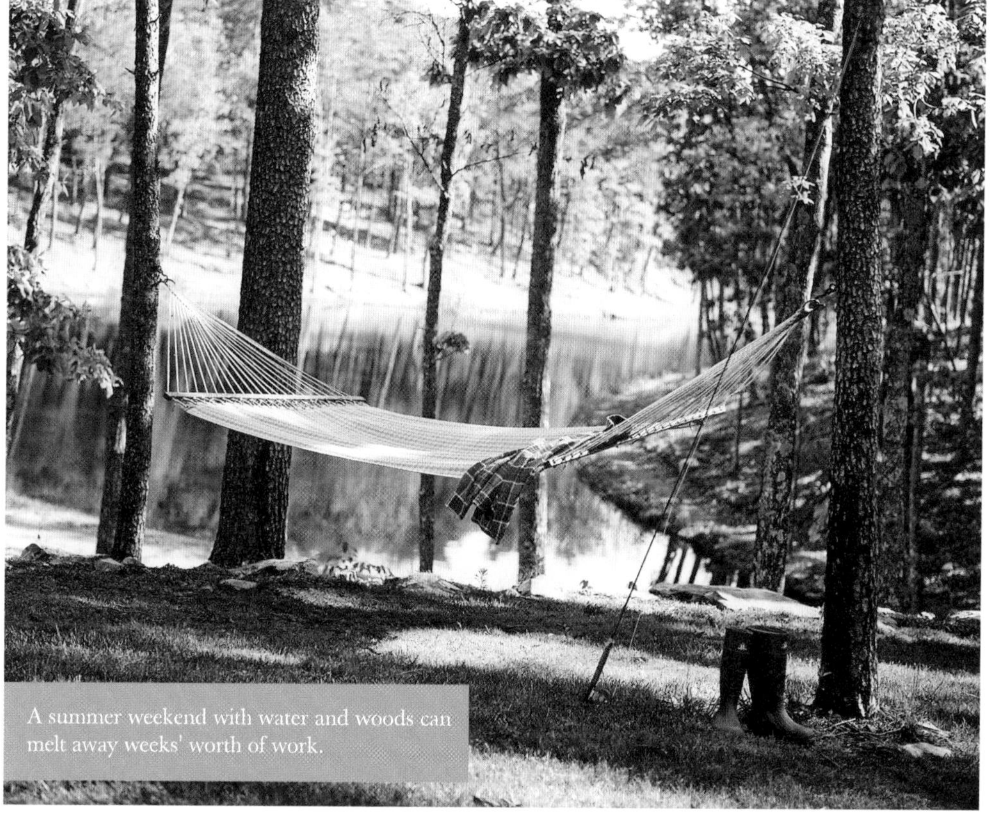

A summer weekend with water and woods can melt away weeks' worth of work.

CABIN STORIES

THE CABIN

To write about our little cabin in the woods on Orcas Island, I must first give myself a talking to—first tamper down my enthusiasm so that I don't wax poetic to the point that I come off sounding like some rhapsodic fool. It is no easy task.

Our first little cabin, on the raw five acres of overgrown fir and madrona trees we purchased in 1988, was a 9-ft. by 12-ft. structure erected with the help of friends—so that we might enjoy a little glorified camping. We called it "The Birdhouse" because of its steeply pitched roof that allowed a cramped sleeping loft accessed via an exterior ladder.

We had water: a spigot at the end of the driveway. Who needed electricity? Although novices at furniture building, we managed to cobble together a dining room table and a couple of funky benches from some charmingly twisted fallen madrona branches. A wooden box fitted with an oak toilet seat positioned over a deep hole served as our commode. Sun showers, heated by a sometimes noncooperative sun and hung from a nearby juniper branch, took care of our daily bathing needs.

What happens to us each time we arrive here? It is as though the frayed tentacles of our nerves suddenly shrink sheepishly back into their proper sheaths. It occurs to us that our worries, our burdens will wait. All irritations become petty.

For 10 years, we made the hour-and-a-half drive from Edmonds to Anacortes, where we hopped the ferry to spend as many days as we could manage away from our busy city life. From April to October, rain or shine, we did our camping, spending the days cleaning the decades of debris from the forest floors as we communed with nature and sought, above all, to make our footprint minimal. For the rest of the months, we rented a room in town and still spent the days playing on the property, for never did we consider the clean-up work to be work.

Because our long-range plans were to retire on the property, we decided to take a second step and build a slightly larger cabin that could become our guesthouse once we managed to build the "big" retirement house. Our model for the house you see in the photo was a garage we had spied on a walk. With the help of experts, we poured our hearts into making it a little gem that would capture the spirit of the property, the overwhelming sense of peace we feel the moment we step foot on our special piece of land.

We're not quite sure how we managed to do this so thoroughly to our liking, yet we feel that the tragic loss of our 22-year-old son had a great deal to do with it for, as such losses do, it caused us to look ever more closely at the world around us. His love welcomes us each time we open the door.

What happens to us each time we arrive here? It is as though the frayed tentacles of our nerves suddenly shrink sheepishly back into their proper sheaths. It occurs to us that our worries, our burdens will wait. All irritations become petty.

We have no TV. We listen to an ever-widening

array of music from Pat Methany to Diana Krall to John Mayer, Neil Young, and whatever the Canadian public radio station chooses to serenade us with. We sit at the dining room window and watch—never knowing when a doe and her baby will choose to wander by, or a brown mink will scurry up the driveway, or an eagle will land in one of several tall fir snags, or an Anna's hummingbird will stop to gather fuzz from the lamb's ear just next to the window.

We remember a crow from our days in the old cabin. It would miraculously appear in a nearby tree each time we arrived, waiting for us to lay bits of pancake along a madrona branch. The moment he thought we weren't looking, he would sneak down to cram as many pieces into his beak as it would hold. Jake, we called him. Then there was Humphrey the seal who would follow us as we canoed, his head popping up here and there as we paddled around the bay or sat near the shore, pleasantly exhausted from our day's "work."

We have a couple of rituals that crop up often. In the mornings, we take our cups of tea and head down the long driveway to our one little fenced-in garden, charmed anew by the daily changes of the crabapple blossoms, the draping white wisteria, the delicious-smelling honeysuckle. Our evening ritual occurs just at dusk when we meander down the path toward the water to a glorious viewpoint to the west and sit in the small, open garden that is a memorial to our son.

We hold in our minds the last lines from a favorite childhood book of our son's about a little mouse: "Before I go to bed at night, I watch the lovely sun go down."

—Phyllis Caisse is a part-time resident of Washington State's Orcas Island; loves gardening, writing, and hiking; and is currently busy designing the Caisse retirement home to be situated near their current cabin.

Nobody loves a weekend at the lakeside cabin better than kids, who, deprived of television and video games, actually find something to enjoy in nature.

creating a blueprint, floor plan, and the architectural drawings that provide a trigonometrical version of your dream. I'll help you evaluate important variables and decide on such essential practical matters as heating and cooling, plumbing, the pitch of the roof, and the best design for hauling groceries from the car park to the pantry. (Graph paper, cardboard, scissors, tape, and glue for three-dimensional modeling are required.)

Chapter Five: Assembly Required is all about choosing your building materials, common framing techniques (log, timber, or stick), prefabrication systems, foundations, siding and roofing, doors and windows, fireplaces and woodstoves, appliances and lighting fixtures, and wells and septic systems. One thing you learn is that even remodeling or building a small cabin requires more information and experience than you needed to build that fort as a kid.

"VOYAGE UPON LIFE'S SEA,
To yourself be true,
And, whatever your lot may be,
Paddle your own canoe."

—Sarah T. Barrett Bolton

AN ANCESTOR'S CABIN

Not long ago, I learned about a cabin built by my great-grandfather shortly after he settled in America. An immigrant from Sweden, Sven Anderson built his cabin in the early 1850s, before Minnesota was even a state. Recently some of his descendents restored the structure as a historical site in the historic town of Marine on St. Croix.

These are drawings I did in preparation for restoration of Sven's settler cabin. He lived here for a decade with his wife Stava and three children in this two-room plus loft, 18 x 26 structure. With four windows and two doors, this basic shelter is less then most of us would demand for weekend use.

Chapter Six: God Is in the Details gets down to the nitty-gritty, the fine points, the details that will make your cabin unique. This is the stage where your personality shines through in the furniture you buy for the living area and the antiques you pick up in town to accent the front porch. This may be the last chapter in the book, but it's just the beginning of developing the cabin history that will be passed down from generation to generation.

I've rounded out the text with drawings and photos–of my work and the work of others–to illustrate and highlight many of the points I'm making. If you're looking for additional visual examples–or additional inspiration–you should check out two of my earlier books on the subject: *The Cabin* and *The Getaway Home,* both published by The Taunton Press and available in most bookstores. Between the two of them, you'll find more than 60 structures, old and new, located in a variety of settings across North America.

Finally, as you set out through the following pages, I want to offer a thought I share with my university students when they begin a new assignment: No idea is a bad idea–it just may need a lot of work to get it just right.

You're probably not another Frank Lloyd Wright, but in designing your new cabin or an addition or remodel of an old one, you'll have a chance to let your unsung talents shine. And you'll connect to that simple world that all of us, for many generations back, have longed for.

CABIN MATTERS

FOR FURTHER READING

The Cabin, written with Susan E. Davis, features 37 buildings, both new and old, rustic and modern, but all with less than 1,300 sq. ft. of floor space. *The Getaway Home* focuses on 24 retreats, all of them new and of various sizes and complexity.

The cabins in both books show a wide variety of geographic settings, ranging from a backyard to a mountaintop and from prairie to stream to lakeshore.

"LOOK DEEP INTO NATURE,
and then you will understand everything better."

–Albert Einstein

CABINOLOGY 101

CHAPTER TWO

MORE THAN 20 YEARS AGO, when my oldest daughter was in her teens, Jan and I bought a tiny lot on a lake outside of the Twin Cities. There, about an hour's drive from home, we built a cabin.

So in the humid summer heat and without much building experience, we dove in: the architect testing out ideas in the real world. The goal was to create a minimal habitation with a minimal investment, a basic shelter where we could store food, sit in a chair, and stay overnight for a weekend or more.

Over the summer we built a frame, bolted on exterior-grade plywood, got the screen on and shingled the roof with cedar. Electrical power from a neighbor ran the saw (we didn't add electrical service for three or four more years). By the end of the year, we had a shelter we could use the next year.

For the second summer, I cadged an outhouse from a dentist whose new clinic site had an old outhouse on it. Jan and I borrowed a pickup truck, tipped in the outhouse, and hauled it to the cabin.

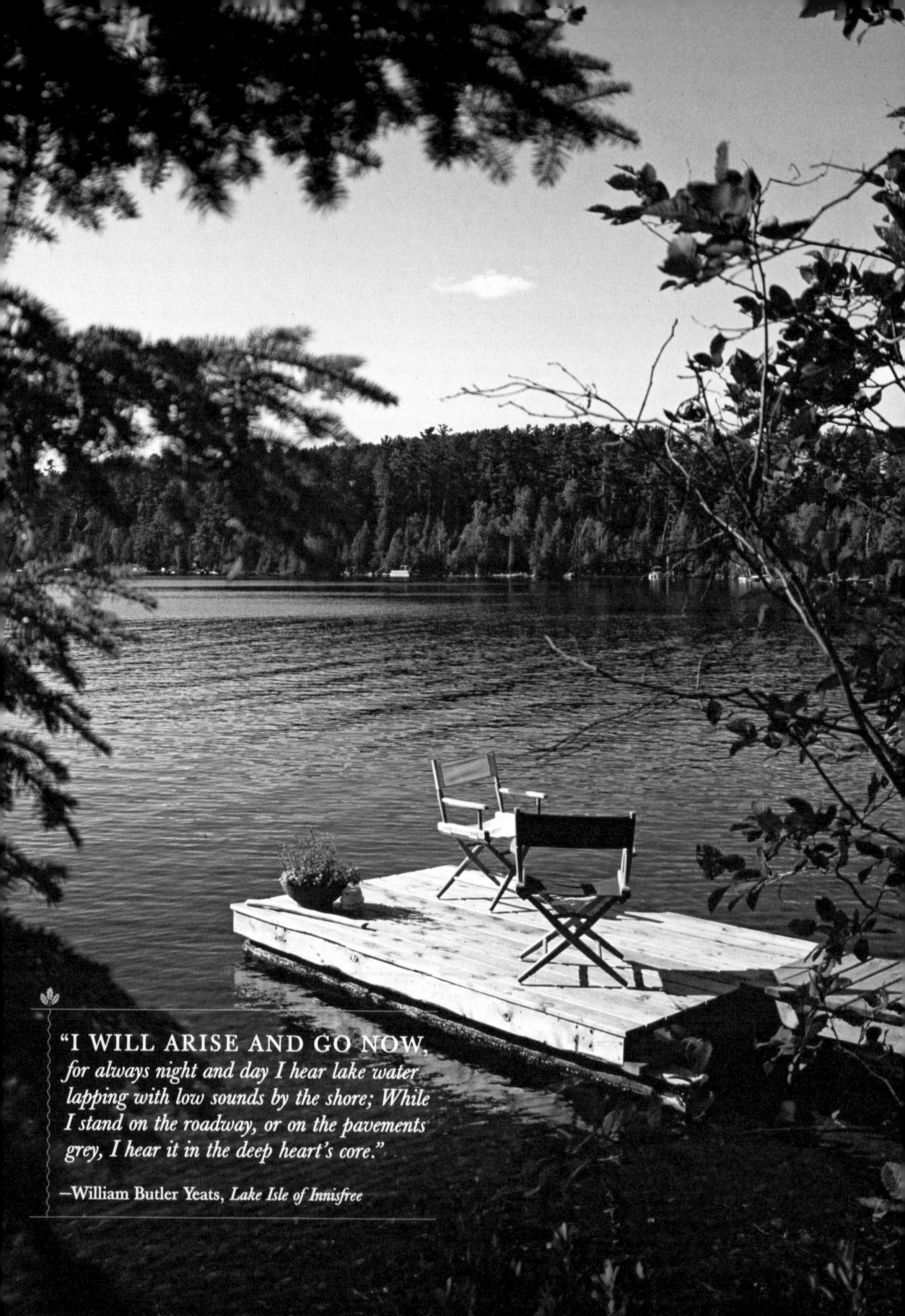

"I WILL ARISE AND GO NOW, *for always night and day I hear lake water lapping with low sounds by the shore; While I stand on the roadway, or on the pavements grey, I hear it in the deep heart's core."*

—William Butler Yeats, *Lake Isle of Innisfree*

We'd dug a hole and lined it with treated timbers beforehand, so we set the outhouse on it and were ready for business.

We bathed in the lake, cooked on a Coleman® stove, and slept in the tiny, screened cabin, which we christened *Le Porch*. And life was good. On that nice little lake we perfected our swimming and learned how to sail and windsurf. And that little structure and plot of ground provided many a fine escape from urban life in the summer. We learned that on successive rainy days we tended to get cabin fever, so we perfected our skills at garage sales and flea markets whenever that occurred. Cabin fever is something we've never experienced since.

BOILING IT DOWN

After studying all things cabin for the better part of my career (now through two cabins of our own and another 50 or so for others), I've come up with some fundamental questions that can help you take that smoky image of a cabin you have in your mind and turn it into just the cabin you want in exactly the location that fits your needs.

I wish I'd had this list of questions when I got started. Knowing what I know now, I would have done some things differently. For instance, I would have designed it to take windows (i.e., no big trapezoidal areas of screen), sleeved the roof for an eventual

RIGHT: This isn't the actual outhouse we first used as the sanitary facility at our weekend cabin dubbed *Le Porch*—it's actually much nicer—but it illustrates an option you might consider for your cabin instead of standard plumbing and a septic system.

BELOW: From late spring well into fall, my family enjoyed *Le Porch*, our little mild-weather lake cabin, where walls of screen kept out the bugs and let the wind wash away our blues.

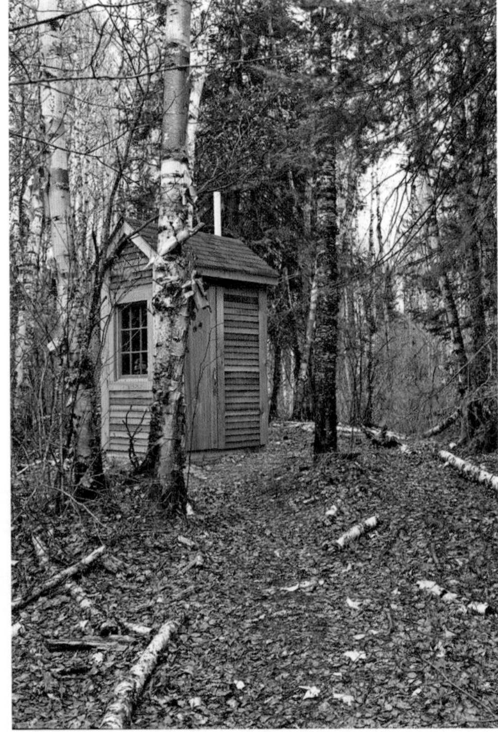

woodstove to extend the cabin's use, and put some Z-flashing on the exterior plywood to better protect it from moisture. And I would have put on an inexpensive metal roof. All in all, we got what we wanted, but it could have been better.

Getting it right really just boils down to thinking it through.

WHAT DO YOU WANT TO DO AND WHERE?

The first question to ask yourself has to do with how you'll use the cabin, as in what you'll do when you're there (fish, swim, ski, hike, bike, nothing at all). Answering that question in turn helps you determine where your cabin is (lake, forest, mountain). And once you know the general where of your cabin, I'll ask you to deal with specific questions connected to the place that have to do with the lay of the land, its dimensions (large lot or small? deep or shallow?), the soil (sandy, clay, rocky?), the views (what will you see from the porch or bedroom?), and plant and wildlife. Finally, I'll ask you to think about much more basic things like access, the availability of electricity, gas, and water, and local zoning regulations.

TOP: The old iron stove is a relative newcomer to this Pennsylvania cabin, believed to be built by Swedes in the mid-1600s. As old as it is, the cabin shares characteristics with what we love in our cabins to this day, a well-worn sense of comfort and coziness.

BOTTOM: Your cabin vision may be sleek and contemporary or it may be cluttered and basic, like this one-room rustic cabin with exposed roof framing.

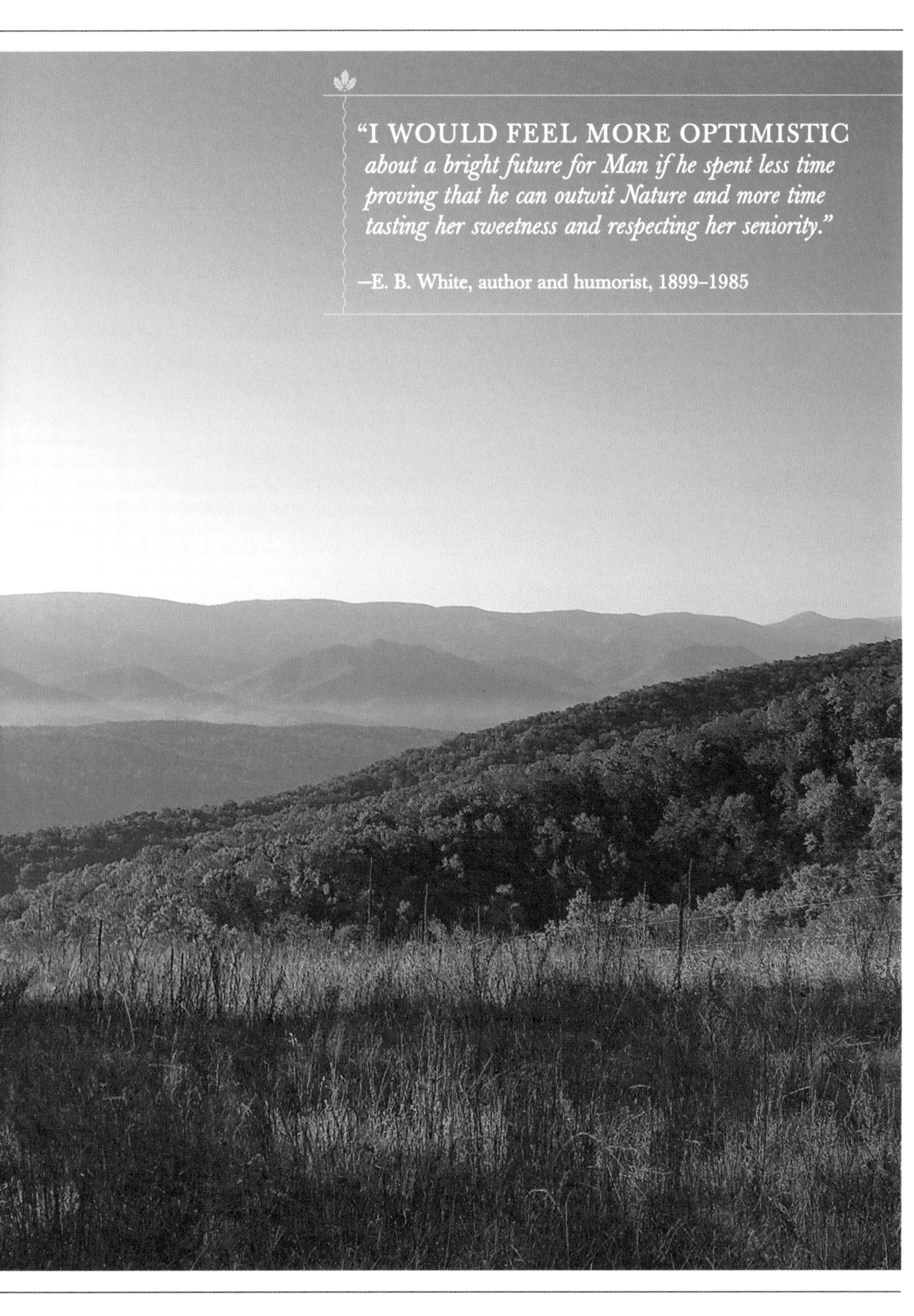
"I WOULD FEEL MORE OPTIMISTIC
about a bright future for Man if he spent less time proving that he can outwit Nature and more time tasting her sweetness and respecting her seniority."
—E. B. White, author and humorist, 1899–1985

CHOOSING THE SPOT

Identifying and choosing the place you want for your cabin can be more complicated than you think. It can even be maddeningly difficult.

For openers, when searching for a cabin or the perfect place to build it, you have to remember that almost nothing is more important than location. You know the old saying about property: What are the three most important things about real estate? Location, location, location. Well, that's almost always true.

As your personal architect, I can design a lot of different types of cabins for a particular site, but I can't, in any significant way, change the site itself. I can't create a mountain view or add a gurgling stream. And I can't make it snow so you can enjoy the cross-country skis you got for Christmas. Which is why it's important to have a good idea of *why* you want to own a cabin and a sense of *what* you want to do there.

If you know how you're most likely to use the place, you can tailor your search for the right location, either expanding or narrowing the possibilities from the get-go. Say your objective is tranquility. In that case, you want a cabin where you can nap, read, relax, ruminate, and watch the sunset. If that's your main goal, you'll have a wide range of choices when it comes to location. If you want to fish, swim, and sail, you'll still have a lot of choices, although not quite as many. And if

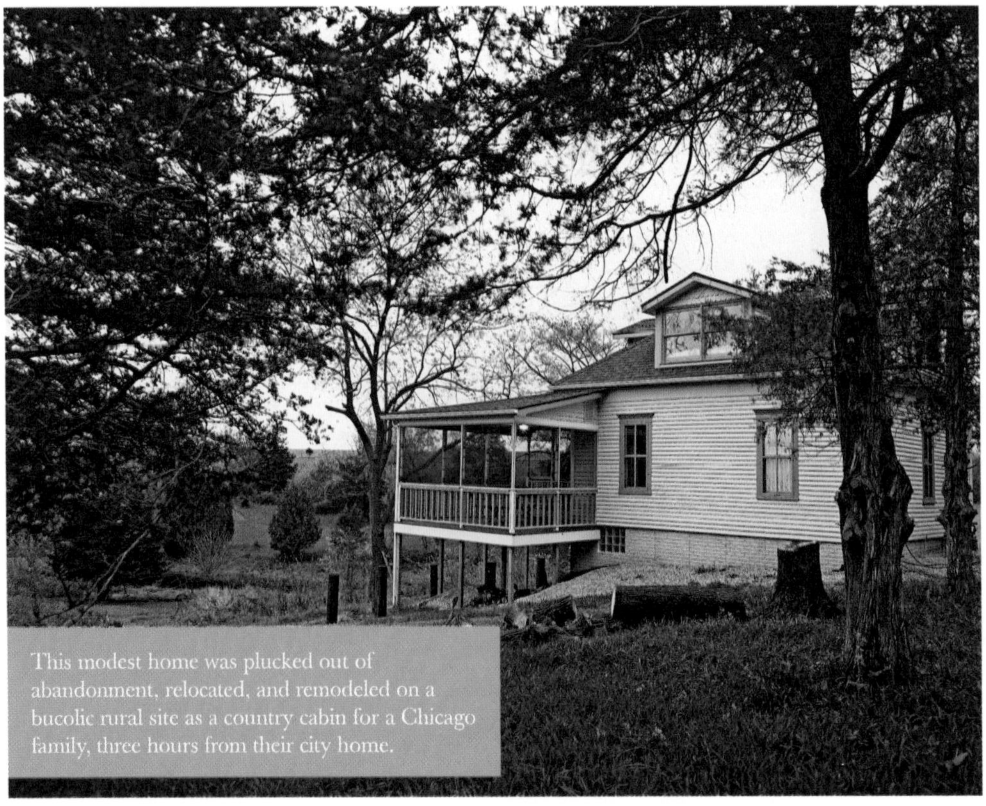

This modest home was plucked out of abandonment, relocated, and remodeled on a bucolic rural site as a country cabin for a Chicago family, three hours from their city home.

CABIN MATTERS

BEFORE YOU BUY THE LAND: THE ESSENTIAL CHECKLIST

Here are 10 key questions to ask before you buy your land.

1. Does the real estate you're considering give you the access you want to the activities you're interested in as well as those of family and friends?
2. What's the site like at different times of the year? How cold does it get in the winter? How hot in the summer? How much rain or snow can you count on? What's the typical length of the building season in that part of the country? What's the state of forest-fire protection?
3. How will you access the property during the seasons you intend to use it?
4. Will you need support services–snowplowing, for instance–to maintain access to the site?
5. What utilities–water, sewer, electricity, gas, telephone, etc.–are readily available at the site? What about power generation, propane gas, and septic system alternatives? What kind of investment will be necessary to make those essentials available?
6. What about the actual building site characteristics? You have to take into account such diverse but important items as soil, drainage, wind, solar access, and the ability of a construction crew to get onto the site.
7. Are there builders in the area to help realize your dream? How about a lumberyard, building supplier, appliance dealer, and miscellaneous craftsmen?
8. How is the land surrounding your property being used? What are the plans for it? Are there controls on future development that will affect your land and/or the land around it?
9. What are the local zoning restrictions? You'll need to know how many buildings you can build on your site, where they can be located and how tall they can be constructed, and just what uses of the land are permitted by local statute. (Most zoning jurisdictions have that information available online.)
10. What building code will be applicable to new construction on your site? Who will enforce that code? And what's the procedure for acquiring permits?

you also want your cabin to be within easy driving distance of a first-run movie theater or four-star restaurant, your options will naturally be much more limited.

TAKE A HARD LOOK

Look at prospective sites with a hard eye because it's easy to let your imagination run away with you. Before we built our more permanent second cabin, some years ago I decided I wanted a particular little rundown cabin on the Mississippi River an hour and a half from our house.

The cabin needed a lot of elbow grease and a lot of care, but I was charmed by the thought of sitting on the porch overlooking the river and, when I got hungry, walking to the quaint little village nearby for a burger and a beer. Jan had no such romantic illusions. She was not impressed. She heard the persistent railroad and highway noise that, in my imagination, I'd overlooked. Nor, she made it abundantly clear, was she interested in a regular diet of microwaved bar food.

My wife was right, of course. Wives usually are. They're the objective balance to our delusional fantasies; lord only knows what I'd do without that balance. That place would not have been a smart purchase, which proves, among many other things, that a wise partner may be at least as essential in these matters as a savvy real estate agent.

Instead, we chose the site of our current cabin. Although it's a bit of a haul, we're fond of the area and of the people who live there. We bought land from an old friend and we've made many more friends since.

We certainly had more convenient choices (the cabin is on Lake Vermilion in northeastern Minnesota, a four-hour drive from Minneapolis). But the opportunity to swim, boat, fish, hike, and snowshoe with old friends on a quiet, wooded site, plus access to a cheerful little town with a grocery store, hardware store, bait shop, restaurant, and movie theater, *plus* the nearby amenities of tennis, golf, downhill skiing, and historic areas made our choice a near no-brainer.

THE VIEW AND YOU

For many people, including some of my clients, their number-one cabin characteristic, or demand, is a view. (And if it's not number one, it's at least among the top three.)

View may seem a benign, relatively unimportant part of the cabin decision, but it can have a very powerful appeal, both in the cabin owner's imagination as well as in actual fact. You might be surprised by how many people, when they're thinking about their cabin (whether they own it yet or not), picture the sun rising over a mountaintop or setting across a lake.

In some cases, view is so important that it changes the way the cabin is described. The "front" is not where your guests drive up and enter; it's the side that faces the mountain or the lake. In those instances, the "front" is often and more accurately called the "view side."

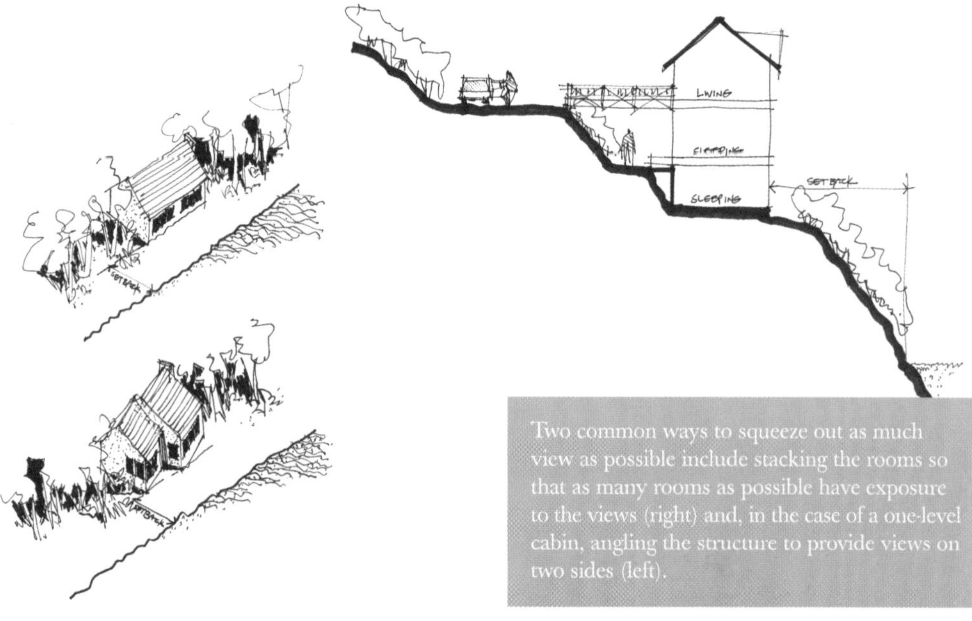

Two common ways to squeeze out as much view as possible include stacking the rooms so that as many rooms as possible have exposure to the views (right) and, in the case of a one-level cabin, angling the structure to provide views on two sides (left).

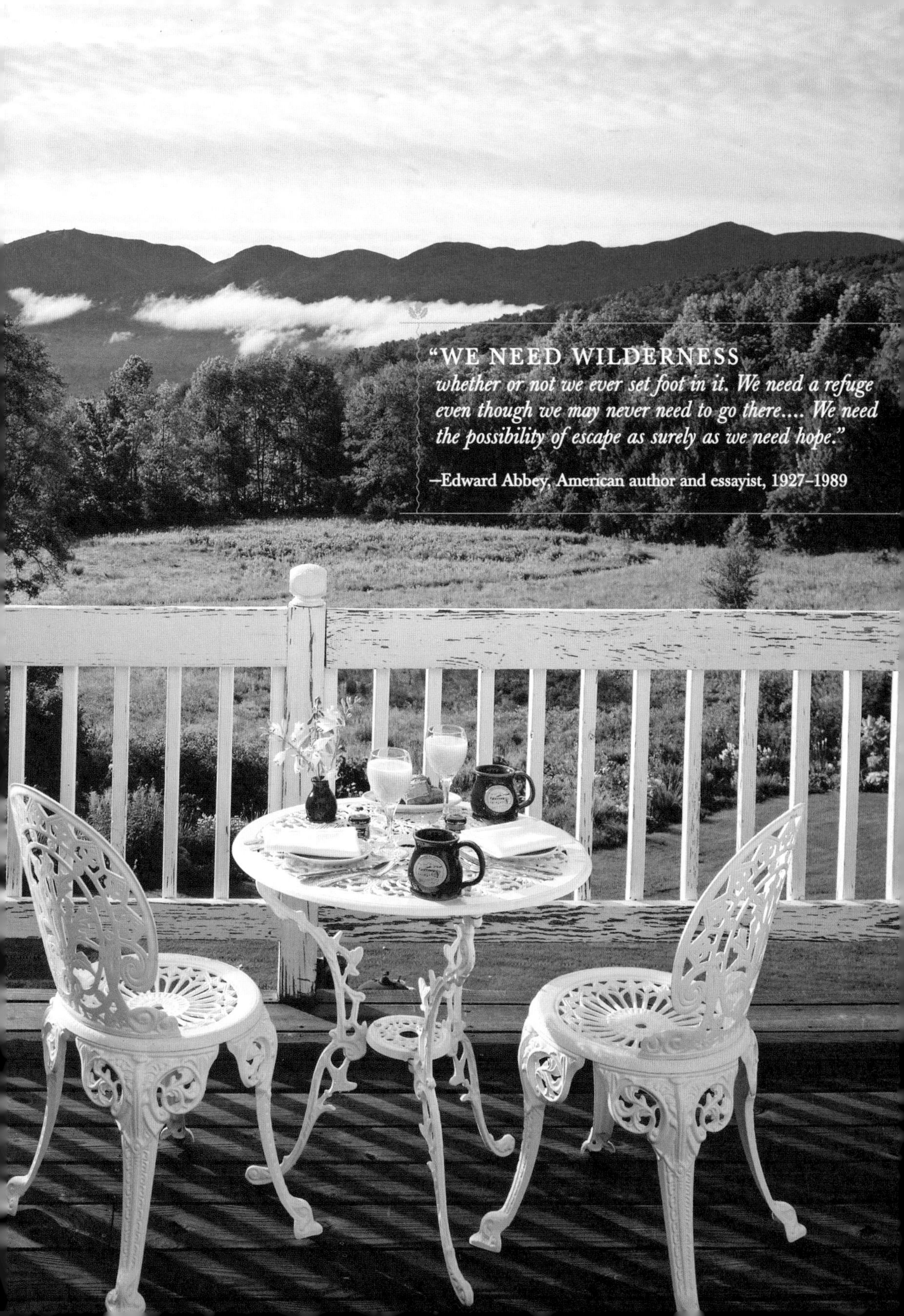
"WE NEED WILDERNESS
whether or not we ever set foot in it. We need a refuge even though we may never need to go there.... We need the possibility of escape as surely as we need hope."
–Edward Abbey, American author and essayist, 1927–1989

ABOVE: A top priority for most cabin owners is to take best advantage of the view through as many windows as possible.

BELOW: With some imaginative design, every room in this four-bedroom waterfront cabin gets exposure to the views as well as direct access to the outdoors.

VIEW VISION

View may eventually be an important factor in the cabin you buy or build. For example, steep sites may not be everyone's cup of tea, but they sometimes allow a spectacular view–if everybody involved uses their imagination. On one such site, a client and I designed his cabin "upside down," creating a bridge between the area where he parked his car and the topmost of three levels (where the living area is located and from which you descend to the bedrooms). A door on the second level opens to a path along the lakeshore that connects with a guest cabin 50 yards away.

Legendary northwoodsman Hod Ludlow designed and built a cabin back in 1949 that's still a great example of how to choose a site and design for the view. Ludlow strung the cabin's rooms along an exterior corridor like an old-time motel. Waking up in one of those rooms, a guest has direct access to the lakeshore outside without having to pass through the living room, kitchen, or porch, and best of all has an unimpeded view of lovely Lake Vermilion (*my* Lake Vermilion).

I advise clients to look for property where imagination and ingenuity will be needed, where the inaccessible can be made accessible, and where the unbuildable can be built. Keep an eye peeled for that unlikely spot where sweat equity can transform a ramshackle hut on a weedy or steep lot into a handsome cottage on a slice of grassy heaven.

So what's most important? Figuring out the answer to that question is the first step toward deciding where you should buy or build.

GETTING GOOD HELP

Real estate brokers in the locality you've settled on should be quite familiar with the area and can quickly help you find what you're looking for, whether it's the raw land or an existing cabin with appealing charm. Developing a personal rapport and working relationship with a knowledgeable and trustworthy agent–someone who understands and appreciates your wants and needs as well as the local real estate market–is close to essential and at least a great place to focus your quest at this point.

The more insightful and savvy your real estate agent, the better your chances of finding the right place and making the best deal. You may also want to talk to and create relationships with other businesspeople in the area–a Main Street banker, the guy who owns the hardware store or lumberyard, and established local builders. They may know about opportunities that haven't come on the market yet. Local newspapers and websites can also give you leads on private sales and a heads-up on forfeited property.

MAKING THE DEAL

The real estate you want will never be cheap on the day you actually buy it, but within a few short years you'll be happy you bought when you did because, as Mark Twain famously observed about land, they're not making any more of it. And what with global warming and rising ocean levels, the land that Earth has to offer is only going to grow more precious.

Even so, you don't want to settle for less than you want (anything short of your dream). You'll also want to make the best deal, so expect to put time and effort into the process. Luck helps, but don't count on it.

CABIN MATTERS

A FIVE-YEAR PLAN

One of my client couples set aside five years to find the site they wanted for their retirement cabin. They had decided on the climate they wanted, determined the maximum distance the cabin could be located from their favorite art galleries, health-care provider, and a major airport, identified the recreational opportunities they wanted, and listed the attributes they would require in their adopted "hometown"–all, of course, within their projected budget.

They ended up buying their dream cabin at the foot of an Appalachian mountainside in Georgia, where, if the spirit moved them, they could theoretically step out the door and begin a hike that would take them to Nova Scotia or could drive to a baseball game in Atlanta.

DOWN ENDION ROAD

The drive down Endion Road was a journey to another world. Having left Long Island six hours earlier, my family and I turned off Route 30 just past the town of Long Lake, New York, onto a dirt and gravel road that led us to a cabin on the lake. The headlights of the Northway, the highway that leads into the Adirondacks, were now replaced by dozens of shining eyes that peered out from the Adirondack woods–fox, deer, possum, owls, bears. My brother and I stared back out the window, hoping one might dash into full view of our headlights.

A mile farther down, we made a left turn onto an even narrower road and then a right where a handmade sign read "Blazing Birches"–a grandiose designation rarely used for the modest cabin we were headed for. If anything, it was called "Blazing Bitches," a name jokingly used by Peggy Ryan and

her three daughters, our neighbors back home, who owned it.

When we pulled up to the cabin, the intense darkness of the woods was broken by the soft gleam of the lake. Like alpenglow, it had its own muted luminosity that subtly brightened the night.

There was nothing beyond the basic necessities that (barely) separated us from the woods outside. Yet that simplicity, finally, was its secret.

This, combined with the glow of the Coleman lanterns coming from the cabin, contributed to the magical feel of the place. And, as the cabin was not electrified, it was a conduit for the coming and going of natural light, creating a rhythm we easily fell into while we were there: waking to blinding sunshine, morning swims in the dark currents of the lake, fishing and waterskiing, late afternoon horseshoes, cocktails for the adults, gutting and frying fish for dinner, gin rummy next to the fire, and comic books by flashlight. This routine lasted for four weeks with little variation. Conversations ebbed and flowed and it seemed easy to get to know everyone who stopped by. Our dogs, too, came and went, sometimes disappearing for days and then returning as distinctly different and wilder creatures.

The cabin was built by Peggy's husband, Jack, who had died a number of years earlier. It was a simple one-story dwelling with four bedrooms, a large fireplace and, in the early years, no working plumbing. It had a gas stove that gave off a distinct odor, one that mixed with the smoky smell of the fireplace and the lanterns that hissed throughout the evening.

In hindsight, it is amazing that such an unremarkable structure could have held us in such thrall. There was no attic to play in or basement to explore. There was nothing beyond the basic necessities that (barely) separated us from the woods outside. Yet that simplicity, finally, was its secret. Who needed a rambling old farmhouse or mansion when I could put my ear against the cabin at night and hear the slapping of rain, rustling of trees, mysterious growls and cries, the breaking of branches and thunderous wind–in short, the incomprehensible news of the universe–occurring right outside my room?

On any given morning, we might wake up to a gaping hole in the screened porch and find scat and hair and orange rinds and ribbons of plastic bags where bears broke through the night before.

"Well, at least you've had this," I seem to remember my father saying, referring to the days of unbroken light and darkness before the cabin was inevitably electrified, when not even a single scratch of radio static touched our ears for half a summer. It was one of those early evening conversations–sitting in front of a window, his silhouette completely engulfed in shadow until his voice became the only thing that defined him.

"At least you've had this," he said. Or should have said, because it was true.

–Chris Kingsley lives with his wife and two children in New Hamburg, New York.

GOING ONLINE

Access to the Internet allows you to do much of your research at your convenience and from the comfort of home. In addition to Realtor.com®, virtually every real estate agency in the country, large or small, now offers a searchable database of property for sale or at the very least a scrollable listing.

If you haven't looked lately, pick an area, Google™ it for realtors, and start clicking (don't forget to bookmark your favorites). Create a folder on your computer in which to store the listings that are to your liking, with subfolders for raw land, "handyman's specials" (cabins that likely need a lot of work), and cabins that are move-in ready. Over time, you'll get a sense of what's for sale, what real estate prices in a given place are doing (going up, down or steady), and what type of land or cabins are available.

Even if you're not ready to buy, once you're armed with the information you've found on the Internet you might think about taking a drive one weekend (equipped with your digital camera) to conduct an exploratory mission. A firsthand look at property you find on the Internet will help you develop an instinct for what's what. You'll learn to read between the lines of property postings. You'll also get a sense of the area and whether it offers the kinds of things you really want nearby, such as decent restaurants, a hardware store, and maybe even a good coffee shop.

WHAT IT'S CALLED DEPENDS ON WHERE IT IS

Whether you call it a cabin, cottage, or camp–the three most common generic designations for the structure–usually depends on where you live.

The same building situated in, say, northern Wisconsin may be called a cottage if the owner lives in Milwaukee and a cabin if the owner comes from Minneapolis.

If it's somewhere in the Maine woods, it would likely be called a camp. But if you put it on a flatbed truck and transplanted it nearly anywhere along the Atlantic shore, you'd probably describe it as a cottage.

Generally, *cabin* is the more common term in mountain locations, whether you're talking about the Appalachians or the Rockies, while *cottage* has a greater association with water, whether a lake, river, or ocean.

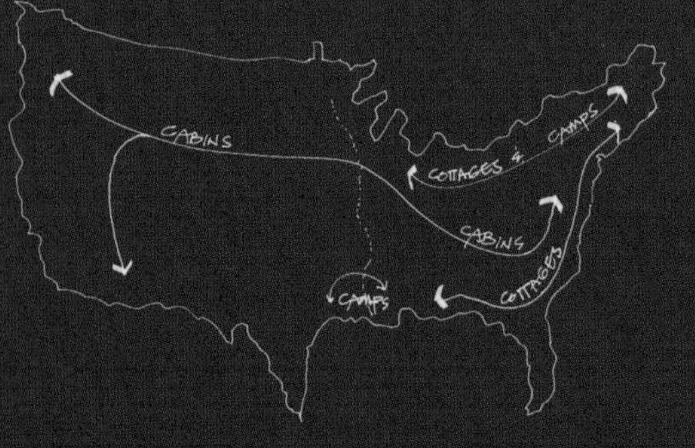

"THE CLEAREST WAY
into the universe is through a forest wilderness."

–John Muir, American preservationist, 1838–1914

To best understand the property you own or want to own, find a copy of the U.S. Geological Survey's topographical map for the area and, with compass in hand, walk it all, looking for hills and rock outcroppings, views and access points.

UNDERSTANDING YOUR SITE

Okay, fast-forward a bit. Now you've bought the real estate you want for your cabin and you need to develop a plan for the site (if you're going to build) or for the cabin you want to remodel.

If you're going to build or seriously remodel (including adding on), you'll need a thorough understanding of the property. This understanding begins with solid information. Contour maps produced by the United States Geological Survey (USGS) are available for most locations, and aerial images can be found online (check out Google Earth™) and ordered in high resolution.

State, county, and other jurisdictions also have valuable information for the asking. Start by checking the appropriate government websites. The University of Minnesota's extension service, for example, offers a "Lake Home and Cabin Kit" that's full of helpful information on everything from water quality and vegetation to septic-system requirements. The kit also lists contacts to help deal with pesky cabin concerns like mildew, radon, and pest control. It also tells how to preserve water quality through shoreline management and how to take other important steps to maintain a healthy cabin environment. Check with a state college or university in your area for similar packages.

Something else you'll want to consider is flood risk. Floods happen more than you think and often to people whose houses have never flooded before. The Federal Emergency Management Agency (FEMA) maintains the National Flood Insurance Program mapping system, which maps the entire country to show the likelihood of flooding. Somebody in the courthouse in whatever county you're considering will be able to direct you to the local flood maps. The last thing you want is to find out just before the closing that your area is prone to flooding and that you have to take out FEMA flood insurance. You might want to do this anyway, but you want that knowledge to factor into your decision to buy—well beforehand.

Nothing helps you more at the beginning, though, than a detailed USGS topographical site survey, which will be invaluable as you plan for a new cabin or for adding on to an existing one, as well as for building additional structures, roadways, landscaping, septic system, and other important components. With your map in front of you, your vision will become more vivid and

Most states don't offer such a publication, but luckily for Minnesotans, the University of Minnesota's extension service publishes a "Lake Home and Cabin Kit" that contains a wealth of great information for the would-be cabin owner in the state.

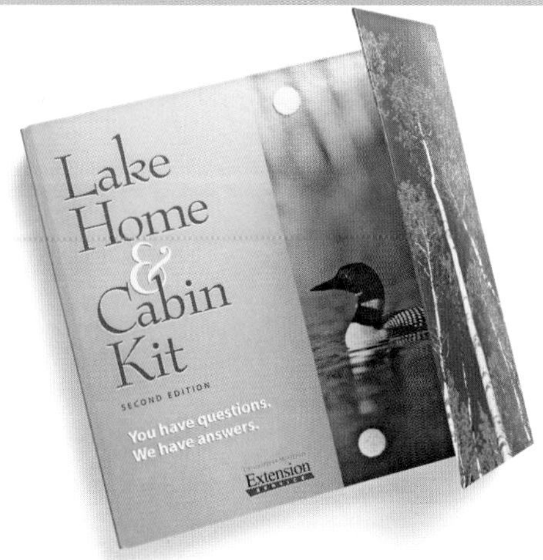

CABIN MATTERS

BEING YOUR OWN SURVEYOR

If you can't afford, or don't want to work with, a professional surveyor, you can produce a working survey of your own by following a series of steps:

1. Establish on your site a grid with 50-ft. intervals, and place a stake at every grid intersection. Using a compass, orient the grid to a clearly marked property boundary or off the axis of a building that will remain on the site. Make sure the diagonal dimensions are equal in the grid's squares. (You can make your grid larger, say, 100 ft., or smaller, maybe 20 ft. A smaller grid will take more time to make but will give you more precise information.)
2. Beginning with the lowest stake on the site, mark the added height of the ground at each stake. Use the designation *Elevation 100* as your starting point. (You don't need to guess at the added height. Use a hand level, laser level, GPS vertical positioning device, or water-leveling clear hose or tube.)
3. Record the grid on a sheet of grid-lined paper, with a letter or number corresponding to each stake.
4. On the lines between grid points, find the location of even integer elevations above your starting point. Connect the points to create a topographic line.
5. Locate and record on the grid paper all of the site's important features, including the shoreline, existing structures, trees, and rock outcroppings. You can also note the location of stream beds, electrical power lines, desirable vista points, prevailing wind direction, and other relevant data.
6. You and/or your architect can now add whatever you're planning to build on the property, using the appropriate scale. (Make photocopies of the original map for your planning to allow for trial and error.)

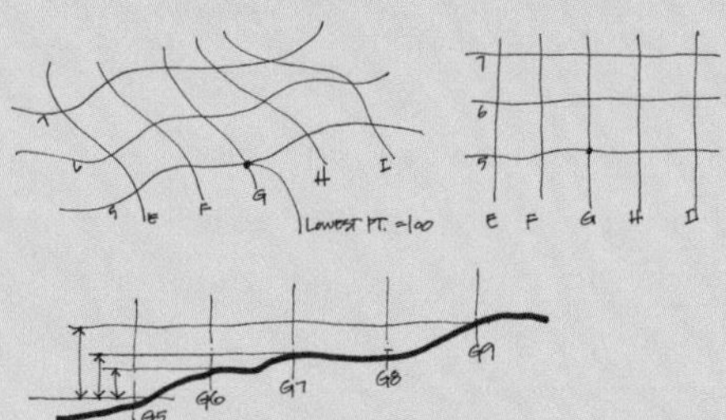

7. Create a final topographic map with your cabin, driveway, and outbuildings, redirecting the topography for positive drainage away from buildings.

TIP **WHAT'S UP, DOCK?**

If fishing and sunbathing are important cabin activities, you'll be looking for a spot where you can build a good-size dock on the north side of a great fishing lake. The cabin itself can be constructed on any practical site near the dock and be large enough only to store your fishing gear, a beach towel, sunscreen, a stove for cooking up the day's catch, and a couple of bunks. A large, well-designed dock will function nicely–at least in good weather–as a waterside living and dining room.

precise. *Here's* where you'll sit and tie your fishing lures. *That's* where you'll come and go on your cross-country skis. *There's* the best spot to plot the garden.

LOVE THE LAND

In any case–and this is a crucial point–the site and the cabin should create a happy relationship between you and the property's ecosystem. Author and architect Christopher Alexander, in his book *A Pattern Language*, offers the following advice: "On no account place buildings in the places which are most beautiful. In fact, do the opposite. Consider the site and its buildings as a single living ecosystem. Leave those areas that are most precious, beautiful, comfortable and healthy as they are and build new structures in those parts of the site which are least pleasant now."

When you're at the cabin, you'll likely spend a lot of time outside, whether chopping wood, waxing skis, building a campfire, or whiling away the afternoon in a hammock. The structures you build or find on the property will create the frame for these activities and help define your cabin experience. Your building (or buildings), whether a gabled retirement home with a three-car garage or a humble cottage, storage shed, and outhouse, will be as much a part of the local ecosystem as the lake, trees, and rocks. The better everything works together, the happier you'll be.

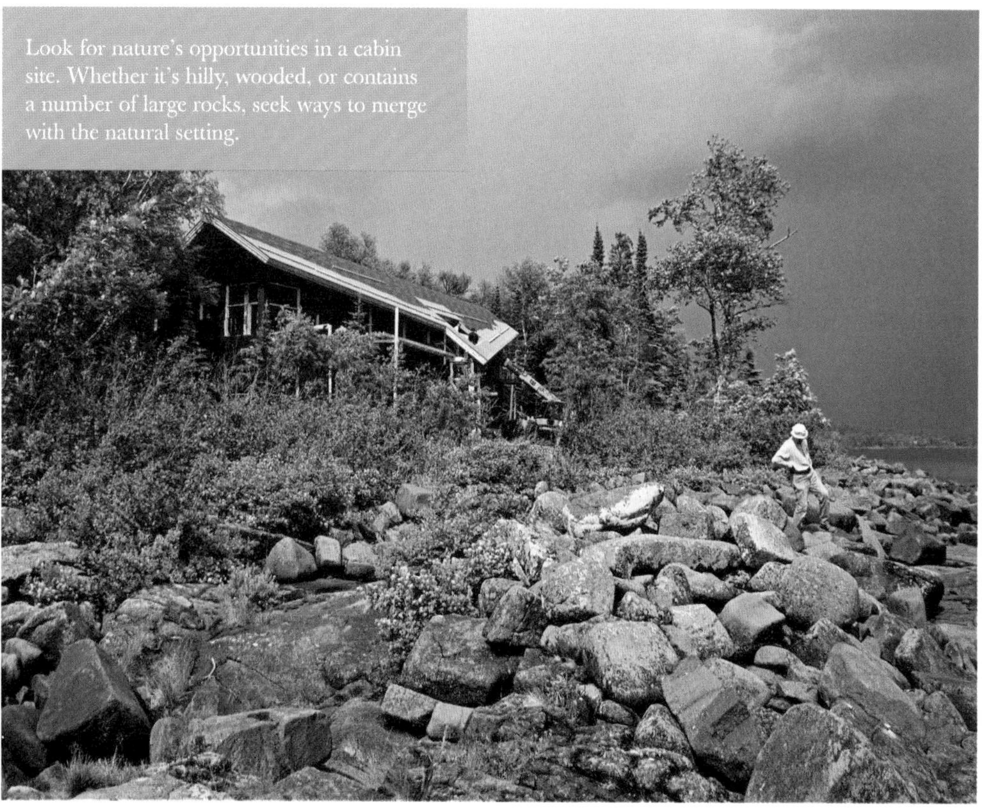

Look for nature's opportunities in a cabin site. Whether it's hilly, wooded, or contains a number of large rocks, seek ways to merge with the natural setting.

CABIN MATTERS

ADDING THE WOW! FACTOR

I'm currently working on ideas for a land developer who's worried that his least attractive lots will be tough to sell without really imaginative designs. I told him we'll use modest structures to add *wow!* to one site (bottom drawing) and charm to another (top drawing).

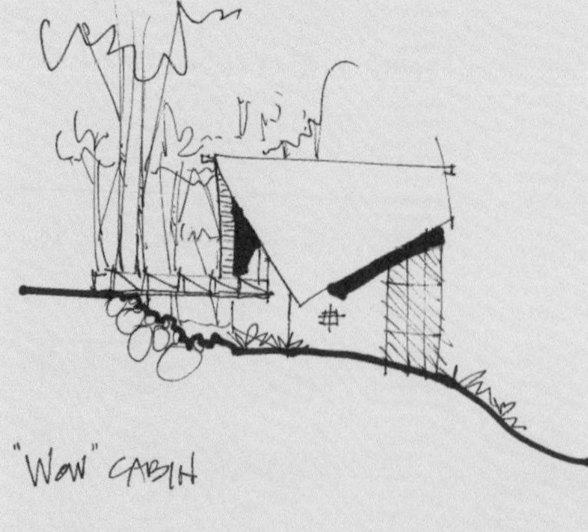

IN PARTNERSHIP WITH NATURE

Every piece of land on earth has a specific solar orientation and set of seasonal wind directions. If you enjoy rising with the sun streaming in your bedroom window and warming the kitchen as you brew the morning coffee, the sun's route across the sky will help determine your cabin's position on the site.

In the Upper Midwest, where I live, a porch strategically placed on the south side of the cabin is warmed by the sun and protected from the northwest winds, giving us a couple of extra months of use every year that we wouldn't have with a shaded porch on the northwest side of our cabin.

The sun's path overhead is predictable throughout the year. You can probably find a chart similar to the one on p. 43 at your county agent's office. But not all choices will be so clear. You may want to position your cabin so that a large oak tree shades it in the summer and lets the sun stream through come winter. But then again, if you build too close to that oak, you may harm its root system and kill it unless you take extraordinary precautions (and its roots won't do your foundation any good either).

You can also turn the most mundane challenge into an opportunity. Large rocks sticking out of the soil may get in the way of construction, yet moved only a few feet away add to the beauty and interest of the yard.

NATURE'S PALETTE

When I walk a building site before designing a cabin on it, I collect leaves, twigs, pinecones, and stones, which I take back to my drawing

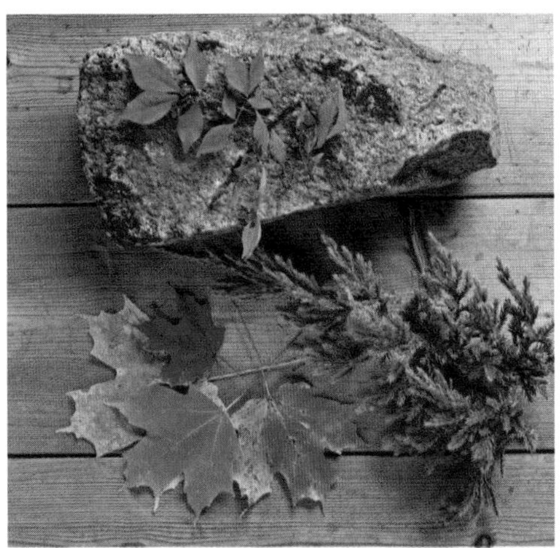

Local stone, berries, leaves, and a small branch from a fir tree can help you choose the palette for your cabin that fits its natural surroundings.

board (yes, I still use a drawing board) for inspiration and ideas about textures and colors–a combination that's often unique to a given location.

To me, these tangible, three-dimensional pieces of landscape are as important as my photographs and sketches. They give me the real colors, textures, and feel of the place that the best photos can't. Those red dogwood twigs, for instance, might be what I need to come up with the color around the windows. The blue-green of the spruce needles may be just right for the roof shingles. The maple leaves may provide the shape for cutouts on a stairway handrail, while the mottling on a rock may be just the look for the kitchen's stone countertops.

SHADE & SOD

Sites with lots of trees provide their own challenges and opportunities. If you're building a new cabin, the woods have to be cleared for

CABIN MATTERS

LOOKING INTO THE SUN

Designing to the arc of the sun means accounting for a heat and light source that changes by the hour, day, and season.

Such a design has to pay less attention to the conditions at high noon on June 21 than to those at, say, 2 p.m. on August 1. The sun angle you want to capture at 10 a.m. on April 21 may be the same you want to repel at 2 p.m. exactly four months later.

Luckily, a range of solar conditions can be easily modeled on your personal computer.

To best orient your cabin for the best natural light or shade, do some homework to understand solar conditions at your site

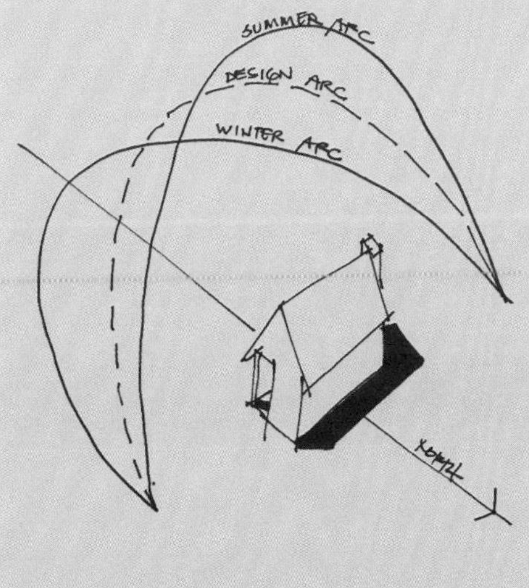

This is a cabin annex attached to a larger garage and workshop.

the cabin, the driveway, and septic field. But, in cold northern climates, opening the forest for those purposes is how you infuse a dark, moist environment with sunlight. Position that septic field southeasterly of the cabin and you've created a clearing that brings in the morning sun.

Soils may vary from one site to the next, although they usually follow regional patterns. Trees and vegetation can tell you a lot about the subject, but, depending on your plans, you may need an expert's opinion. You may even need some soil engineering; sites atop mountains that look solid as rock can hide moving plates that only a professional can discover.

YOUR OTHER NEIGHBORS

Then there's the wildlife. One of the great joys of being at my cabin is watching the abundance of animal life that share our wooded neighborhood. I may look up to see the aerial dogfight between an eagle and an osprey as they battle over a fish. Or a glance out the kitchen window might reveal a half dozen young deer dining on a bucket of corn. Later, a red fox prowls the backyard looking for prey, while out front a gaggle of birds–jays and crows on this occasion–squabble around the feeder. Just beyond the end of the dock, a brood of ducklings glide past in single file behind their mother, ever watchful for a hungry otter or muskrat–all of it much better than an Animal Planet documentary.

You don't have to be Thoreau to wax poetic about your own personal Walden. In fact, the best response to the cry of a loon and a chorus of frogs that bring down the curtain on a summer evening is respectful silence. If you're not saying it, you're certainly thinking it: *Does it get any better than this?*

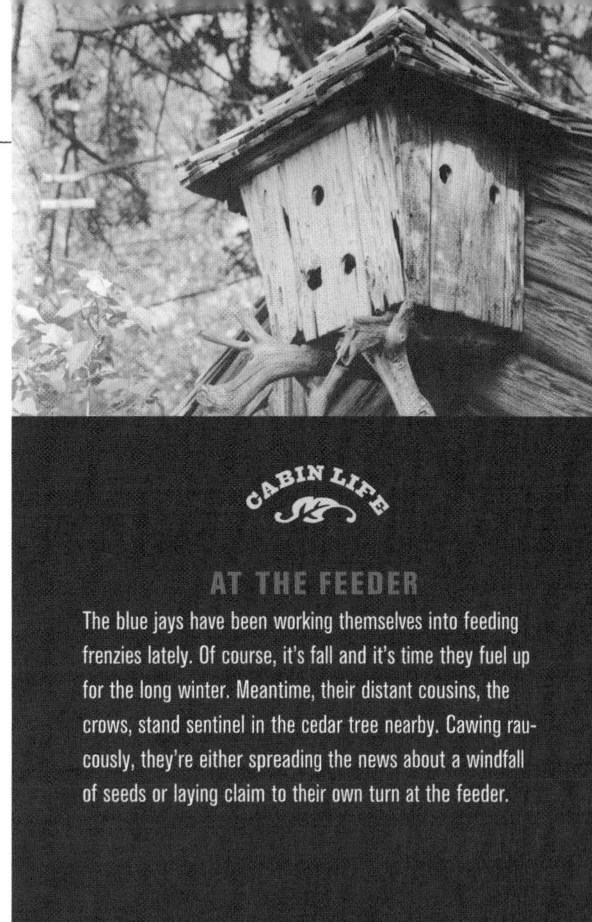

CABIN LIFE

AT THE FEEDER

The blue jays have been working themselves into feeding frenzies lately. Of course, it's fall and it's time they fuel up for the long winter. Meantime, their distant cousins, the crows, stand sentinel in the cedar tree nearby. Cawing raucously, they're either spreading the news about a windfall of seeds or laying claim to their own turn at the feeder.

CABIN MATTERS

NATURAL IDEAS

Nature has her own ideas about cabin design, and those ideas are often worth noting.

Tall pines may suggest, for example, a steep roof, rock outcroppings, a stone foundation, prairie land, a low horizontal roof, and horizontal banded windows. The availability of warm sunshine and cool breezes may also influence the form your cabin takes in certain parts of the country.

Flat sites lend themselves to certain designs that mountainsides do not.

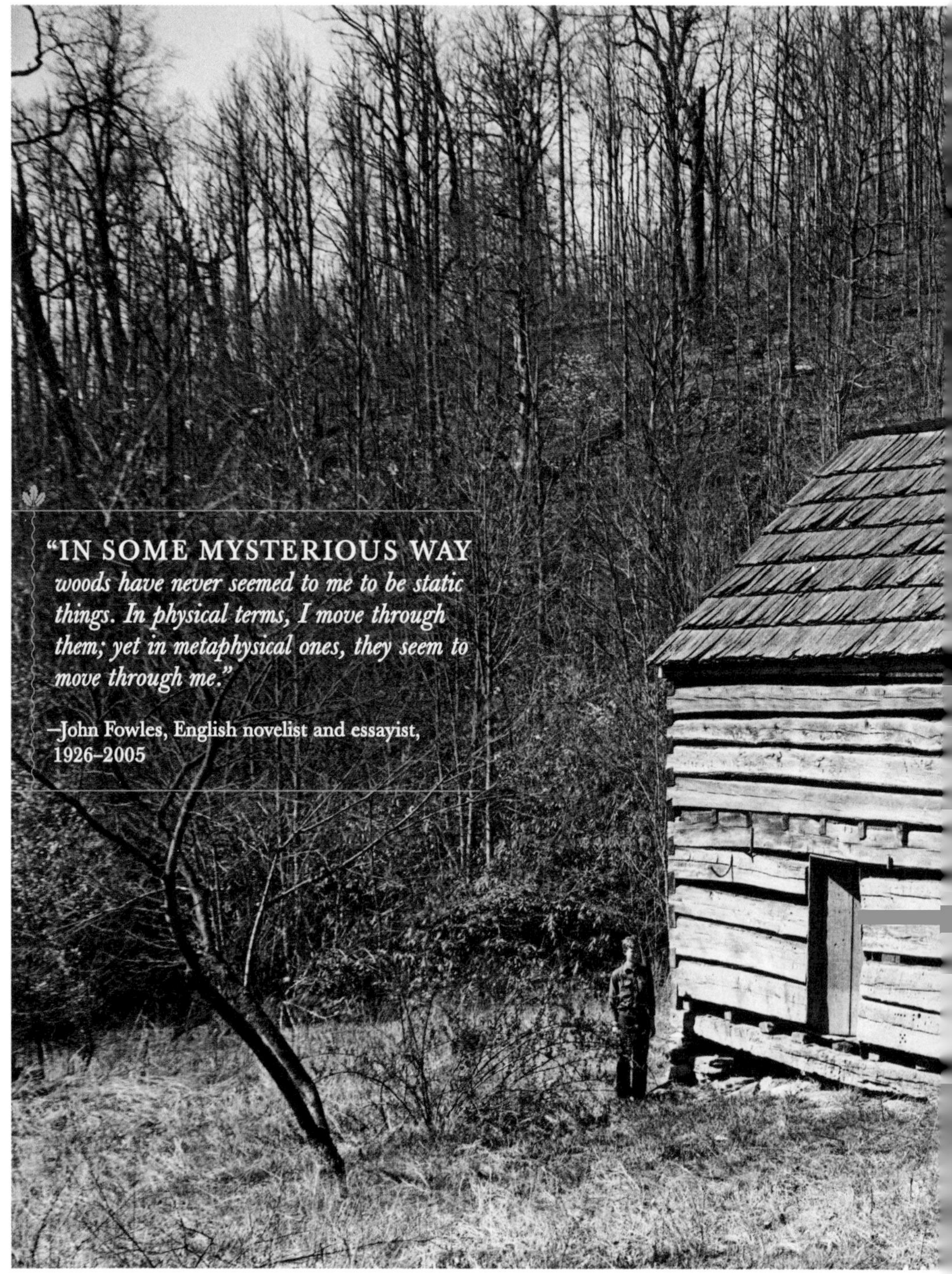
"IN SOME MYSTERIOUS WAY
woods have never seemed to me to be static things. In physical terms, I move through them; yet in metaphysical ones, they seem to move through me."
–John Fowles, English novelist and essayist, 1926–2005

IT TAKES A VILLAGE

Even in the most remote places, you'll be part of a community of some kind. This might not seem compatible with your dreams if your sole objective is to get away from it all, including other people and their rules. The fact is, though, nearly any place you want to buy or build a cabin falls within some state, county, municipal, or neighborhood jurisdiction, each with rules you'll be obliged to follow. I advise my clients to get used to the fact that, no matter how deep into the woods they go, they will never have absolute freedom to do what they please.

KNOW THE RULES

Not all local rules will make a lot of sense to a newcomer (or even to a longtime resident for that matter). Many of them may, in fact, be a pain the neck. Also, they can be open to various and confusing interpretations. A local covenant might require, for instance, that the exterior of your cabin be painted–like everybody else's–a "natural" color. Well, look around. There aren't many colors that are not found in nature. So will the pink found in the lady slipper (the Minnesota state flower) that you spotted in the woods a few yards from your cabin be acceptable?

I naively thought that the silver-gray of the metal roof I had specified for a client's cabin was close enough to the silver-gray of the surrounding birch trees. Yet the homeowners association thought otherwise and I was asked to "de-silver" the roof.

The challenges are endless, so be forewarned. Here's another for instance: According to local zoning regs, your garage can't be built closer than 10 ft. from your property line. But is that 10 ft. measured from the garage wall or from the edge of its roof overhang, which could be a difference of a foot to a foot and a half?

If the rules say your sunset-watching or meditation tower can't be more than 30 ft. high but you're building on a slope, from what point is the tower's height "legally" measured? A 75-ft. setback from water's edge generally means 75 ft. from the "ordinary height water elevation," which is not necessarily the water level you saw when you walked the site with your real estate agent during a stretch of dry weather. Most of the rules you'll encounter are easy enough to interpret, but you'll need to be flexible in both planning and building if you want to build a new cabin or add on or significantly modify an existing one.

Walk the land and try to picture your arrival down a curvy driveway, treated by glimpses of your retreat before you pull up at the front door.

This four-story cabin nearly breaks the vertical zoning limits but only its chimney ultimately rises to the heavens, and chimneys are exceptions.

When I inspect a client's raw land, I visualize the eventual placement of the cabin and think about, say, how somebody will approach it by car. Will the driveway follow a series of curves that give you and your guests welcome glimpses of the cabin ahead? I believe that, after you've driven for three to four hours, the final approach to your getaway is both psychologically and emotionally important. But even the driveway–and thus those first impressions–will probably be determined at least in part by the community's rules.

KNOW YOUR LIMITS

Buying a site with an existing cabin may get you grandfathered into pre-zoning regulation conditions for your property, which are not applicable when building a new cabin today. On my lake there are old cabins 30 ft. from the water, whereas, today they would have to be 75 ft. away from the water line.

Altering or adding on to such a cabin can be a challenge and will require a "variancy." Variances by definition are not guarantees. Often, a unique hardship on you along with

TIP **HOWDY, NEIGHBOR!**

Neighborliness at the cabin can take many forms, one of the best of which is a simple sharing of the land. The trespassing of strangers should not be encouraged, but many cabin dwellers happily share informal paths that cross adjacent properties along a lakeshore. Shared paths are perfect for sunset strolls, bird watching, and, of course, connecting with the neighbors when you want to borrow an electric drill or share a slice of blueberry pie.

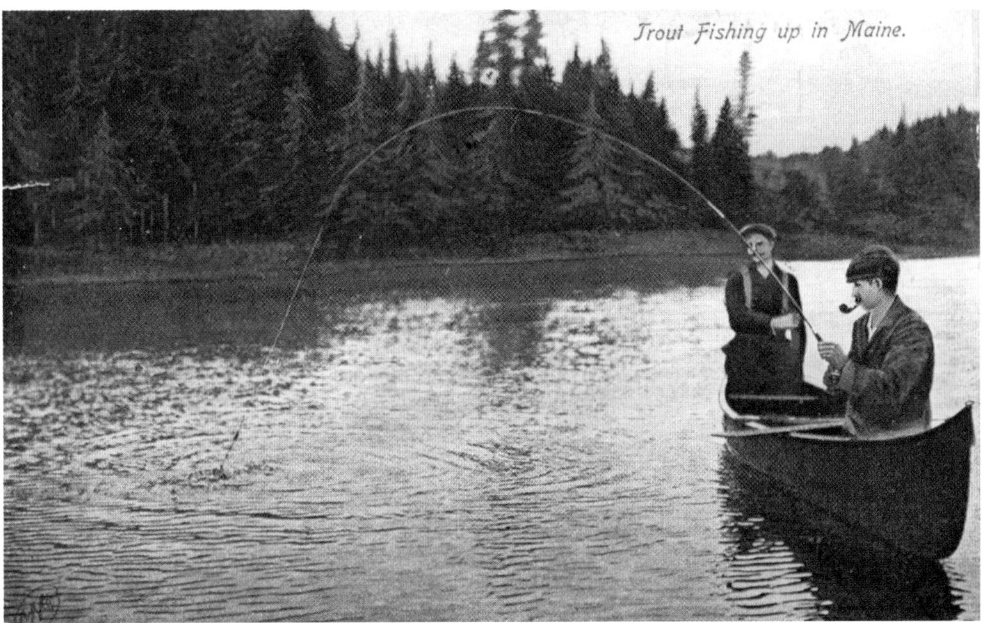
Trout Fishing up in Maine.

your neighbors' support is required to secure one. Even then, you will have to present your case to the zoning board and argue on behalf of the variance you want to secure. Again, no guarantees, although with your neighbors' backing, your odds are markedly improved for getting variance approval.

A CIVIL RESPONSIBILITY

Beyond the township ordinances and regulations, neighbors need to be civil and courteous to each other just as they are (or should be) in the city. And it shouldn't matter whether the neighbors are right next door or a half mile down the road. Newcomers have the responsibility to learn the rules, make an effort to fit in, and become a responsible member of the community. If you don't, you not only miss out on the opportunity to make friends and connections, but you also may give the impression that you're arrogant and uncaring (so if you are, at least try to hide it). Remember, in purely practical terms, as a stranger in these parts, you need your neighbors more than they need you–and in more ways than one.

As in the city, neighbors can be good, so-so, or awful, and you usually don't have much say in choosing them. But, with luck and a little cultivation, neighbors can be a wonderful addition to the cabin experience.

For several years, the neighbors at our cabin were rarely around when we were. We reveled in the solitude, the absence of extra noise and light, and the frequent presence of deer and other wildlife emboldened by the relative lack of humans. Recently, however, the people next door have been showing up more often, and we've become good friends.

Sure, it's a tad noisier and there's more electric light at night, but we like being able to borrow a cup of sugar, having an extra oven available when we have a lot of company, jointly booking a fishing guide, and comparing notes about a particular tree trimmer or plumber. And the deer, birds, and other critters seem as happy to hang around the place as ever.

TO CLAIM OR MERGE

Once upon a time, a cabin was almost always an organic part of the land. That's because it was typically made of materials harvested on the site–foundation stones dug from the soil, logs shaped from the trees that grew in the clearing, shingles made by the mill on the other side of the lake. The form a cabin took was more often than not that of a simple gable box, and the cabin was the domicile required for a homesteader's claim. Everything was of a piece.

In his book *The Place of Houses,* Charles Moore, the late architect, professor, and dean of the Yale School of Architecture, distinguishes between two historic ways of looking at the land and the way we live on it. One is what he calls *claiming.* Our pioneering ancestors claimed the land, and the structures they built of wood or brick on it were similarly objects that could be claimed, that is, something to be owned or occupied.

Claiming's counterpart, Moore said, is *merging,* in which the land is not so much occupied as engaged, or joined. A pioneer family's sod hut, for instance, was an organic extension of the prairie, less something built on top of the land (as, say, a brick house or a log cabin) than an organism rising from it. But merging refers to more than sod huts. In the 20th century, many of our most sophisticated architects and builders–Frank Lloyd Wright is a notable example–designed their structures in such a way that they consciously merged with their natural settings at least as much as they claimed them.

THINK IT THROUGH

This is more than shop talk for architects and designers. It is, or should be, an important part of the discussion you have with your

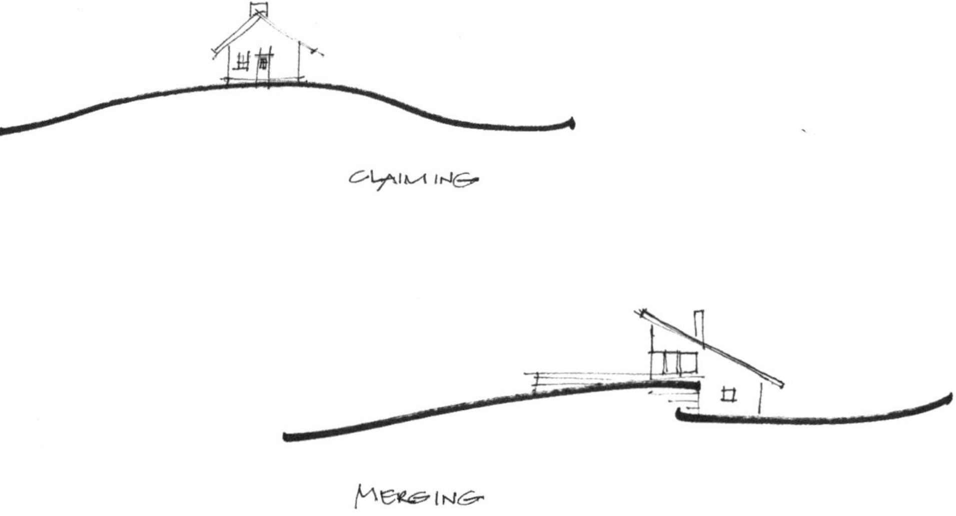

Merging with the landscape can be extended to merging with local materials as this lodge does with local stone.

GETTING THERE

The drive from our home to our cabin takes four hours if we don't stop for a burger and milkshake en route. In the three and a half of those hours spent on the interstate, we can pick up our favorite northwoods radio station and listen to DJ "Rainbow Trout" for only two. Of course, it's the final half hour on a two-lane highway that takes forever and forces us to ask the question, "Why do we live so far from a place we love so much?"

But then, five minutes before we actually reach our cabin, we approach the lake. The dirt road, still rutted from the spring thaw, now takes us into deep woods. We see deer grazing in the meadow clearing created by a power line. Then the road runs along the shoreline before becoming the mini-roller coaster that leads up to the cabin.

Finally at the cabin, we step out of the car, stretch our stiff limbs, and open our senses to the fresh air, excited greeting of the birds, and the scent of pine riding a light breeze off the lake.

And we ask ourselves the other relevant question: "Why did we stay away so long?"

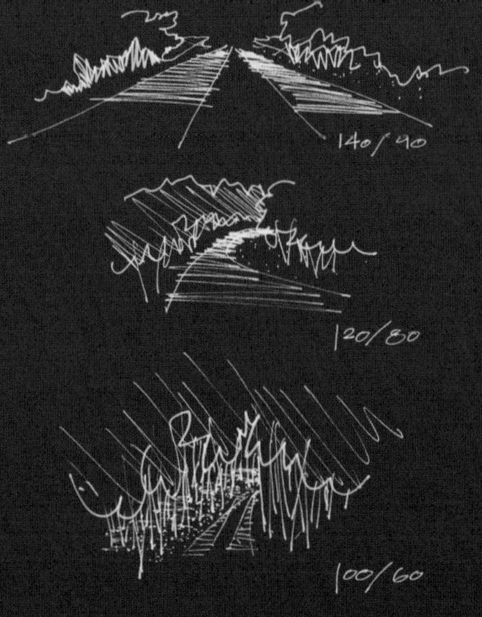

spouse, partner, architect, real estate broker, and other advisers when considering the cabin you want. Part of it, for sure, involves aesthetics. But thinking about and working with the environment–merging with it rather than claiming it–can give you some practical advantages. I can't tell you, for instance, how glad I am that I built our cabin into the ground's natural slope. That merging with the land–taking advantage of the earth's natural insulating capacity–helps keep the place nice and toasty on the coldest winter nights.

Truth be told, though, most of my clients believe that claiming is just fine. They want to make the most of their cabin setting and be sensitive to its natural surroundings. But they're okay with the idea of occupying the land that they love. They're more than happy to claim it as their own.

YOUR CUP'S HALF FULL

Your land purchase (or your inheritance) may find you with both land and an existing cabin, charming or otherwise. Architects might fantasize about their heroic, even stellar inventions, but many of us get just as excited about the challenges of restoring, remodeling, or adding on to something that has been there for a while.

Working with clients and their existing houses often takes me places I might never have gone on my own, which is a professional joy. As a bonus, I get to measure and assess existing cabins and, in the process, understand the constructive logic of an earlier era.

The reality is that, for many architects–at least those of us who are business realists–we understand that for every new cabin we design and build, 50 more are going to be remodeled or added on to. Many of these existing cabins may not require an architect's ingenuity but, when one does, I hope to be there.

Where it's adding to a double A-frame, restoring a historic dovetailed square log cabin, transforming a smelly stable into a charming rural retreat, or rethinking a basic clapboard-sided handyman's special, my response is not "will I?" but "when can I start?"

In truth, most of the issues that are present for a remodel exist for a new cabin, issues such as space and how that space will be used; electrical, insulation, heating, and ventilation concerns; cooking and eating and sitting; wells and septics; access to the site; and all the architectural details that make any structure special. The difference is that half of the responses to those issues are already given by the existing conditions, a structural shell, a sand point well, or a beautiful fieldstone fireplace.

Depending on what you want to do to your old cabin, how much of a remodel you're up for (including adding on), you'll ask yourself how much of the work can you do yourself (and how much are you willing or have time to do). Also, ask yourself, "How much do I know how to do?"

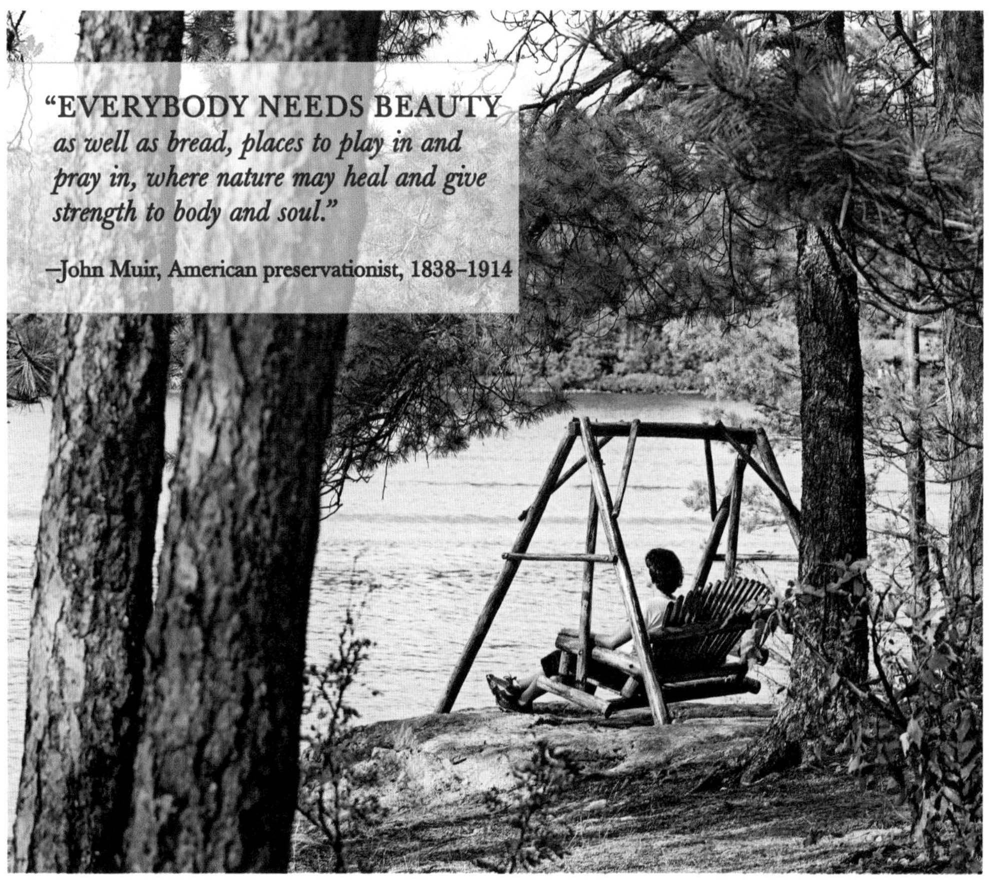

"EVERYBODY NEEDS BEAUTY *as well as bread, places to play in and pray in, where nature may heal and give strength to body and soul.*"

—John Muir, American preservationist, 1838–1914

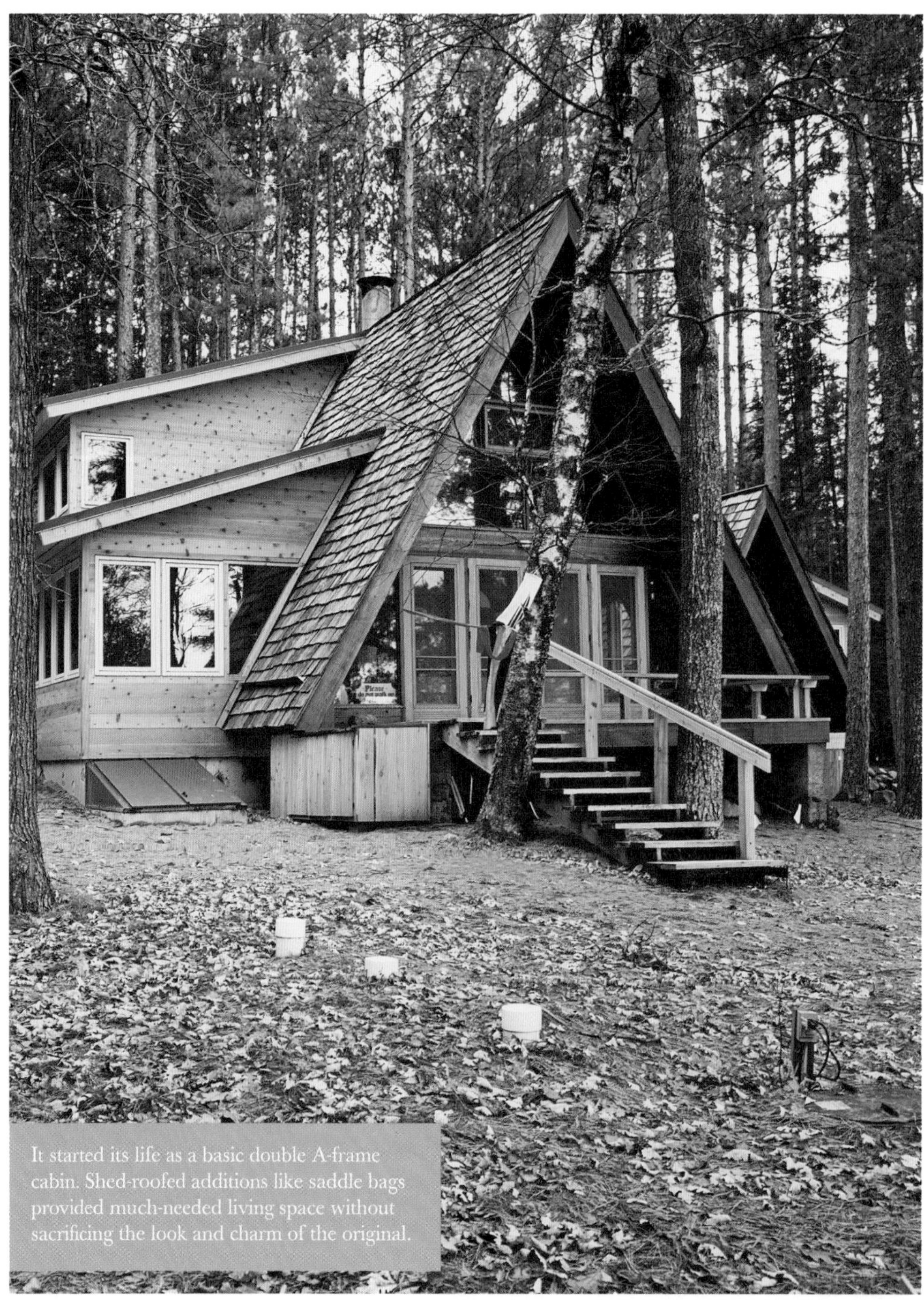

It started its life as a basic double A-frame cabin. Shed-roofed additions like saddle bags provided much-needed living space without sacrificing the look and charm of the original.

DECIDING WHICH WAY TO GO

Sometimes, new and remodel can come together, such as when a building lot already contains a cabin. If the existing cabin is fairly new (say, no more than 30 years old) or has been remodeled or updated more recently, it may work just fine for your short-term needs.

Often, however, the old cabin is not adequate for modern requirements. In such a case, you can remodel it, remodel and add on, tear it down and rebuild, or leave it alone and build a new cabin nearby if local zoning laws allow. We pursued this last option with the cabin we built on a lake in northern Minnesota.

For us, an old hand-hewn log cabin sitting on the lakeside lot we bought was definitely a keeper. I believe it was an old settler's cabin, probably dating from the 1800s, which had possibly been relocated to the site in the 1930s. So it had been on the site for a long time, had seen several owners, and had lots of modifications.

Right from the beginning, we considered a variety of possibilities that included the old log structure, which had three rooms–two tiny sleeping compartments and a common kitchen-eating area. It had an outhouse, and

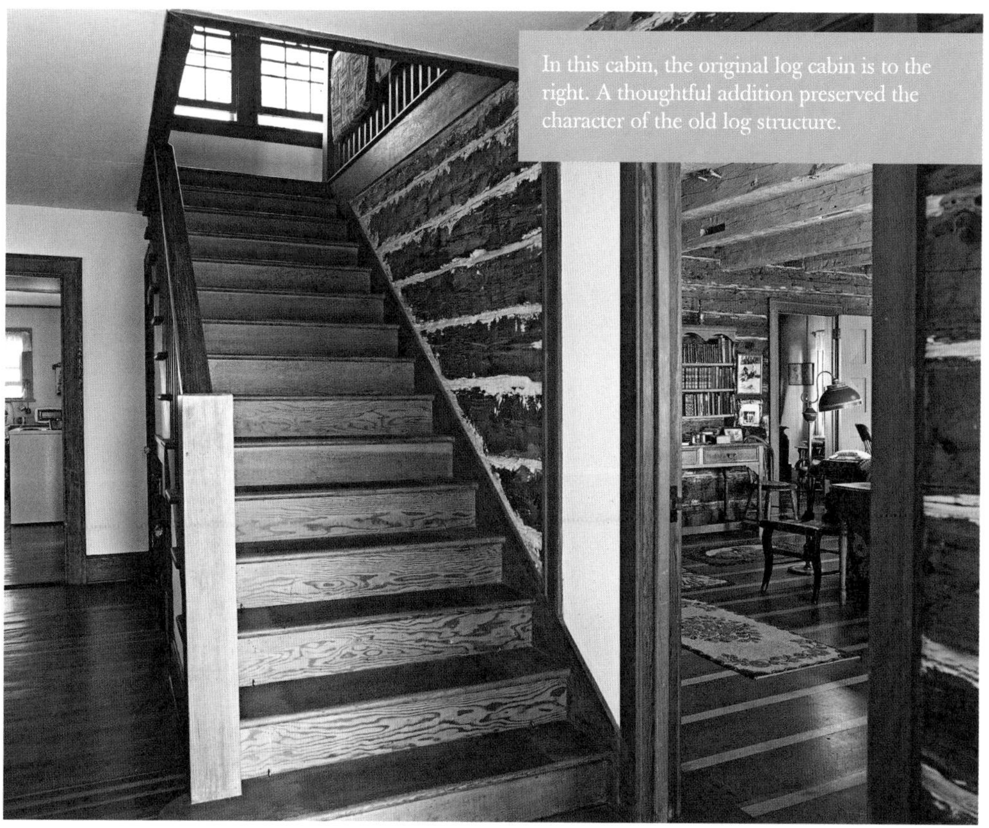

In this cabin, the original log cabin is to the right. A thoughtful addition preserved the character of the old log structure.

CABIN STORIES

ON FOREST LAKE

It seems every Minnesotan family has a cabin. Not a lake home, mind you, but a cabin.

A lake home would signify some luxurious house atop a lush green hill overlooking a vast body of water. And while I'm sure there are plenty of families who do spend their summers enjoying such a home, my family is certainly not one of them.

Nor do we want to be.

Our cabin is just that. A cabin. A crumbling cottage that's been in our family seemingly forever.

Which is why it's perfect. Because it's ours. Because it's crumbling due to the countless memories made both inside its four walls and outside in the brisk waters and on the sandy shores.

I loved Saturday mornings at the lake—I'd sneak my leftover DQ Oreo Blizzard from the night before out of the freezer and sit too close to the television as I watched all my favorite Saturday morning cartoons.

Before I was born, before my parents were even married and my dad was raising his other four children on his own, for a time he lived there with my siblings.

Sure, there were enough bedrooms, but the cabin itself is no bigger than my Manhattan studio apartment. And all four kids plus my grown-man father managed to survive and thrive in our perfect crumbling cabin on Forest Lake.

Up until age 13 when I became too cool for family and started spending my weekends hanging with friends, every Friday, when my dad would come home from work, we'd load up the car and head to the cabin.

We'd spend the entire weekend there, fishing, swimming, skiing, grilling, and swatting mosquitoes, and we wouldn't leave until Sunday evening at sundown, after we'd watched the lake wholly swallow the descending blazing-orange sun.

I loved the fact that, unlike in my "pristine" room at home, at the cabin my dog, Tiger (and later, Zipper), was allowed to sleep in my bed with me.

I loved Saturday mornings at the lake—I'd sneak my leftover DQ Oreo Blizzard® from the night before out of the freezer and sit too close to the television as I watched all my favorite Saturday morning cartoons.

I'd wait patiently—or rather, impatiently—for my parents to wake and my older siblings to arrive at the lake with their friends. I loved tagging along with the big kids no matter what they did.

I'm convinced this is why I learned to water-ski so young (the age of 5). They all water-skied, and water-skied well, so I had to learn, too.

In the meantime, after eating Blizzards for breakfast and watching cartoons, I'd run over to my neighbor's house and spend a few hours pretending I was an Olympic trampoline jumper as I practiced all my death-defying feats (butt-sits and aerials, respectively) on their trampoline.

As it goes, through the years everything changed.

My family shifted. My sister lives in Chicago and I moved to New York, so it's no longer just

Marissa Kristal and a stringer of pan fish in days gone by.

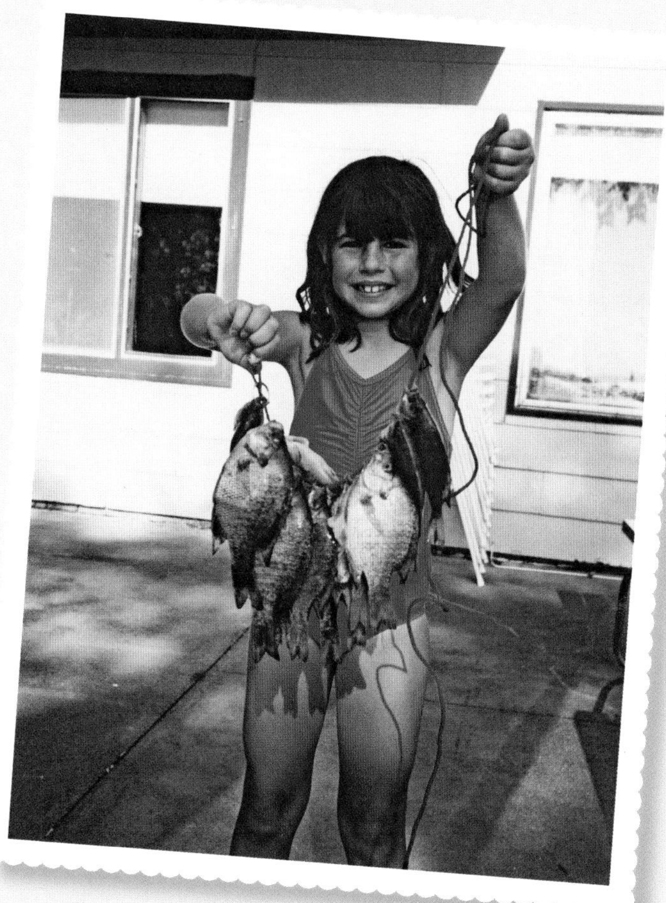

the five of us. And my immediate family has grown extensively.

I no longer spend my summer weekends at my cabin in Forest Lake. Sadly, I no longer spend any weekends at my cabin on Forest Lake. Except for one. I always manage to make it out for the Fourth of July.

The years might fly, the family will continue to transform, the future may see us all living in different locations, but the one thing that will forever remain the same is Forest Lake on the Fourth of July. Fireworks, parades, bonfires, barbecues, family.

And our perfect, crumbling cottage filled with infinite memories inside its four walls, and laughter and love lapping the shores of our sparkling, brisk waters.

–Marissa Kristal is a writer living in New York City (reprinted by permission of the Forest Lake Times, *Forest Lake, Minnesota).*

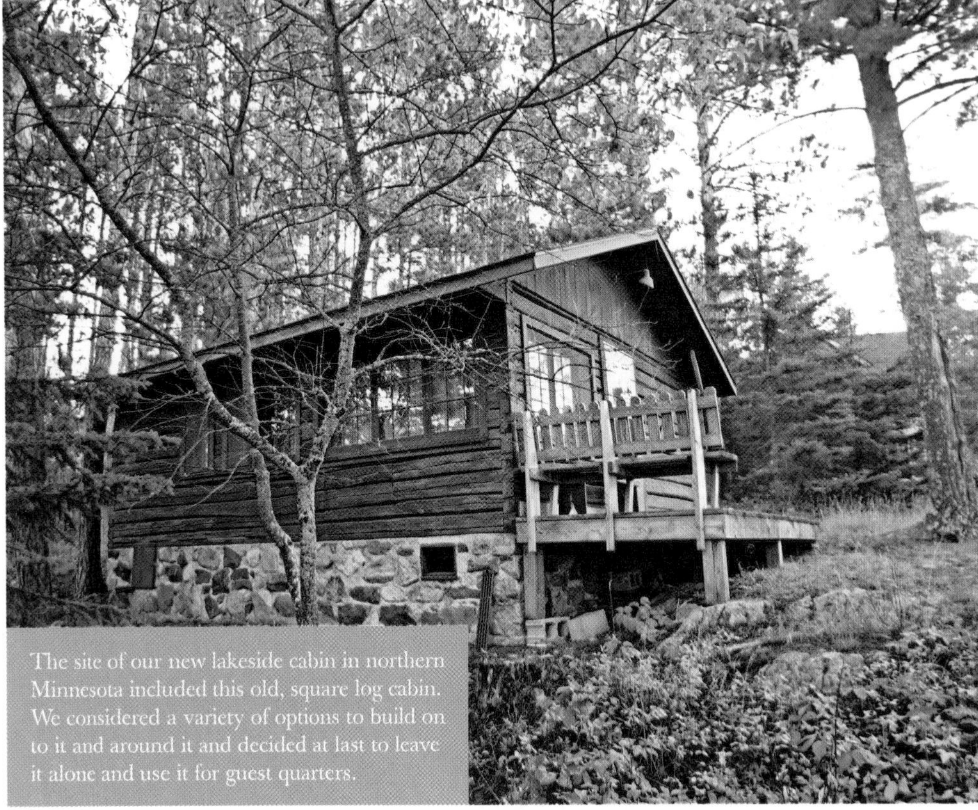

The site of our new lakeside cabin in northern Minnesota included this old, square log cabin. We considered a variety of options to build on to it and around it and decided at last to leave it alone and use it for guest quarters.

we used that for two years. First, we explored various design scenarios that included an addition to the cabin. For instance, one solution was to treat the log cabin as a room. We would gut it and, in the rebuilding, construct other rooms around it with the old cabin as the core. We looked at this option in a variety of ways and with a variety of additions.

The old cabin has logs on the outside but is sheathed over with cheap paneling on the inside. My thought was to reverse that. If we were creating an insulated environment, we could sheathe it on the outside and open it up to the logs on the inside. By removing the partition walls, it would've made a nice living space. It has nice views to the water. It's placed on the site just beautifully. The addition would've been on the opposite side of the cabin from the lake, away from the water. I would've left the window side alone and gone out the back side, up two stories. We looked at building on top of it. We thought through a variety of scenarios.

It was probably our partner in the cabin (an architect/professor at the University of Minnesota, where I teach cabin design) who explored the possibility of leaving the old cabin alone and building the new one near it.

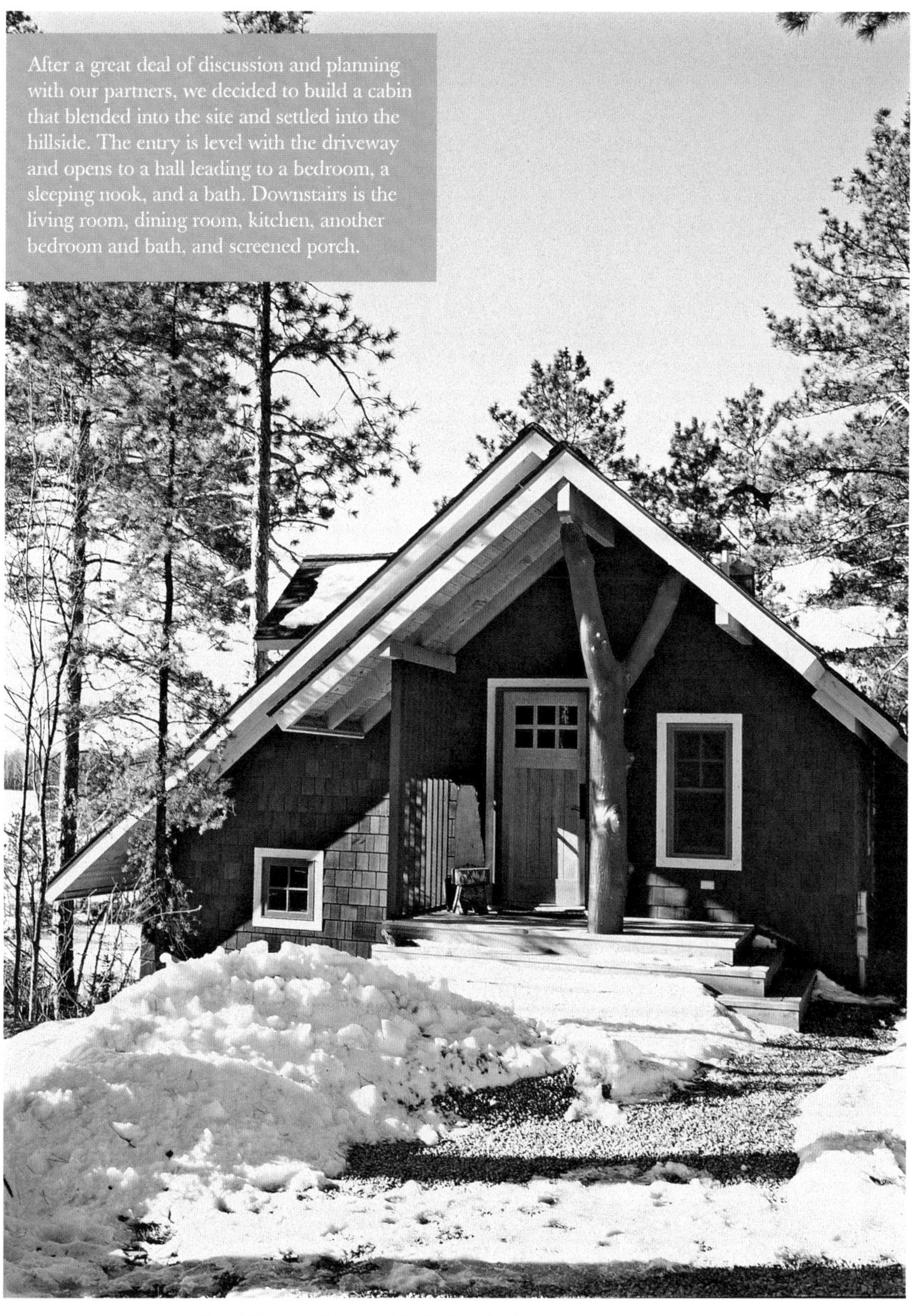

After a great deal of discussion and planning with our partners, we decided to build a cabin that blended into the site and settled into the hillside. The entry is level with the driveway and opens to a hall leading to a bedroom, a sleeping nook, and a bath. Downstairs is the living room, dining room, kitchen, another bedroom and bath, and screened porch.

"What sets a canoeing expedition apart is that it purifies you more rapidly and inescapably than any other travel. Travel a thousand miles by train and you are a brute; pedal five hundred on a bicycle and you remain basically a bourgeois; paddle a hundred in a canoe and you are already a child of nature."

–Pierre Elliott Trudeau, former Canadian Prime Minister, 1919–2000

Suddenly, we were no longer constrained by designing something that fit with the old cabin; we were freed up to explore all sorts of possibilities. Ultimately, we decided that the old cabin lacked many of the attributes that were of critical importance.

IT'S REALLY YOURS

If your experience is like mine and that of countless others (some of which you'll find in the "Cabin Stories" throughout the book), your cabin site will quickly become something personal and unique. It will be the object of your daydreams when you're away and your objective when you need a break from the everyday.

Eventually, if you're lucky, the cabin will be your year-round home when you retire or a seasonal retreat where you spend the better half of every year.

Whatever spot you choose and whatever you decide to do at the cabin, once it's yours, it's a very special place. All the money in the world can't buy the memories and experiences you'll have in your own private hideaway. And although you might still think you'll live forever, there are worse bequests than leaving a cabin to your kids along with a heart full of great memories.

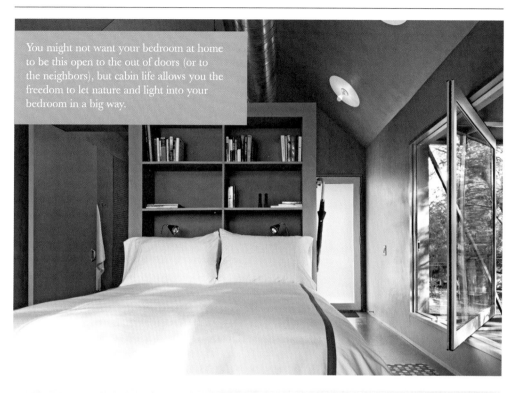

You might not want your bedroom at home to be this open to the out of doors (or to the neighbors), but cabin life allows you the freedom to let nature and light into your bedroom in a big way.

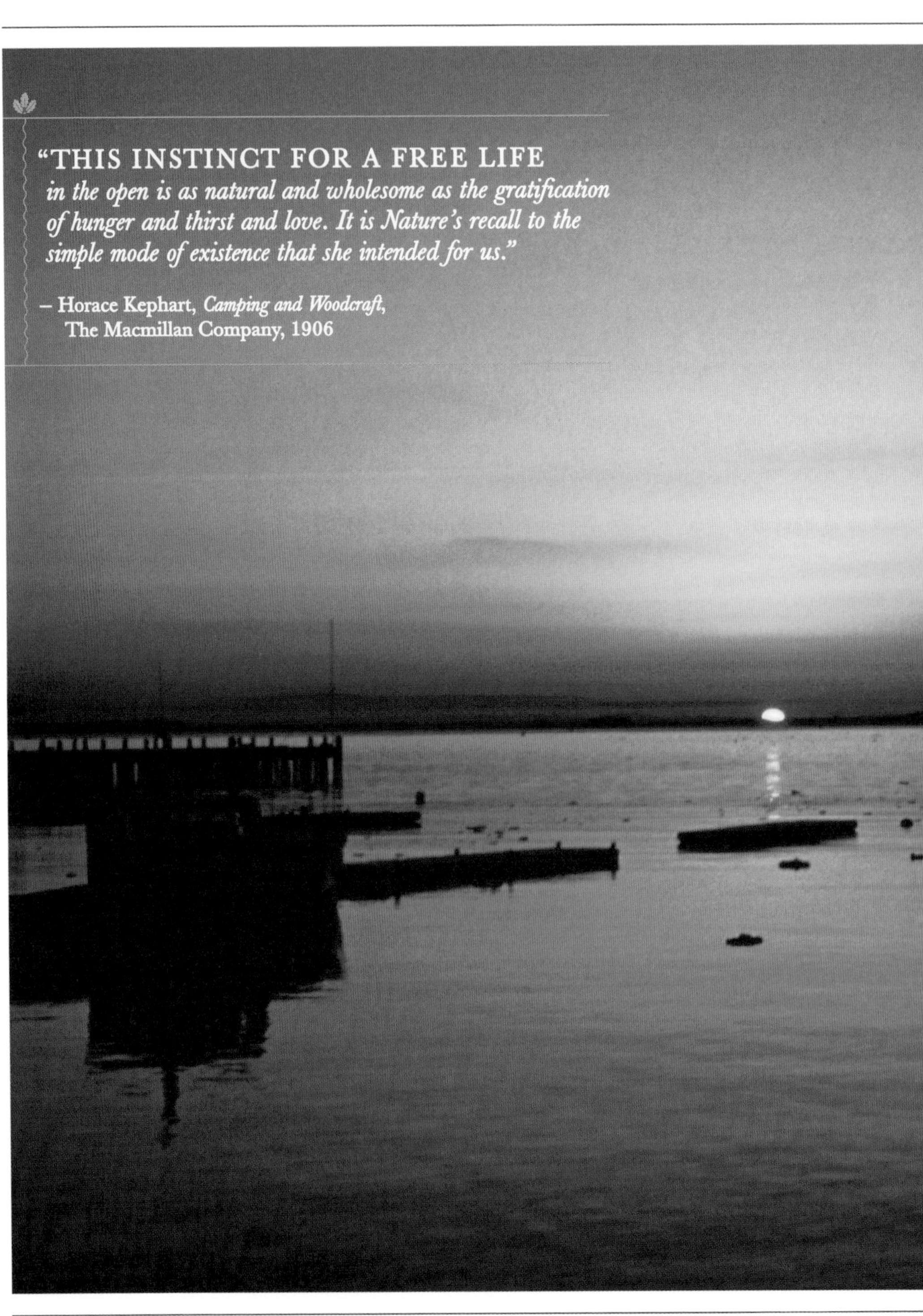
"THIS INSTINCT FOR A FREE LIFE
in the open is as natural and wholesome as the gratification of hunger and thirst and love. It is Nature's recall to the simple mode of existence that she intended for us."
– Horace Kephart, *Camping and Woodcraft*,
The Macmillan Company, 1906

MAKING THE CABIN YOUR OWN

CHAPTER THREE

THE SEARCH IS OVER. After months of driving around and getting lost, researching, e-mailing, studying maps, talking on the phone, Googling, hiking up muddy dead-end roads, running from dogs, and drinking bad coffee with realtors, you found the cabin you want (or the land where you want to build).

You're ready for the fun part: the cabin itself.

For now it's not important whether you're building or remodeling. What's important is to focus your creative efforts, to think in practical terms about that cabin vision you've got stuck in your head–to channel it, to fashion it, to realize it. To make it yours.

You need to have a frank discussion with yourself, to ask yourself lots of questions, and to answer yourself honestly (hopefully, you'll know if you're telling yourself the truth). Your goal is to figure out what your cabin will be, how big it will be, and how it will be built or remodeled. It's time to consider which way it should face and whether

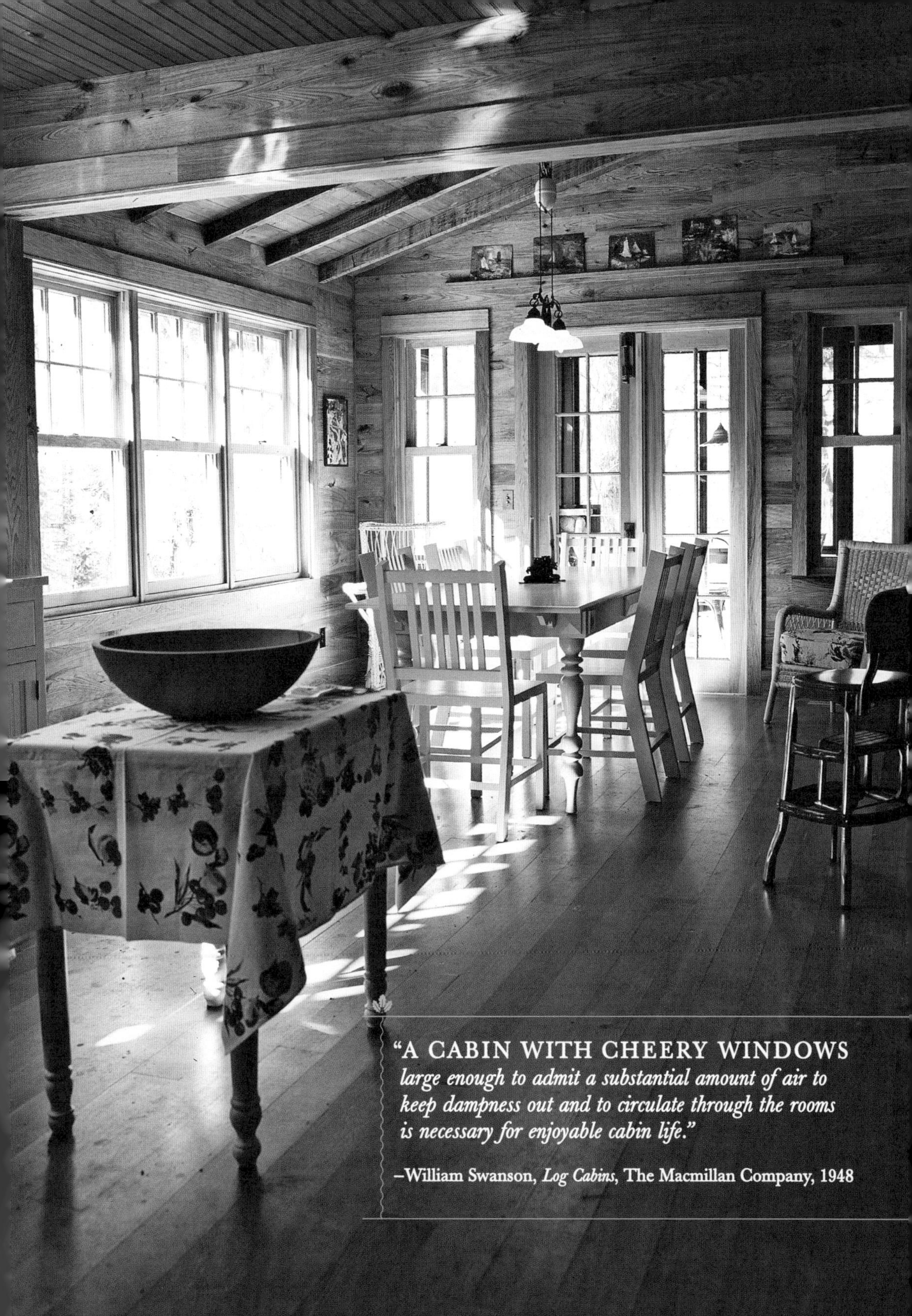

"A CABIN WITH CHEERY WINDOWS *large enough to admit a substantial amount of air to keep dampness out and to circulate through the rooms is necessary for enjoyable cabin life."*

–William Swanson, *Log Cabins*, The Macmillan Company, 1948

it should have two bedrooms or three. If you add on, do you go up or out or both? Does it have a screened porch or a deck? Indoor plumbing or an outhouse? A fancy, full-size, regulation kitchen or just a small galley large enough for one?

HOW DO WE GET FROM HERE .... TO THERE

As important as these questions are, however, they are secondary. First, you'll ask yourself more primary questions. Those answers will help you narrow your choices–in a good way.

WHO'S GOING TO USE IT?

So who's going to use your cabin? That's a stupid question. You'll use it, of course. But who else? Your spouse and kids. Maybe your grandkids and your brother and his kids.

Perhaps your next-door neighbors. Not the ones who can't stop talking about how much money their son makes, but the other ones. The ones with the boat. And maybe your college roommate when he happens to pass through.

Or maybe the cabin is to be your Fortress of Solitude, your personal and private getaway, your special spot, to be shared with only that very special person–or perhaps with no one at all.

Whatever your answer, the *who* question is an important starting point when thinking about and planning just what kind of cabin your cabin will be. Along with your budget, these answers will help you figure out most of the decisions that are to come.

WELL, WHO ELSE?

The *who* question is more complicated than it seems because it's a two-parter. The first part is who, specifically, will be using the cabin? What are their names?

Part two is who, in a general sense, are those folks? Grown-ups? Grown-ups and kids? Young adults, older people, a crowd large or small or somewhere in between? Big kids or little kids? Maybe business associates? And how many of whomever they are will be using the cabin at a given time or during a typical season? And what in the world will they do while they're there?

Dealing with these questions isn't just you having idle chitchat with yourself. It's actually an important part of the planning process. For instance, I'm rarely at our cabin by myself. It's even a memorable occasion when my wife and I have the place to ourselves. Sometimes we're there with the couple we built the cabin with. More often than not we're there with some combination of family and friends, a group that ranges from old

ABOVE: A stormy day will keep the kids indoors. To keep them out of your hair, be sure to have places where the kids can play, nap, or read.

BELOW: As you're planning your remodel or new cabin, imagine all the people you'll regularly invite to enjoy it with you and create a list. This list will affect your decisions on the kitchen, sleeping facilities, and baths.

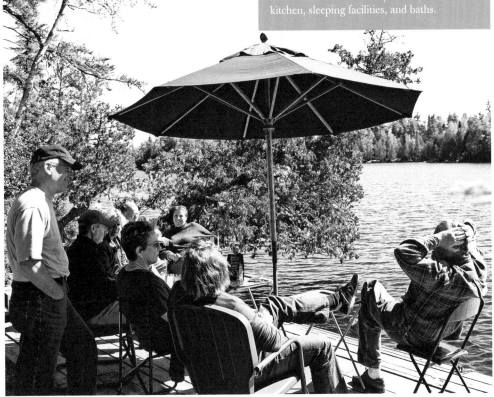

folks to infants, with a dog or two thrown in to keep things interesting.

At our cabin, a typical Fourth of July dawn breaks to a dozen or more kith and kin scattered throughout the premises–on the porch, in the loft, on a hideaway couch, and, of course, filling every bedroom and, often, filling every square foot of floor space with sleeping bags. If the group gets any larger, we pitch tents in the yard–and it's happened. Although it's tempting to associate a cabin with privacy and solitude, most of the cabins I know are more often temporary centers of great and diverse activity and lots of people taking part.

AND WHAT WILL THEY DO THERE?

Hard on the heels of *who* comes *how* and *when*. How will you and your guests–or, for that matter, just you all by your lonesome–use that cabin? And when are you most likely to be there? Will you likely spend most of your time outside? Is your idea of a great time at the cabin to be in, or on, the lake?

Do you plan to go to the cabin year-round or mostly during the summer? Will your cabin be where you get away from all the hiking, birding, golfing, skiing, and snowmobiling, or will it be the center of that activity, your clubhouse in the woods? Is solitude what you're seeking? Will the cabin be like a real home (and maybe, eventually, be your full-time home) or "merely" a home away from home?

Questions, questions, questions. But it's important to have this conversation now. I've found that the wisest step at this point is to make a list of who you expect to use the cabin, how they're likely to use it, and when they're likely to be there. Like other parts of the cabin experience, the list will be subject to change, or at least some tweaking. In some cases, dreams will have to bow to reality. A freestanding "dormitory" for the cousins may be neither practical nor affordable. Or maybe you'll decide that having a place for your in-laws and their kids is not something you want at any cost. Maybe they're part of what you're getting away from.

STAY FLEXIBLE

If you're like me (and I'm probably like most cabin owners), your cabin will be many things to many people. What's important is that you either buy, or design and build, a cabin that meets as many of your needs as you can afford–as well as those of the folks who will share the cabin with you. It's a pretty big investment of time, money, and personal energy, and you might as well squeeze the most out of it.

Given the informality of cabins, the wise and happy cabin owner is flexible and adaptable. When it comes to getting the group together for a weekend at the cabin, you've got options. You can expand. You can improvise.

Say you have two kids under the age of 10. If that's the case, then a bedroom (for you and your spouse) and a pair of bunks should do you for the time being. But then your kids have cousins and then they get older and have friends they want to bring along for a long weekend. Even if you don't have another bedroom, you've created the space and have the resources (a hide-a-bed, porch sofa, air mattresses, sleeping bags, tents, etc.) to accommodate others when necessary–to expand your guest capacity.

I will arise and go now, and go to Innisfree,
And a small cabin build there, of clay and watt
le:
Nine bean rows will I have there, a hive for the
bee,
And live alone in the bee-loud glade.
And I sh
e some peace there, for pea
Droppi
the veils of the morning t
There
s all a glimmer, and noon
he linnet's wings
BIRD WATCHING
Hoopla
Yahtzee
CRANIUM
the game for your whole brain

This interesting niche contains a wood-burning stove along with flexible accommodations for sleep, play, and storage. The quotation on the wall is from *Lake Isle of Innisfree* by William Butler Yeats.

You generally have more options in the summer, when people can sleep under the stars or out on the porch. You'll have fewer options come winter, when the temperature dips below freezing and your fieldstone fireplace becomes the big draw. But being able to adapt to contingencies and opportunity, whenever they arise, is an important characteristic of a well-designed cabin.

The bottom line is that the choices you make about the size, design, and configuration of your cabin follow from the answers to your *who, how,* and *when* questions. And they apply to all the cabin's basic functions–that is, to everything you and your guests are going to want to do there, from the moment you arrive.

BEDS, BUNKS, AND SLEEPING BAGS

Whatever big plans you have for your cabin, everybody who shows up will need a place to sleep. Because no matter how energetic you all are, no matter how much time you spend fishing, exploring, hiking, swimming, or skiing, you and the folks you've invited to stay will spend more time in or on a bed, bunk, futon, sofa, or other horizontal surface than anywhere else on the premises.

It's amazing, when you think about it, how many places a sleepy person can crash when the last game of Scrabble® is played at the end of a long summer's day and the sound of crickets overtakes the fading conversation. Sure, there are beds and sofas. But how about that broad window seat where just this morning your wife was reading Stephen King and at dinner Uncle Billy messily enjoyed those fish you all caught that afternoon? If that window seat is long and soft enough, one or

I created this diagram to help figure out where everybody who might possibly come to our cabin at any given time might find a place to sleep. Note the different numbers for summer and winter.

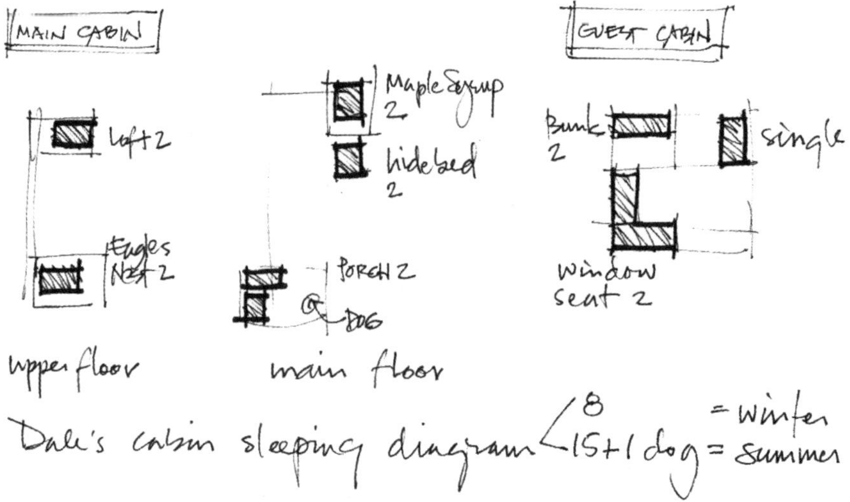

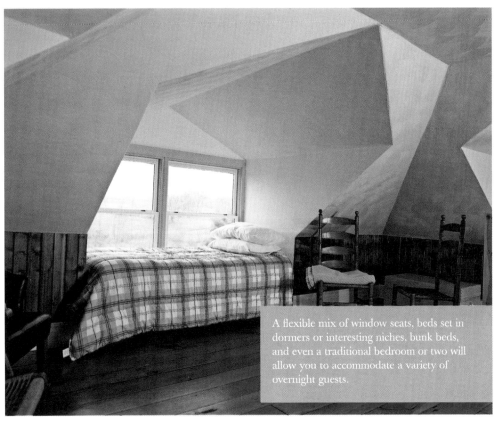

A flexible mix of window seats, beds set in dormers or interesting niches, bunk beds, and even a traditional bedroom or two will allow you to accommodate a variety of overnight guests.

more of the kids will be more than happy to sack out there.

Adults long accustomed to king-size Select Comforts at home may get a kick out of a night or two in a bunk bed or in a sleeping bag on the living room floor (sweet memories of childhood).

Just like dogs, kids usually find their own nighttime spots. We have a small loft in our cabin, just large enough for a queen-size mattress. This is the "bedroom" of choice for our grade-school-age grandchildren. Far from keeping them awake, our muted late-night banter in the sitting room below has an uncanny way of lulling them to sleep. It's a comfort to them: The adults are on night watch and nothing bad can happen.

If you expect a range of both ages and relationships, you'll want even more flexibility in your sleeping accommodations. Some folks will want to arrange themselves by family and gender and some by whether they rise early or sleep late. In general, the larger the cabin, the more diversity of type and activity the sleeping accommodations can comfortably handle.

SLEEPING ALL AROUND

Cabin life is blessedly informal, so rules that usually decide when and where we sleep (or nap) don't strictly apply. At the cabin, even a fussbudget can't possibly expect the peace and quiet he's used to at home. On the other hand, if kids are likely to share the same general area with adults, some degree of privacy must be possible. That may mean separate bedrooms, a loft, a sleeping porch attached to the cabin, or perhaps a freestanding bunkhouse or sleeping space in the attic above the garage or boathouse. Or, weather permitting, a screened-in gazebo or a flat space for tents in the yard.

Essential as they are, however, cabin bedrooms don't need to be large or nearly as well equipped as their full-time counterparts at home. That's because most of what you do at the cabin takes place somewhere else, inside or out. You generally need only a bed, a nightstand for a lamp and a book, and space enough to maneuver around them.

PLANNING THE ACCOMMODATIONS

Most cabin visits are short (often only a night or two), so guests will be okay living out of packs, suitcases, and overnight bags. Instead of a closet and dresser, wall pegs and a bench usually suffice. If you really want a closet, maybe it has a colorful draw curtain that requires less space than a door (that needs room to open), adds color, and saves you bucks.

At a cabin, you don't need a special linen closet or anything of the sort for sheets and blankets–they only need to be accessible

TIP **THE PRIVACY NONISSUE, PART I**

I know of a small cabin where the "sleeping quarters" was an unusual bunk bed consisting of upper and lower *double* beds. A pair of septuagenarian brothers and their wives have used the bunks happily and without reported strife for many decades.

Here, sleeping is informal and out in the open. A small twin bed in the corner and a set of bunk beds work for the owners of this three-season cabin.

CABIN MATTERS

GUEST QUARTERS

In your eagerness to share your getaway with family and friends, you may be tempted to build your guest cabin (or, say, guest quarters above the garage) before you build anything else. That's fine, but beware of overbuilding.

I know of several new cabin owners who equipped the guest areas with everything they had in mind for the main cabin—only to discover that they could no longer afford what they had in mind for the main place.

ABOVE: The guest structure can be anything from a small dormitory to a fully formed small cabin with its own kitchen and bath.

LEFT: This interesting closet has no doors but does have built-in storage and ample room for hanging clothes. And I could imagine, in a pinch, a child sleeping on top of the built-ins on a small pallet of blankets.

BELOW: If you think "outside the box," you see the benefits of a doorless closet. It can combine pegs for coats and hats, a shelf above, and drawers below, or it can contain a sleeping or reading nook with a large cushion above built-in drawers.

(at our place, we color-code them according to mattress size). My wife and I chose bed platforms with built-in storage that make the most of otherwise wasted space underneath. That space is especially handy for blankets, luggage, and out-of-season cabin clothes.

Even given the availability, a bedroom may not be the sleeping space of choice for some of your guests. When my daughter and her husband steal away to our cabin in midwinter, they open the living room hide-a-bed and sleep in front of the fireplace. (In cold weather, a cozy cabin seems even cozier.) During the day, they play Scrabble and read on the bed's soft, spacious surface, warmed by a crackling fire.

ADDING A BUNKHOUSE

The only obvious exception to the size rule for sleeping places pertains to bunkhouses, especially if you want one for your kids, their cousins, and their friends, who would appreciate getting away from the adults.

The bunkhouse could be freestanding, either a few feet away from the cabin or on the far side of the property. Or it could be a "house" in name only, situated in the attic above the garage, or a simple log lean-to set just into the woods. (Many cabin garages are constructed with storage trusses overhead, so an ever-ready sleeping area is preengineered into the space.)

Wherever you put it, that separate sleeping space often becomes the site of some of the happiest cabin memories that you, your kids, and friends will file away in that mental scrapbook of favorite places: pillow fights, ghost stories, and adventure books read under the covers by flashlight long after Mom or Dad calls, "Lights out."

THE BARE BEDROOM NECESSITIES

- When you're reading in bed, you'll need enough electrical illumination to complement whatever ambient light you might have.
- As a charming, practical, and cost-saving alternative to air-conditioning, a ceiling fan may be all you need to keep cool on warm nights. Or pick up an old oscillating fan or two at a garage sale (they're generally much quieter than new mostly plastic fans) and let it blow.
- Natural light and ventilation are important considerations (and not only for places where people sleep). Windows on two walls provide sunshine and cross breezes. Dormers and skylights can be interesting variations to achieve the same pleasant effects.
- Extra sleeping space can be found in nearly every room, from hide-a-bed sofas in a living room, window seats in dining rooms, and a book nook on the stair landing.
- Cabin bedrooms are usually just for sleeping so keep them small and intimate with built-in storage.
- Mine the roof volume for multiple lofts. The children in your family will adore you for it.

“YOUR CABIN-IN-THE-WOODS
can be a perfect cure for restlessness. If you are restless today, you may be even more restless ten years from now, unless you do something about it now. Life brings increasing cares. So going to your dream-spot month after month, year in and year out, you will experience a re-charging, a rehabilitation, a re-creating . . . In this way after each visit you will return to your city life rested, stronger, revived.”

–Conrad Meinecke, *Your Cabin in the Woods,* Foster & Stewart Publishing Corporation, 1945

A cabin kitchen can be big and fancy or, more appropriately, relaxed and functional. Storage can take the form of display or can be cabinets with doors–built-in or freestanding. All you really need is a place for everything and a couple of places for people to work, such as a countertop and a table.

COOKING, EATING, AND HANGING OUT

If you're my age, the next most important thing you do at your cabin after sleeping is cooking and eating. Everybody loves to eat–and nowhere does eating become such an all-consuming, day-and-night, not-just-at-mealtime preoccupation than at a cabin. Cooking and dining need an appropriate amount of space, but so do food storage, cleanup, and garbage disposal.

While you're figuring out what kind of kitchen you'll have, it's a good idea to again consider the *who* question. Who's going to cook (chances are, it won't be only Mom or Grandma) and who will they be cooking for? Are you talking about intimate little gatherings around a candlelit table, or mass meals on which every flat surface in and around the cabin is groaning with good things to eat and drink?

Is the "chef" sophisticated and creative? Is the "clientele" worldly and discerning? (The latter questions have to do with equipment and resources more than space and configuration. The rarely used wedding present percolator may not be good enough for modern, Starbucks®-trained coffee drinkers craving an after-dinner espresso.)

It could be that yours is a meat-and-potatoes crowd that believes the more there is to eat and drink the better. But then you may have a few oddballs who need special treatment. For instance, will there be special requests from a vegan son or daughter-in-law, for example, who drinks only soy milk? Or meals to accommodate a diabetic? Or maybe you'll find yourself entertaining the simply finicky? These types of considerations are no different at the cabin than they are at home. It's just that maintaining a sufficient supply of "natural" or "organic" products requires more planning at a location 80 miles from the nearest co-op health-food market than it does in the city.

YOU CAN'T HAVE TOO MANY COOKS

Whatever your and your friends' tastes, fixing food is a team sport. Instead of the old caution about having too many hands stirring the pot, at the cabin, the more the merrier.

Today, cooking and eating are group activities, which truly couldn't be more so than at the cabin, where breakfast, lunch, and dinner (and all the places where you eat all this food) enjoy a freedom of expression that can't be matched at home. Even if everyone

A log ripped lengthwise, sanded, finished, and bolted to the island countertop seems an appropriate serving area for this cabin kitchen.

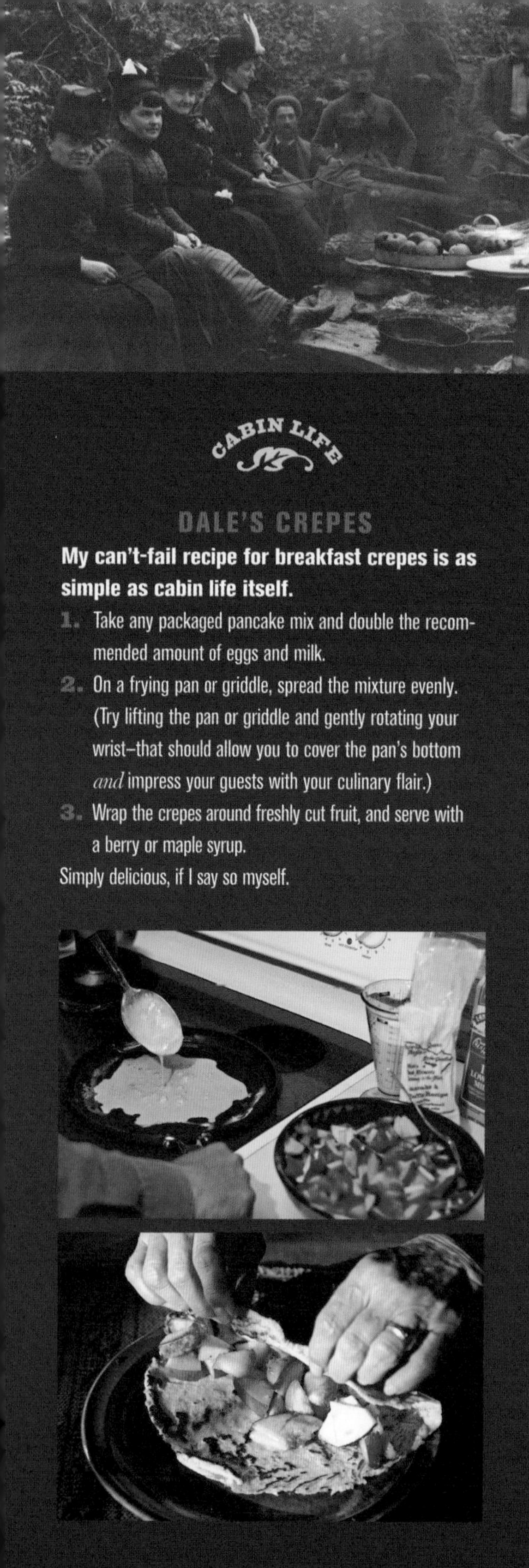

CABIN LIFE

DALE'S CREPES

My can't-fail recipe for breakfast crepes is as simple as cabin life itself.

1. Take any packaged pancake mix and double the recommended amount of eggs and milk.
2. On a frying pan or griddle, spread the mixture evenly. (Try lifting the pan or griddle and gently rotating your wrist–that should allow you to cover the pan's bottom *and* impress your guests with your culinary flair.)
3. Wrap the crepes around freshly cut fruit, and serve with a berry or maple syrup.

Simply delicious, if I say so myself.

isn't actually helping get the food ready and on the table, everyone seems more than happy to hang out and be part of the energy.

In our family, my wife–an exceptional cook–cooks just about everything we eat. At the cabin, however, I pull the chef's hat over my big head at breakfast time, when crepes are the house specialty. I love both the cooking and the conversation that starts burbling as our guests smell the coffee, rouse themselves from their bunks and bedrolls, and straggle into the kitchen–without even a thought about how their hair looks.

In our modest cabin, the dining-room table and chairs are just a few feet from the kitchen work area, not separated by walls and doors. We also put out stools around the countertop for those who want to keep a sharp eye on the cook. (Not a bad idea.) When my crepes are ready, I serve them buffet-style from the counter, and to those more formal breakfasters seated at the table, I actually walk over and roll one out of the skillet and onto their plates. Providing seconds (and thirds) and cleaning up afterward is just as casual and easy.

KITCHEN ESSENTIALS

Our kitchen is L-shaped, with an island in the middle, the most popular configuration I see nowadays in cabin kitchens. The L can be stretched out in large cabins or compressed for smaller cabins like mine. I've found that when the total countertop, appliance space, and storage area combines for at least 20 linear ft., you've got the bases covered.

In our cabin, the kitchen is designed to allow one or two of us to cook at the same time. The island allows greater movement and flow than, say, a peninsula, and it reduces the potential traffic jams when more of us are working in the kitchen. In an L-shaped kitchen, the large appliances (refrigerator and oven) are typically at either end of the L, with the stovetop, sink, and dishwasher in the middle. In our kitchen, the sink and dishwasher are built into the island, which suits us fine.

For us, the kitchen island is essential. It's the center of our little cabin life and serves a wide range of functions, both at mealtime and throughout the day. Think of it as the cabin's (Starbucks) coffee shop–the place where people enjoy hanging out. With its handy stools, it's where people come together to talk, make plans, and organize the day.

When I'm by myself, I sit right there at the island and read the paper and pay the bills. When suppertime arrives, we come together in the same spot and get to work. Because it's right in the middle of things and is breezy and open, it keeps whoever's working there (or loafing there) in the middle of the conversation and at the center of attention. When it's time to eat, the island is either the buffet table or the dinner table.

Cleanup, likewise, centers on the island. The countertop is raised and wraps around one end of the island, which means that the dishwasher is positioned 6 in. higher than normal (which in this case means 6 in. higher

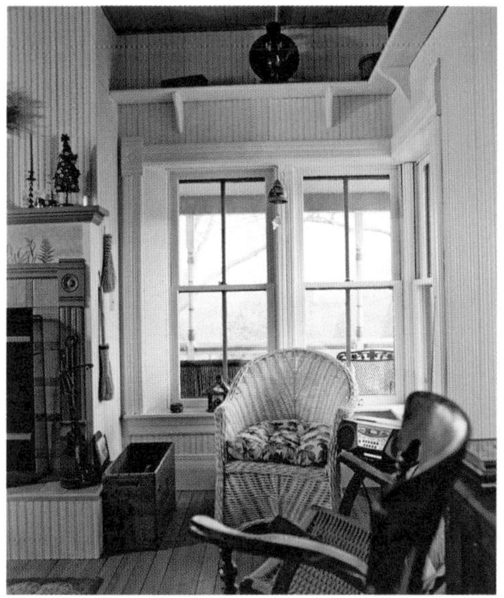

ABOVE: A small sitting area is incorporated into the kitchen/dining area of this cabin.

RIGHT: A two-story ceiling soars above this dining area, which is bounded by the living area, kitchen, and a corner filled with windows.

ABOVE: Even ordinary cups and saucers, glasses, and plates seem special when displayed in open kitchen shelving. An additional benefit is that you always know where everything is.

LEFT AND BELOW: This kitchen provides multiple eating and work areas. A long table acts as an island and eating bar and the more formal dining table is set apart, off the wood floor, for a traditional dining experience.

than it is at home). I didn't come up with the idea, but I'm happy to accept the compliments of ad hoc cooks who think I'm quite clever to have created this higher workspace, which reduces stooping and bending.

At the open end of the island is a microwave oven that's convenient to the cooks and to the grandkids who want to make popcorn. And it's built in, which frees up valuable counter space.

WHERE WILL YOU EAT?

The island is dandy for little groups eating lunch or dinner. It's great for eating on the fly. It's the preferred dining venue of the early riser and the latecomer, as well as the day-round snacker. Big dinners, though, need an official dining table.

In our cabin, the dining table is only a few steps away from the kitchen. This is where we serve the big dinners (walleye, beer bread, fresh blueberries over homemade ice cream). It's the spot for Scrabble and Monopoly® competitions, giant jigsaw puzzles, and my granddaughter's paper-doll project.

With the place full of guests (the overnight variety, along with our cabin neighbors and local friends), we move out to the screened porch where a trestle table provides extremely comfortable dining al fresco (by this I mean that the screen keeps out the bugs and the ceiling fan on low above the table keeps things cool even when it's unseasonably hot).

(I don't want to go overboard about the sweetness of cabin life, but there's quite honestly nothing like the taste of pan-fried sunfish–flour batter or cornmeal–that you caught in the afternoon served beside green beans and peaches you bought from a farm stand a couple of hours before dinner. Close your eyes and you can actually be there: a breeze perfumed by pine coming lightly off the lake, the peaceful soundlessness of a canoe slipping across the water, a loon crooning out its lonesome cry, the light sound of children playing nearby knitting itself into the background noise of ice settling in glasses, plates rattling, and burdens lifting. It's heaven.)

Sometimes the meal truly is al fresco–right out in the fresh outdoor air and bright sun (or not-so-bright dusk). Eating breakfast off a tray on the dock and wolfing down chicken sandwiches and potato salad during a shore lunch–everyone loves it. Who wouldn't look forward to drinks and appetizers on the pontoon boat as the sun bows out for the day?

PUTTING THINGS AWAY

Are you inclined to keep coffee pots, the toaster, and food mixer out on the kitchen counter or neatly tucked away in cabinet storage? Will the counter need space for a favorite cookie jar, sugar tin, and pencil basket? And where will the vases for the wildflowers, the extra scouring pads, and the baking trays be stored?

Walk through your kitchen at home and make a list of what you will need to store at the cabin and where. You might not need the Thanksgiving turkey roaster or the fall canning jars, but you will need to cover the basics.

Because there's not a supermarket around the corner, food storage is especially important. You'll want a cupboard or pantry that provides lots of shelf space, yet doesn't get in the way. Many practical cabin owners like open shelves, which tend to increase efficiency and make it easier for visitors to find things. Some, however, think the open shelves require more cleaning and make life easier for ants and other pests.

MORE MESSY KITCHEN DETAILS

If you bought an old cabin, updating its electrical wiring will allow you to enjoy all the appliances you have in the city. (If you choose to live without electricity, you have little choice but to rely on propane if you want refrigeration and at least limited cooking.)

Really remote sites require careful choices. For instance, when it comes to the appliances you put in your cabin, you'll probably want to purchase popular brands, for instance, to increase the likelihood of parts and service being available nearby. That exotic $10,000-a-lineal-foot cast-iron French stove won't be much good if it sits idle for weeks while you have to wait for a part to come over from Le Havre.

Then there's the often messy issue of garbage. The gnawed remnants of all the food that arrived in a dozen grocery bags and several coolers must now, at week's end, be hauled out. That includes too many aluminum cans, glass bottles, and other recyclables to count and way more ripe refuse than you care to think about. In most areas, you can incinerate wastepaper out back, but composting will be difficult unless you spend enough time at the cabin to formulate biological digestion using grass clippings and other organic matter. Meanwhile, you don't want your garbage to attract bears, raccoons, and other scavengers. If we're at the cabin for any length of time, we make a weekly run to the town dump for sanitary disposal and recycling.

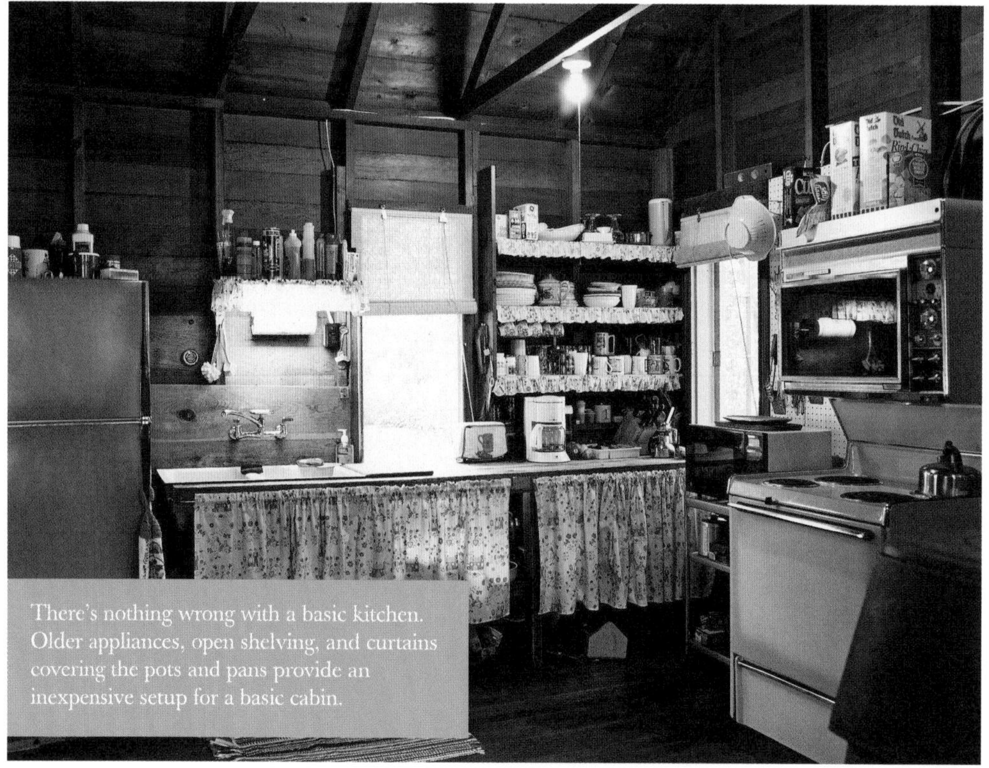

There's nothing wrong with a basic kitchen. Older appliances, open shelving, and curtains covering the pots and pans provide an inexpensive setup for a basic cabin.

What a spectacular place to have lunch, surrounded by incredible views of forest and water and cooled by breezes drifting through the screens.

CABIN STORIES

RAISING LOST LIVES

In the forest, I'd always been a mere visitor. Hiking. Hunting. Enjoying the fall colors. In 2001, however, the opportunity finally came to experience more.

We bought a patch of Pennsylvania mountainside where the Poconos bleed into the New York Catskills. Generations had logged this land and stacked the stones of two bluestone quarries into a variety of old foundations for houses that still stand or that once stood along the road. Men chopped and dug and carried with dirty, thick hands. When I close my eyes, I see teams sawing timber and hear horses pulling logs down the steep, rocky roads.

Their ghosts lurk under our feet. Like a calm, patient ocean, the soil swallowed pieces of them. Ax blades and shovels and chains for pulling felled trees—when your fingers curl around them, the vast span of years almost falls away.

I work in Philadelphia, and in many ways, that life of streetlights and orange nights seems imaginary. Cut the power, and the wonderland disintegrates. I chose to build a log cabin in the old way to feel what it was like to face the frontier. I wanted a little of that lost life to rise again.

So I went to work, and the first thing I learned was the beauty and danger of simple forces: gravity, height, friction, and the power of a strong piece of rope. Machines rip and wrench and can correct nearly any mistake we make. But when you are alone, respect for the simple forces gets the job done. For example, pulling a log downhill is manageable but uphill will grind away your energy for the day. Finding straight trees is not enough. You must find them in the right place.

I chose to build a log cabin the old way to feel what it was like to face the frontier. I wanted a little of that lost life to rise again.

I proceeded slowly, using the ax I found to cut the saddles of simple Swedish joinery. One by one, the logs rose, and each course was an achievement.

Today, I sit eating a green apple from an ancient tree. I'm finishing the cabin with my family now. Hopefully, our children will remember how it felt to raise a shelter with their own hands. The memory will be bittersweet, I'm sure, like the taste of the apple.

Simpler, kinder days are behind us, but future generations will say the same of our time. My experience is a gift to them, and I hope they will pass it on.

– Jason Evans is an attorney in Philadelphia.

I cut the logs and notched the corners in the old way–by hand.

Along with the sense of achievement, the small handmade cabin takes shape.

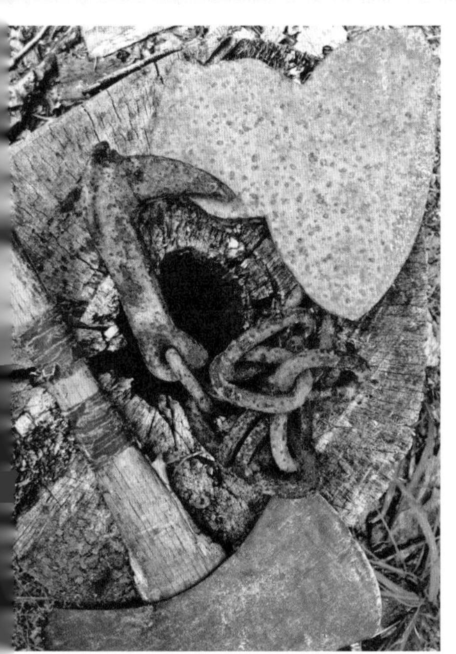

Ax blades, chains, and other old logging iron appeared out of the past.

THE ROOM WITH A VIEW

I'm reluctant to call the sitting area of our cabin the "living room" because we "live" everywhere on the premises. Our cabin has no television, so the sitting area is where we sit (around the fire), read, and engage in the old and distinguished pastime called talking. It's where the grandkids play on rainy days and where adults are given to simply staring out the big windows in silent contemplation of the lake beyond.

Your sitting area doesn't have to be especially large or come with a great view. You may find that the fireplace and your family or friends are all you desire for surroundings. Again, it comes back to wants and needs. If you paid a premium for the view of the mountain, valley, or lake outside your window, you'll want to enjoy it.

SQUEEZING OUT THE MOST VIEW

You may want to highlight the view with a window wall, perhaps in the popular prow shape that juts out and offers a spectacular panorama of the natural world. If the view is of a lake, let's say, a horizontal wall of windows is what you want because a lake is essentially horizontal. If the view is toward a mountain peak, a vertical window wall is what you want. Window walls can be whatever you want them to be (and can afford): They can be designed in an arc, following either a series of bow windows or forming a broad, curving wall, or they can be ganged together in a straight line. With the materials and windows available today, almost anything is possible.

Another, less costly, option is to angle a rectilinear window wall toward the view. I learned the technique from Minnesota architect

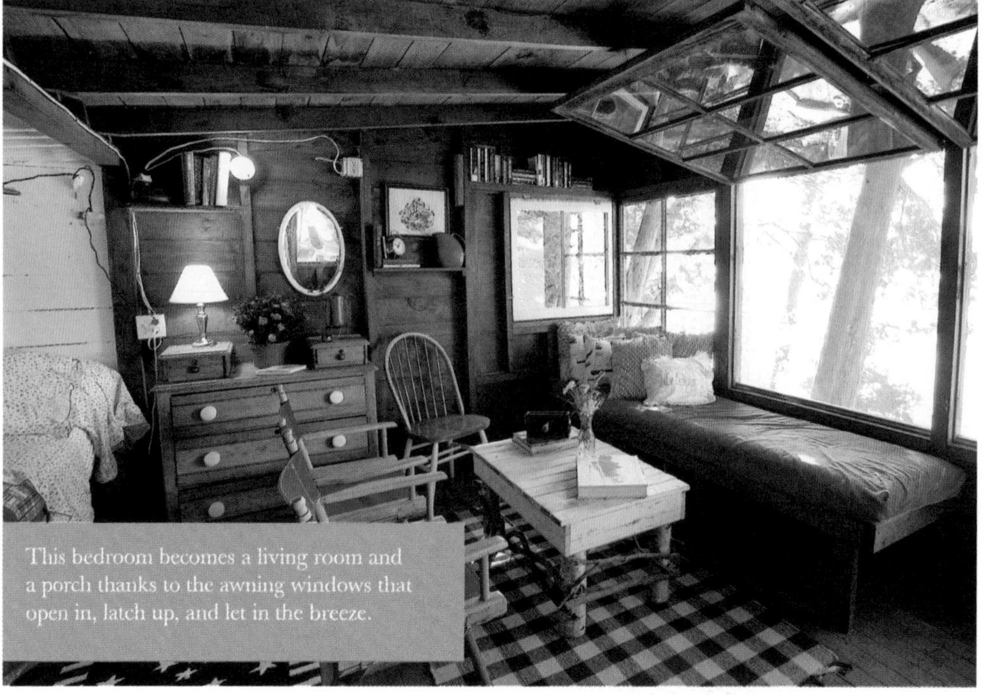

This bedroom becomes a living room and a porch thanks to the awning windows that open in, latch up, and let in the breeze.

This impressive room opens right up to a view of the forest, serving as both a sitting area and a porch.

CABIN LIFE

HAVE A SEAT

Among our cabin's motley furnishings, one of my favorites is the British officer's camp chair. Made up of eight sticks, two canvas slings, and two canvas arm straps, it comfortably accommodates an adult of even my girth. When not in use or when in transit, it can be easily disassembled, rolled into a tube, and stowed away until next time.

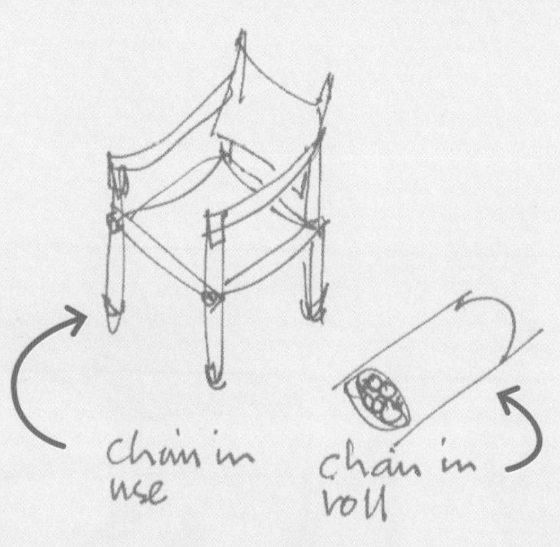

Edwin Lundie, who died just about the time I was getting started in the business. His simple, Scandinavian-styled cabins are located on the majestic North Shore of Lake Superior, with the broad side of the rectangular wall overlooking the vast water and horizon, while the shorter side opens to a closer view of the shoreline.

All things considered, though, the view is ideally best designated a part of the overall attraction of the cabin, available from most locations on the property, and not relegated to the focus of only one spot.

A GOOD PLACE TO SIT

View or no view, in the sitting area you'll want comfortable furniture, plenty of natural and artificial light for reading and playing games, and enough storage for the books and games when you're not using them.

When it comes to sofas and chairs, comfort should trump style if you have to make a choice, and they don't have to be either oversized or overstuffed. Window seats are popular with young and old. And is there anyone who doesn't love a rocking chair?

THE BEATING HEART OF THE CABIN

Ever since we were kids, for that matter ever since as a species we've been able to make a spark and ignite dry leaves, fire has fascinated us. It's no wonder that fire is one of the magic ingredients of cabin life.

It's not a question of why we love staring into a fire. All we need to understand is that we love it–whether we sit and stare into the flames in solitary rapture or whether we're with a

CABIN MATTERS

LUNDIE'S LOVELIES

Edwin Lundie designed several beautifully modest cabins in the Scandinavian tradition of timber framing. Because these cabins were used only during warm weather, they required no insulation and thus exhibited their frames inside and out. The exteriors were painted to protect the wood. With its turned post, this cabin beautifully illustrates Lundie's ability to import rich Scandinavian details into an American setting.

group of friends. Whenever the pull of the day weakens or the conversation lulls, nothing works quite like looking into the flames.

Although some cabin owners opt for the convenience of a gas flame, most of us still crave the glow, crackle, scent, and ritual of a wood fire. And the old adage that "wood warms twice" is all the incentive we need to split that wood with an ax. Gathering and storing firewood to keep it available and suitably dry is one of the primal chores–and pleasures–of cabin life. Building a warm, efficient, long-lasting blaze is one of its arts.

For pure heating efficiency, the best bet is a woodstove positioned in or near the center of the cabin. Woodstoves burn well, radiate their heat around the room, and keep the coffee pot warm. They come in all shapes and sizes, and can be wrapped in soapstone for some degree of heat storage. For late-night arrivals to a cold, damp cabin, the woodstove offers a dependably cheery welcome, heating swiftly and fragrantly while you unpack.

Yet, even for most woodstove devotees, the big stone fireplace remains the irreplaceable icon of cabin life. I've learned that many cabin owners will forgo every other popular amenity while insisting on a large, distinctive fireplace. No matter who uses the cabin and how, you, too, will probably reach the conclusion that the hearth is where the heart is.

With your fireplace comes the prospect of a mantel and a big stone mass from which to project it. Is your favorite picture of the bass catch going to sit on the mantel? Is the elk rack going to hang on the fireplace or will you put the flat-screen TV up there? Would you like some twinkling sconces hung here or a projection of some black iron brackets for those two beautiful kerosene lamps you bought on eBay[SM]?

If wood burning is your choice, you will have to think about where you are storing wood. We store a limited amount within the cabin, enough to have one night's fire upon arrival. Bringing in firewood also brings in

"I HAD DAYDREAMS AND FANTASIE*when I was growing up. I always wanted to live in a log cabin at the foot of a mountain. I would ride my horse to town and pick up provisions. Then return to t cabin, with a big open fire, a record player, and peace.*"

–Linda McCartney, photographer, musician, and animal rights activist, 1941–1998 spiders, bark beetles, and other nasty critters, so a big wood storage bin inside may not be desirable. In winter months, we store additional wood in our screened porch. Beyond that, we have a season's supply in the woodshed.

SOUND AND PICTURE SHOW

One of the most controversial pieces of equipment you have to consider at your cabin is whether to have a television. Today with satellite dishes and digital recordings, we can catch the fall World Series or snuggle up to a rerun of *Gone with the Wind* at our remote location in the woods.

I prefer the absence of TV at our cabin and fortunately so do our cabinmates. Our grandchildren arrive and make note of its absence in the first hour, but after beating their grandmother at Scrabble later that day, they grow to appreciate its absence. And they particularly enjoy attending the 60-seat cinema in the little village down the road where we sit among the antiques and boutique items the cinema vendor also sells.

I also give preference to my local radio stations over an exotic CD collection. Listening to the bluegrass music racked up by DJ "Rainbow Trout" or the call-in-hour program called "Green Cheese" all adds to the charm of my up-north getaway.

But if your cabin needs a complex sound system for Jimi Hendrix CDs and a large-screen TV for a big family night at the movies, well, then it's best to plan ahead so seating, wiring, and the popcorn stand can all be accounted for up front.

FIRING UP

The key to a sure-starting fire is the kindling.

Because I spend a lot of time around construction sites, I have access to plenty of 2x4 stud scraps, which I collect, haul to our cabin, and split with a hatchet.

When it's time for a fire, I lay several pieces of the split studs across a crumpled sheet or two of newspaper. Then I lay a few slabs of split birch atop the kindling. (You could also toss dried pinecones on the heap.)

Apply a lit match to both ends of the paper, and enjoy one of the great pleasures of cabin life.

A black iron wood-burning stove and its tall, black stovepipe are set in the middle of this room so that heat radiates throughout the space rather than being drawn up a chimney as occurs with a standard fireplace.

CABIN STORIES

OUR SPECIAL PLACE

Our special place is a small log cabin nestled in the mountains of Cascade, Idaho. Four generations have spent many a beautiful summer day breathing the mountain air, cooking, hiking, reading, boating, visiting, and creating memories in that precious place where Grandpa and Grandma Marshall began a legacy more than 35 years ago.

At the age of 70, our grandfather took on the project of building a family cabin. He was a farmer, not a carpenter, so for him this was a challenging undertaking. Grandma let everyone know just how proud she was of Grandpa, that Oliver could build a cabin.

Traditions are the cornerstone of the Marshall cabin. It begins Memorial Day weekend when as many family members as are able come to "open the cabin." We remove the shutters, sweep out the cobwebs, rake up the branches and pine needles, and check out what needs repairing.

Of course, delicious homemade food is among the most revered of all the family traditions. Grandma Marshall was a fabulous cook, and she passed on her talent and her recipes to her daughter and granddaughters. Sourdough pancakes from the original 50-year-old "starter" and the "big cabin breakfast" are a must. The Fourth of July consists of traditional fried chicken, Aunt Kristin's potato salad, Aunt Karen's homemade rolls, and at least a couple of berry or rhubarb pies along with fresh raspberries.

Food means dishes and everybody pitches in and takes a turn with the hot, soapy water or a dish towel. Lots of great conversations have taken place over the kitchen sink, and the activity includes people of all ages. The little kids have all learned to wash and dry dishes at the cabin—a lost art in many modern households.

Several generations line up in front of the Marshall cabin near Cascade, Idaho.

The cabin is not just for the family. Endless friends have had many a barbecued steak at the cabin. Church groups, friends of the kids, the grandparents' card club, college roommates, distant cousins, people from all over have enjoyed the hospitality of the cabin. You might even have enjoyed a weekend with us.

Regardless of who you are, expect to be part of the family—doing dishes, carrying wood, and changing beds. Everybody gets treated the same. It's the cabin and that's how it is.

Before guests or family members pack up and head south on Highway 55, the final tradition takes place: signing the little brown guest book and sharing yet another memory of our special mountain home.

—Janet Benoit is the granddaughter of Oliver and Ernestine Marshall, the builders and original owners, and the daughter of Lorene Marshall Guentz and Gerry Guentz, the current owners.

THE VANISHING OUTHOUSE

We're witnessing the demise of a little piece of cabin history: the rustic outhouse. Zoning regulations and water-quality concerns have put the kibosh on the legendary "convenience" in many parts of the country. At the same time, cabin owners are opting not only for indoor plumbing but also for multiple bathrooms–at least one on every level and sometimes one for every bedroom.

Although it's not always convenient, especially when it's cold or wet outside, an outhouse does possess a certain amount of nostalgic charm and retains our connection to the biology in nature.

WASHING UP

Bathing at the cabin can take many forms, with significantly different levels of investment. Any room that contains plumbing is, generally, more expensive to build than, say, a bedroom or sitting room. Again, you decide what best fits your needs, wants, and budget.

At our first cabin–a one-room screened "porch" in the woods–we drank from five-gallon jugs we'd filled with tap water at home and bathed in the lake. A recycled outhouse we'd hauled in from another site rounded out our facilities.

That must sound primitive to some modern cabin owners, who want at least as many bathrooms as bedrooms, not to mention spa-quality facilities with separate shower and tub to go with a couple of sinks, a toilet, and a bidet. Our culture today clearly takes its bathrooms seriously–even at the cabin, where the desire for a full bathroom (or several) requires a well and elaborate septic system.

By contemporary standards, a cabin bathroom comprises, at the minimum, a sink, a toilet, and a shower. Often, because several people share the facility, we place the sink outside the bath, hotel- or motel-style.

As your cabin will likely grow over the years, you'll probably want more than one bathroom. If you have bedrooms on two levels, each level should have a bathroom. And, ideally, people will get to the bathroom without having to pass through somebody else's bedroom. Also, you and your guests should be able to easily reach at least one bathroom from outside, without tracking sand and wet footprints through the house. Where there's a beach or simply a lot of water activities, an outside shower is a wonderful idea–for sandy beach babies and their hosts alike.

Hot tubs are popular at cabins. Like their suburban counterparts, cabin owners love soaking in warm, gurgling water while sipping sherry and enjoying the night air. (A whirlpool bath inside the cabin is another possibility.) But hot tubs must usually be kept full of warm water whether anybody's using them or not, so the possibility of high heating costs and the risk of a wintertime freeze-up when someone's not on the premises may make a wood-fired sauna a better choice, at least in northern climes.

Set into a dormer with its sloping, sheltering ceiling and comfortably tight enclosure, a big tub set beneath a casement window seems like the most practical form of cabin luxury.

CABIN MATTERS

BATHING ON THE CHEAP

You can combine a sauna and a solar shower for an inexpensive and pleasantly low-tech means of bathing.

Friends who have used the two methods in tandem tell me that an armful of wood for the sauna and two and a half gallons of sun-warmed water can bathe two adults.

If you use a rain gutter collector and a large storage container, the only water you'll have to fetch is the potable kind for your coffee.

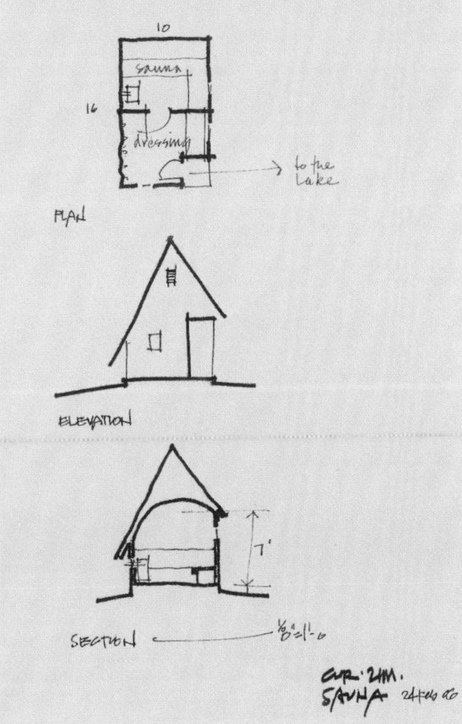

Plan for arrivals and departures by creating a covered place outside to unload the car and, inside, to stash coats, bags, hats, and gear.

ARRIVING AND DEPARTING

Perhaps the least appreciated functions at the cabin are the most basic–coming and going.

You'll have a door or two (or more) and maybe a porch or two. But, given the needs of you, your family, and your guests, you may want to include a mudroom in your plans. If "mudroom" sounds too gritty, maybe "foyer" is a better word. By any name, this handy space will be the place–especially important if the cabin is used year-round–where you set down the luggage and the groceries while you shuck your coats and boots.

You'll want to equip the space with plenty of hooks or pegs. An adjacent closet–or a closet somewhere nearby–will be where you stash brooms, rakes, snow shovels, and other out-of-season essentials.

Folks arriving and departing will likewise appreciate a covered outdoor space, such as a front porch. If you arrive in the rain, you can move from car to door protected from the deluge. On your way out, a covered stoop provides a sheltered assembly area for setting suitcases and packing the car. It's where you take a fond last look at your much-loved cabin and take stock of your gear, making sure you're not forgetting the book you're in the middle of or the glasses you'll need to finish it when you get home.

ESSENTIAL EXTRAS

So those are the major elements of a typical cabin experience–all important pieces of any plan, which I'll cover in more detail later. But keep in mind that with a cabin, especially if you're starting from scratch, almost anything is possible within the boundaries of your space, time, and budget.

Consider a few of my favorite extras, which, to those who own and love them, are not "extras" but essential parts of cabin life.

A WELCOMING ADDITION

I've mentioned the screened porch, but it's such a wonderful feature that I think it deserves its own discussion. The fact is the screened porch was the reason many of our grandparents and great-grandparents sought out the cabin experience–actually bought or built a cabin–in the first place. Fresh air was considered a healthful retreat, a balm for city folk, especially for women and children, who were considered weaker creatures than men. Fresh air was believed to help prevent polio, diphtheria, and other diseases associated with overcrowding and "stale" urban air. A screened porch allowed guests to take in the healthful air of the woods while playing, eating, and sleeping "outdoors."

I love screened porches, so much in fact that, as I've said, our first cabin was nothing but. (My family and I thought of that cabin experience as "going camping," only without the tent.) Attached to your cabin, the screened porch quickly becomes a treasured part of the experience.

Obviously, keeping the rain out and the bugs at bay are the first requirements of porch design. Next is providing enough space for a variety of activities and keeping the porch close enough to the kitchen to allow for quick and frequent refills of lemonade or beer. It's important, too, to position your screened porch where it catches a gentle breeze in the

EVERYTHING ELSE

One of my clients bought a beautiful little cabin that they used only on holidays. They liked the place so much, however, that they eventually decided to move there for good. Living in the structure full-time, though, required more space than the occasional weekend visit, yet they didn't want to destroy its compact character with alterations. The solution? They asked me to design an "everything else building" that included, among other amenities, a garage, shop, office, and sleeping space for guests. Set into the "prow" window of this "everything else" cabin is a light-filled loft sleeping nook.

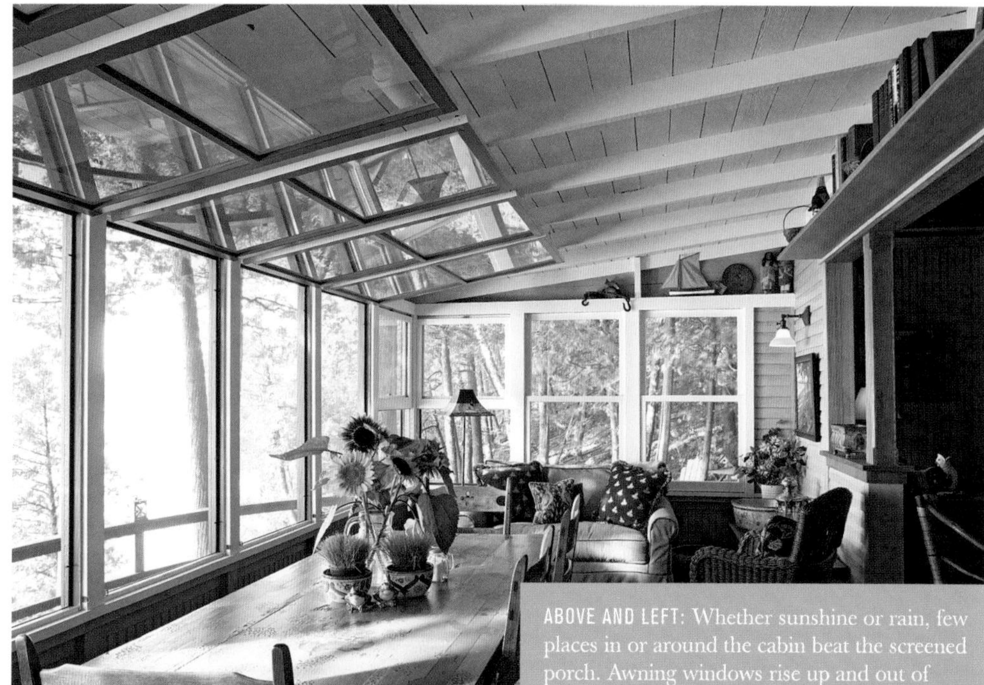

ABOVE AND LEFT: Whether sunshine or rain, few places in or around the cabin beat the screened porch. Awning windows rise up and out of the way to open this porch to cooling breezes (above) while the porch (at left) functions almost like an outdoor pavilion to catch the breeze from three sides and to share it with the interior.

BELOW: Wrapped around two sides of this cabin, this deep porch offers places to nap, sit, talk, eat, and daydream.

summer, yet where the chilly winds at either end of the season won't shorten your cabin year (which brings us back to the issue of siting according to the prevailing breezes). A little morning sun will dry the dew on the furniture. But too much sun in the afternoon may send you inside the cabin earlier than you'd like.

Not that your cabin need be limited to only one screened porch. An entry porch is a great place to dry wet gear and stow everything from your fishing rods to your skis. To my mind, a "living porch" is best when it offers a view, a picnic table, and a swing seat or hammock. A screened porch on a cabin's second or third level is marvelous for reading, sleeping, and airing the linen the next day.

OTHER POSSIBILITIES

Beyond the cabin and porch, you may want a patio, deck, or gazebo. Where bugs are not a nuisance and (depending on where you live) a deck may in fact take the place of a porch as the center of outdoor dining, reading, games, and conversation. Add a gas or charcoal grill, and you have an alternate kitchen–particularly welcome in hot weather. But be careful where you place that deck, lest it interfere with your view of the lake or mountain from inside. If the cabin is built into a hill and has a lower level, the deck shouldn't shade or block the view from the windows.

I've also grown fond of towers, which, odd as this may seem, have been part of some cabin dwellers' experience for at least 200 years.

I designed my first cabin tower about 10 years ago and positioned a sleeping porch at the top, where folks could enjoy the evening breeze and wake to the soft sound of birds in the neighboring treetops. Since then, I've designed several cabins with attached towers–and one tower that is the cabin itself. I've designed towers just for kids and towers that appeal to the kid in adults.

The tower I built for one client has a room at the top with no officially designated purpose. You can read there or spend the night or check the weather from its heights before heading out on the lake to fish. Towers can take many different shapes–round, square, rectilinear,

CABIN MATTERS

A PERCH ON THE PORCH

Everybody likes to sit on a porch. An open, unscreened porch, with only a roof to shield us from the noonday sun and a late-day shower, may be the ideal. But, for most of us, screens that protect us from mosquitoes, flies, and other airborne pests are also essential to our cabin activities. In any climate, a site allowing for a fresh breeze and a wide view of the surroundings is almost always best. Accomplishing all of this with classic cabin style is this porch-like cabin sitting high above the St. Croix River.

octagonal–and they can be flat-topped, domed, or wear a witch's hat. Whatever you imagine.

The challenge in designing any kind of tower is providing enough room to be practical while maintaining its character as a tower. A stairway is essential (and, for obvious reasons, usually preferable to a ladder), but it takes up a lot of valuable space, especially if it's a relatively narrow tower. In other towers I've designed, the tower is attached to a two-story cabin and only the stairs from the second level to the third lie in the tower itself. In yet another, the tower stairs are part of the children's cascading bed platforms. "Skip stairs" (p. 110) and other "slimming" techniques important to tower design are described on p. 130.

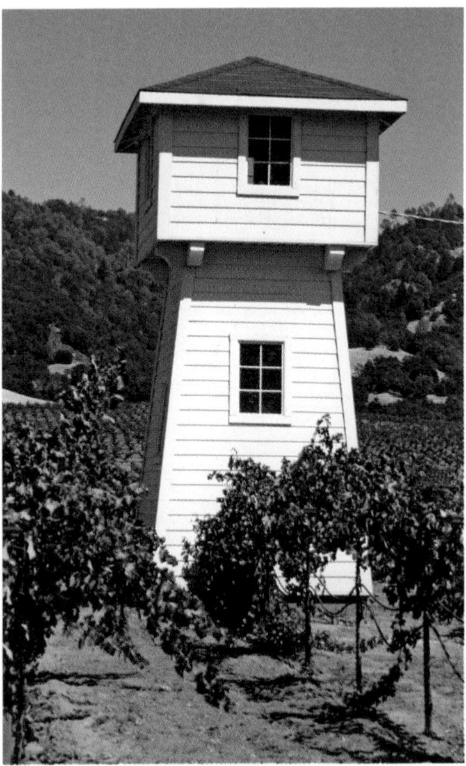

CABIN MATTERS

THE RISE OF THE TOWER

Towers are romantic additions to the cabin experience, rising above the earthbound structure at its base and providing an elevated perspective on the adjacent lake and uninterrupted view of the starry heavens.

Of her own cabin's tower, one of my clients says, "It's a peaceful place to read and drink coffee in the morning, while looking out at the treetops and listening to the rustling leaves. It's also a great place to have cocktails with friends, play board games, and read while listening to the loons and the lake lapping against the shore. We have seen some awesome sunsets from up there, and watched storms–though that can sometimes be a little bit scary! After dinner, we tend to head to the tower because it just feels good to be up there."

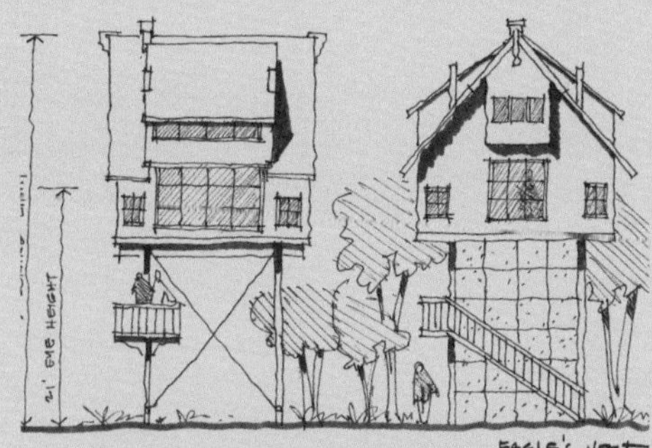

I designed this tower cabin with living on the third level and sleeping on the fourth.

Architect Marlon Blackwell designed this tower escape in the Ozark hills of Arkansas. It doesn't begin with bathroom and utility levels until you're four stories in the air; then up to the glazed living/sleeping space. A walled-in rooftop for spectacular star gazing tops it off.

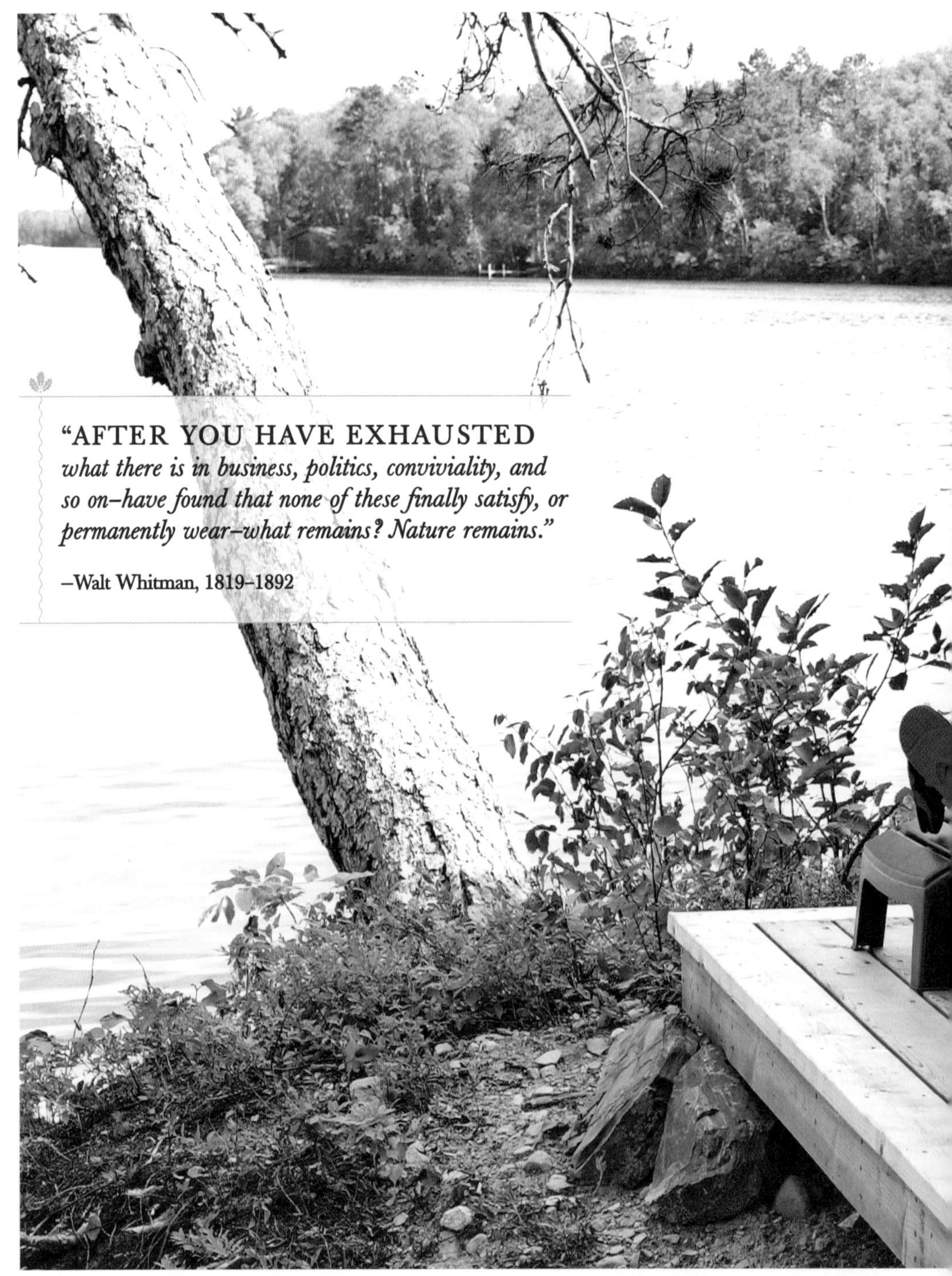

"AFTER YOU HAVE EXHAUSTED *what there is in business, politics, conviviality, and so on–have found that none of these finally satisfy, or permanently wear–what remains? Nature remains."*

–Walt Whitman, 1819–1892

RECOMMENDED READING

For additional information, ideas, and inspiration, check out the following titles:

- *Your Cabin in the Woods* by Conrad Meinecke (Foster & Stewart Publishing Corporation, 1945; reprinted by Bonanza Books, 1979)
- *Log Cabins and Cottages* by William S. Wicks (1928; reprinted by Gibbs Smith, 1999)
- *How to Build Your Dream Cabin in the Woods* by J. Wayne Fears (The Lyons Press, 2002)
- *The Place of Houses* by Charles Moore, Gerald Allen, and Donlyn Lyndon (Holt, Rinehart and Winston, 1974)
- *Tiny Houses* by Lester Waker (Overlook Hardcover, 1987)
- *The Wilderness Cabin* by Calvin Rutstrum (Macmillan Publishing Co., 1972)
- *A Pattern Language* by Christopher Alexander (Oxford University Press, 1977)
- *Cabins: A Guide to Building Your Own Nature Retreat* by David and Jeanie Stiles (Firefly Books, 2001)
- *Modest Mansions* by Donald Prowler (Rodale Press, 1985)
- *The Cabin Book* by Linda Leigh Paul (Universe, 2004)
- *XS-Big Ideas, Small Buildings* by Phyllis Richardson (Universe, 2001)
- And not least, *The Cabin* by Dale Mulfinger and Susan E. Davis (The Taunton Press, 2001)

MAKING YOUR CABIN ONE-OF-A-KIND

Finally, there's the history, perspective, memories, and ideas that you bring to your cabin–the attributes that make your cabin unique.

One client asked me to visit his childhood cabin, which had since been sold, and to record the room dimensions, fireplace characteristics, and truss spacing so we could re-create it in his new cabin. He even split his own rocks for the new foundation so they would look like the originals.

Sometimes what makes a cabin special is the fact that it isn't, or wasn't, a "cabin" at all. I know of cabins that have been fashioned out of discarded railroad cars (especially the caboose), schoolhouses, churches, town halls, even a sheep wagon. A couple of brothers I know are converting a pair of shipping containers into a woodsy getaway. I know of cabins that have been transported many miles and across state lines to new sites to be a new owner's cottage or part of an existing lakeside compound.

Recently I made visual reference to a Greek temple in a cabin design, and I'm currently refurbishing a cabin along a nautical theme and shape. I've seen a cabin that used a teepee shape as its organizing idea and more than one A-frame inspired by a tent. One cabin, which its owners affectionately call the "Brown Bat," took its shape from a bat in flight.

Often a personal artifact influences at least a part of a cabin design. A trestle table that belonged to Great-Aunt Mae determines the shape and size of a rectangular dining area. Brother Bob's prized moose head requires space above the fireplace to accommodate its 7-ft. rack. The pressed-tin ceiling that graced

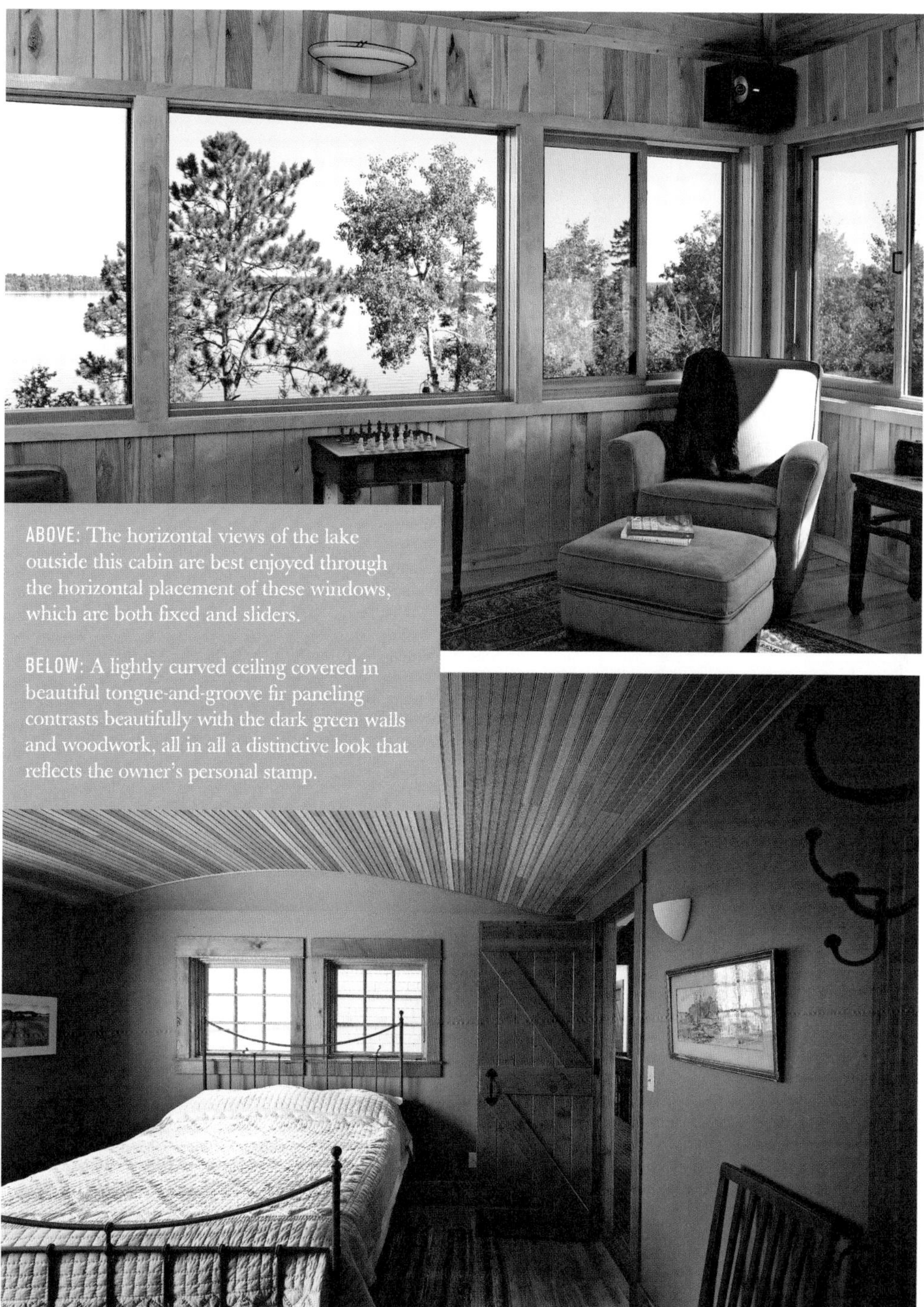

ABOVE: The horizontal views of the lake outside this cabin are best enjoyed through the horizontal placement of these windows, which are both fixed and sliders.

BELOW: A lightly curved ceiling covered in beautiful tongue-and-groove fir paneling contrasts beautifully with the dark green walls and woodwork, all in all a distinctive look that reflects the owner's personal stamp.

Alternating-tread stairs take up less room than traditional tread-and-riser stairs, which makes them a good choice for a thin cabin tower. This stair is hinged to lift out of the way when not needed.

Granddad's hardware store needs an appreciative home, as does a thousand board feet of barn timber from the family farmstead. Gnarly cedar roots exposed by last year's gullywasher would make a one-of-a-kind handrail on the cabin stairs. The rug your daughter brought back from her trip to Tibet is perfect for your cabin's sitting room. And on and on.

You get the idea. The point is to explore all the ways to make this cabin uniquely yours. Some of this you build into your cabin, but the rest can be added in layers over the years. In fact, I dare say you'll have a hard time preventing the accumulation of personal artifacts and personal touches to your cabin. Things get brought there and tend to hang around–indefinitely.

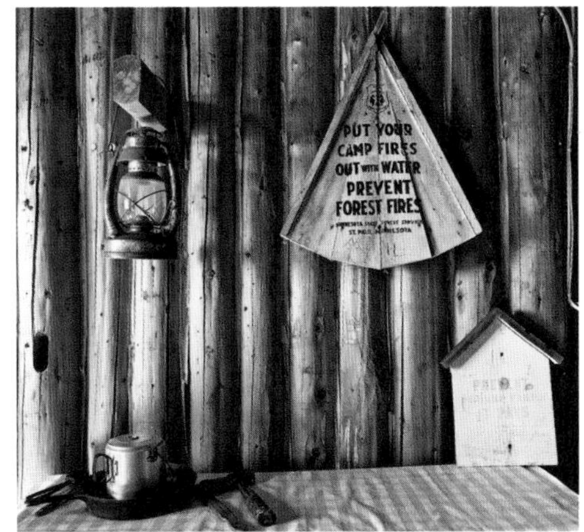

Personalizing doesn't mean hiring a decorator–just the opposite. Artfully, even not so artfully, displaying some of your favorite collectible and junk treasures is a good start to making the cabin truly and uniquely yours.

ULTIMATELY, IT'S ABOUT YOU

I'm partial to materials, colors, and references that echo the world around the cabin. I like to craft rooms with local wood and then name them after local birds, landmarks, or characters. The Spruce bedroom in our cabin features light wood with blue-green accents. The Meadowlark is brightly painted and glows in the morning light. A bedroom in a cabin that has served six generations of a family I know bears the name of Great-Uncle Arthur. It's fun to imagine each new generation asking about the room's namesake and hearing the family's Arthurian lore.

There's obviously more involved in these choices than utility. Just remember that you're the cabin's alpha user. Your cabin should reflect, first and foremost, your needs and wants, your character, personality, history, tastes, and peculiarities. And when it does all that, your cabin will be unlike any other cabin in the world. Then it will truly be your own.

CABIN MATTERS

THE VIEW FROM THE DECK

While sitting on your deck, you'll want the best view possible of the lake below, especially when your kids or grandkids are playing on the beach.

A deck rail built to code stands 36 in. to 42 in. tall, and many rail designs feature a hefty top cap that will get in the way of your view when you're comfortably sunk into your cushy chaise lounge.

For a clearer view, build your deck rail with that heavy top cap, and use cable, pipe, or thin metal bars for the railing below.

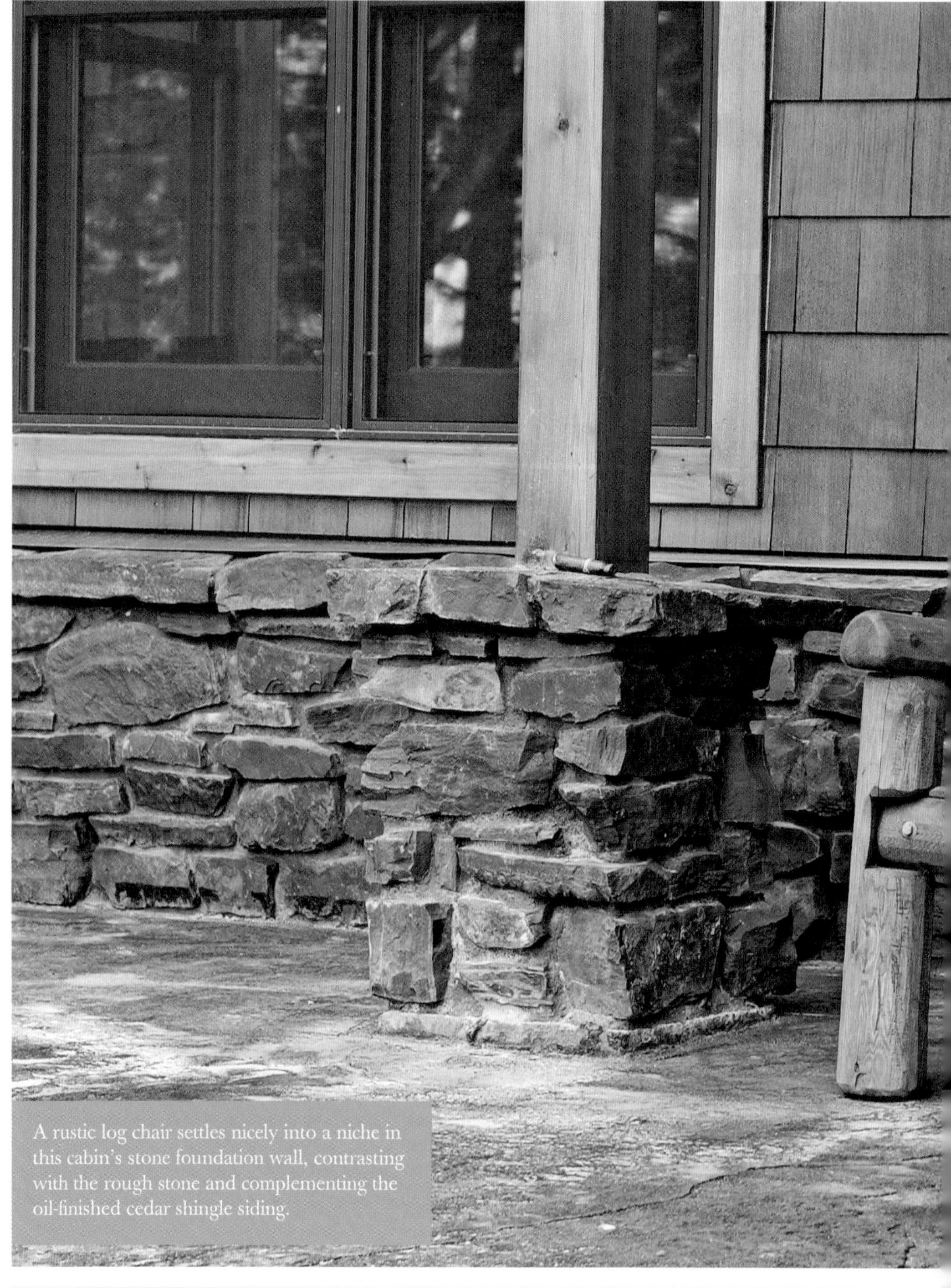

A rustic log chair settles nicely into a niche in this cabin's stone foundation wall, contrasting with the rough stone and complementing the oil-finished cedar shingle siding.

THE MASTER PLAN

CHAPTER FOUR

AS A NATION, OUR CABIN ROOTS GO DEEP. The earliest European settlements were often clusters of impossibly tiny cabins crafted of logs. Trees were plentiful, and a log cabin was the expedient, even emergency solution to shelter. As our ancestors migrated east, west, south, and north, wherever they landed, they cut down trees and built themselves cabins.

In 1852 my great-grandfather, Sven Anderson, built a small log cabin in Scandia, Minnesota. It had two rooms, two outside doors, and four windows. The logs were joined at the corners with dovetails. The roof was hand-split local cedar. I can't even imagine what it was like during a typical Minnesota winter with only a fireplace to sustain life. Just the labor required to cut and split such enormous amounts of firewood would've been a nearly full-time job. I doubt many of us today could stand up to such hardship.

Yet they survived, or at least enough of them survived. We are all obvious proof of it. However, even the roughest, most basic cabins were

"SO, MR. CABIN-BUILDER,

I say plan wisely. Spend a summer on your site in a tent before you build. Study the air currents that flow down the hills; the prevailing winds; the landscape and vista you want to develop. Do you prefer sunrise to sunset? If you do not enjoy sunrise, then set your cabin so the morning sun will not disturb your sleep. You may enjoy the sunset from your porch or big window. Where are the noises from the highways and how can you plant trees to blot out ugly views or even some of the noise?"

–Conrad Meinecke, *Your Cabin in the Woods,* Foster & Stewart Publishing Corporation, 1945

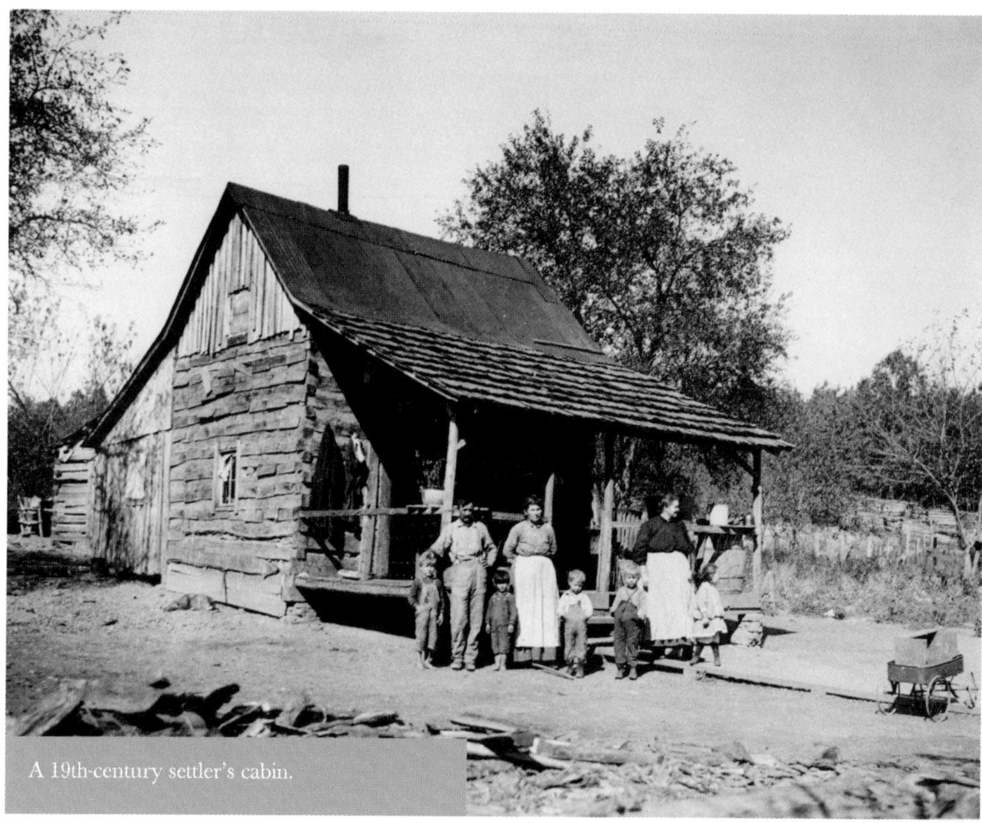

A 19th-century settler's cabin.

built with an understanding of the land, the available materials, and the seasons that has mostly since been bred out of us.

Today, technology allows us to build the most remarkably inefficient and inappropriate structures wherever we want. As your cabinologist, my purpose is to guide you back toward the old way of thinking, that is, toward the way that seeks to understand place, in which a cabin merges with the land rather than dominates it, that results in the creation of a cabin that belongs.

GETTING IT RIGHT

Here's a hypothetical cabinology situation: The land you bought includes an 18-degree slope and is mostly sandy clay soil. It gets from 25 in. to 45 in. of rain and up to 60 in. of snow over the course of an average year. And the temperature ranges from about 95°F in the summer to 10°F in winter.

Site and weather are just two of the practical factors you'd be wise to consider when planning a cabin. While we're being hypothetical, let's also assume that, in addition to those factors, your budget allows for up to 1,500 sq. ft. of cabin space, which is what you'll need to accommodate the family and friends who are likely to visit plus the room to feed them three meals a day and bed them down for the night. Also, you'll want room for a septic field, a small dock on the lake, and a place for several cars to park (as hard as life was in my great-grandfather's day, it was mercifully simpler).

What you need now is a plan that allows you to put these pieces together in a cabin that's comfortably all your own. The plan includes the usual three dimensions–the familiar x, y, and z coordinates of form in space–and a fourth coordinate to represent time, meaning the time of day, the time of year, and the time it will take to build the place. That's all part of the mix.

IT STARTS IN YOUR HEAD

If you were a kid, you'd just pick up your crayons and draw a picture of the cabin you've got floating around in your head. That's pretty much the way you need to start now–by tapping into your imagination. Letting the child inside you take control, sketch the cabin you have in mind, both inside and out.

Imagine your family at the dining table, working on a jigsaw puzzle, playing Monopoly, building a house of cards. Envision you and your pals ringing in the new year in front

TIP JUST IMAGINE

For your first cabin drawings, use the medium you feel most comfortable with or whatever's most convenient. Color helps but isn't essential. Crayons, watercolors, and markers work nicely on plain white paper, brown butcher's paper, or, for that matter, the back of a napkin. The point is to use whatever it takes to let your imagination fly like a child's.

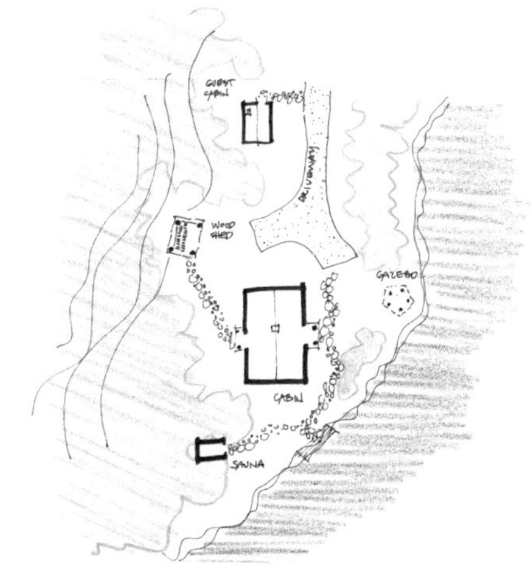

SITE AMENITIES

As you plan, imagine the cabin (that already exists or that you intend to build) in the context of the land, with water, views, trees, paths, roads–everything you'll take into account.

of the fieldstone fireplace. Picture yourself making my no-fail crepes in the kitchen the following morning, or taking a nap, or reading in a window seat, or staring out a window while you shuck off the concerns of daily life back in the city. Place the cabin in context, complete with lakeshore and a stand of pines or with a mountain range in the distance.

Don't worry if you draw like a five-year-old with stick figures and squiggly lines. The important thing is to draw what you see with your mind's eye, how you want your cabin to look inside and out.

For inspiration and ideas, I tell my clients to clip photos and drawings of the cabins, or the parts of cabins, they like. I know folks who have accumulated bulging files full of five to ten years' worth of magazine articles, product literature, and snapshots taken while visiting friends' cabins, cruising along a lakeshore in a boat, or taking a drive through the country.

The particular object of interest may be the entire setting or just a single thing, like a specific window treatment, chimney, porch,

or roof. In any event, the drawings and photos make up a collage of images that give shape, scope, color, and detail to the cabin of their dreams.

Taken all together, that's the cabin you first put down on paper. That's where you start.

NOW GET REAL

From there, you move on to the real thing, the drawings, floor plans, and elevations of the actual cabin you want to build, add on to, or simply remodel.

You need to decide and diagram, if only in the most basic way, how you want to orient your cabin and how you're likely to use each of its levels, if you'll have more than one. Let's say you want the main door to the cabin to be on the northwest side, which is where you have the best sunset views in the summer (when you'll use the cabin the most). And you want the kitchen near the screened porch for convenience. Reflect all this (and any other relevant consideration) in your next sketch. You'll need a sketch for each floor or level, understanding that to make everything "work" the way you want it to, you'll probably have to rethink and redraw the basic details before you're really comfortable with the plan. When planning a cabin from scratch, no one gets everything right the first time.

The rest of your drawings (or doodles, as your rendering abilities may be) need to include all of the parts that will, or should, determine the cabin's ultimate design. Also, instead of simply drawing the cabin in isolation, you might sketch your plans on a site survey map that gives the solar orientation

TIP — FUNCTION AND FLOW

The diagram you want at this stage of your planning is about connections and relationships–not unlike a family tree or a zoning map of your neighborhood. The task is to highlight an activity (cooking, sleeping, etc.) and visually connect it with another activity (serving dinner, going upstairs to the bedroom). Simple labels, lines, and arrows will do thc trick. Your diagram probably won't show everything a builder needs to know about your cabin's function and flow, but it will encourage some basic decisions and stimulate more detailed thinking about how the parts of your cabin should all come together.

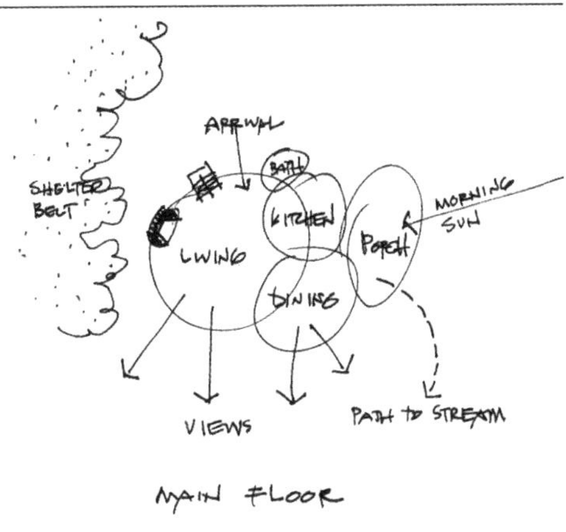

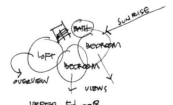

If you're starting your cabin from scratch, add dimensions to your drawings by thinking through a floor plan for each level to correspond with the elevation drawing of the exterior.

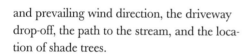

and prevailing wind direction, the driveway drop-off, the path to the stream, and the location of shade trees.

SEE IT IN YOUR HEAD

Be practical now. If you have small children, you'll want to keep your eye on them from the kitchen sink, so you need to position the kitchen wall and window to look out onto the yard or lakefront. If you have trouble climbing stairs, keep your bedroom and bathroom at ground level, opposite the kitchen or sitting room. And so on.

An easy mistake at this point is to cram too much into the main floor of the cabin. I have to remind folks that the size of the main floor and the plans they have for using it greatly affect the overall cost of the cabin because those factors will dictate the extent of the foundation and the size of the roof–the most expensive components of a cabin. Moving a function–sleeping, for instance–from the main floor to either the upstairs or downstairs may help amortize your construction investment. Try reducing costs by sneaking more volume over a smaller foundation and under less roof. Since many of us prefer steeper roofs, we can mine the roof volume for charming sleeping rooms in the sloped ceilings.

Being practical doesn't mean a lack of imagination. Besides saving some money,

Keep a camera with you so if you see a particular roof feature, or a type of siding or window you like, you can snap a photo for your planning file.

you may create a happy surprise by spreading things out. Put the laundry on the second floor, near the bedrooms where the dirty clothes pile up, and you might brighten an otherwise ordinary chore with a lovely second-story view of the treetops and the lake beyond.

As for the drawings themselves, focus on the most important parts of the cabin and the things you plan to do there. Keep your eye on the things you do most often and their relationship to each other and to the site. At this point, don't worry about the fancy stuff such as a linen closet, wine cellar, hot tub, or sauna; they can be added later.

CABIN MATTERS

SMALL WONDERS

Good planning should result in the best use of available space because it allows you to use all (or almost all) of that space effectively.

When I field-measure the cabins I visit, I'm often impressed by how much livable area can be provided in the most modest structure.

To understand and appreciate how this is achieved, read Sarah Susanka's excellent book, *The Not So Big House* (The Taunton Press, 1998). Also instructional is Lester Walker's *Tiny Houses* (Overlook Hardcover, 1987), in which he details, among other things, the scale of Henry Thoreau's cottage on Walden Pond.

Porch cabins like this one surround the central core of the cabin with screened porches on two or three sides, which function as the main living and sleeping areas of the cabin, while the cooking, bathing, and heated areas are inside the main cabin walls.

CABIN STORIES

THE MARCH OF MEMORIES

Northern Minnesota is a land of sparkling glacial lakes and wilderness forests that stretch beyond what the eye can see. Lake Kabetogama is one of those lakes, and, fortunately, civilization has not yet marred its remote and intrinsic beauty.

In any given spot, on any given day, images of Ojibwa warriors riding spotted ponies through the woods come unbidden as past collides with present, luring us into believing life could still be as pure and unblemished as it once was. Shadows of turn-of-the-century French fur traders and hardworking loggers weave like the wind through the pines where they left their mark: small sheltering cabins nestled in the woods. At night, in a secluded bay where moon dances on water and stars shimmer in an ink black sky, the aurora borealis mystifies, intensifying the sense of wonder in this special place.

It is in this magical place that my family is fortunate enough to have our refuge by the shore. Surrounded by towering white pine, birch, and aspen, our little cabin has stood stalwart and serene for nearly eight decades. As a girl, my family went to a nearby resort where we spent many memorable summer vacations. Then, about 20 years ago, a little lakeshore cabin nearby came up for sale, and my husband and I jumped at the chance to own a little piece of this north woods paradise and to continue the cycle of family tradition at the lake.

It's this little bit of heaven that we call "Kabby" (short for cabin). Sadly my parents are now gone, but they dearly loved Kabby, a love that is ingrained in my DNA and that I now endeavor to imprint on our children and grandchildren—so they can pass along to theirs the same emotional and physical attachments we feel.

Every year all make the pilgrimage north to refresh, renew, and recharge in a place that time truly seems to have forgotten. In its totally stress-free (and virtually time-free) zone, the lake comes alive with the sound of our grandchildren's laughter as they play in the sand, squeal over a caught fish, or stare in wide-eyed wonder when they spot a bear lumbering across the road.

New memories. Wonderful memories.

And when the babies are tucked, pink-cheeked and smiling, into their beds at night, I slip outside onto the deck where I listen to the wind and the lapping of the water. And I wonder...was that minuscule light in the forest merely moonlight dancing off a pristine white birch...or was it starlight glinting off the flowing mane of a swift pony as a young brave rode in silent stealth through the trees?

Only at the cabin can such dreams even exist. Only at the cabin can those dreams be nurtured and held in trust for generations to come.

—Cindy Gerard, author of *The Bodyguards* series and other books, is a *New York Times* bestselling author.

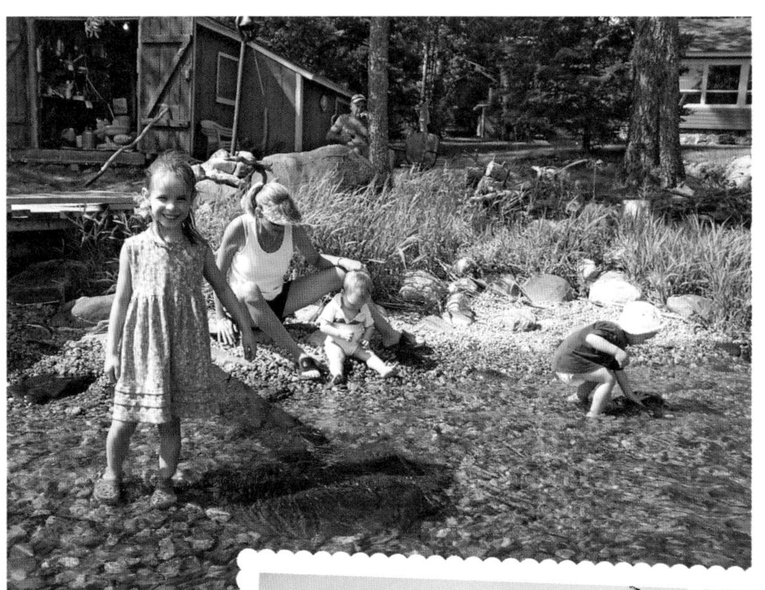

Novelist Cindy Gerard and her husband share their cabin with children and grandchildren at every opportunity.

CABIN MATTERS

JUST THE ROOF YOU WANTED

In the old days, cabin roofs followed hand-framed rafter systems that either relied on trees felled and milled at the site or used standard lumber. Nowadays, the most common roofing systems incorporate manufactured trusses that are engineered specifically for a particular design and provide the character and slope of the roof you want. In this photograph, the sloping roofline of a second-floor bedroom creates a comforting sense of shelter while leaving sufficient headroom in the middle of the room.

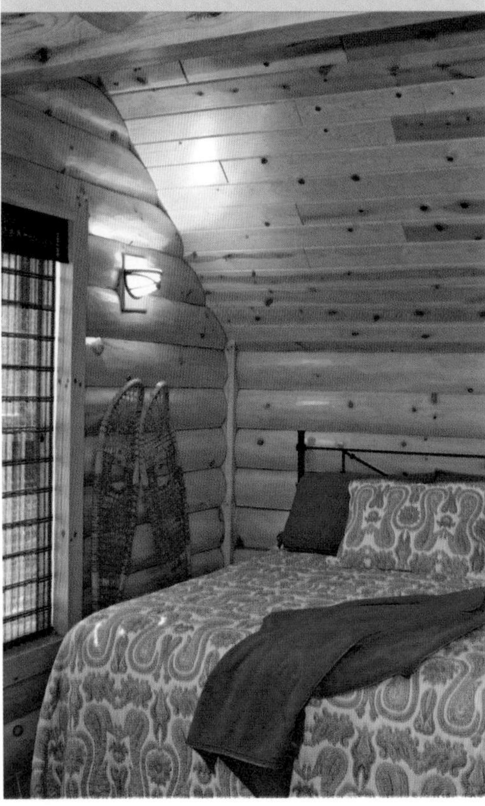

KITCHEN FIRST

Planning the cabin's main floor starts with planning the kitchen. There's a lot to consider. For example, when you bring in the groceries or take out the trash, you want the kitchen—and the kitchen door—to be in a convenient location. Also, it should be only a few short steps from your kitchen to the dining table, the porch, the deck, or wherever else you serve food and drinks.

Preferably, the kitchen is situated so that the cook is part of, if not in the middle of, everything else that's going on around mealtime. And need I say that the cook would appreciate a lake view as well as a view of the rest of the property while he or she labors over dinner?

If the kitchen is, as I believe it should be, the command center of your cabin, then the kitchen's location will command the cabin plan.

If your view looks out from only one side of the cabin, the dining and living spaces would normally be positioned next to the kitchen on that view side of the floor plan.

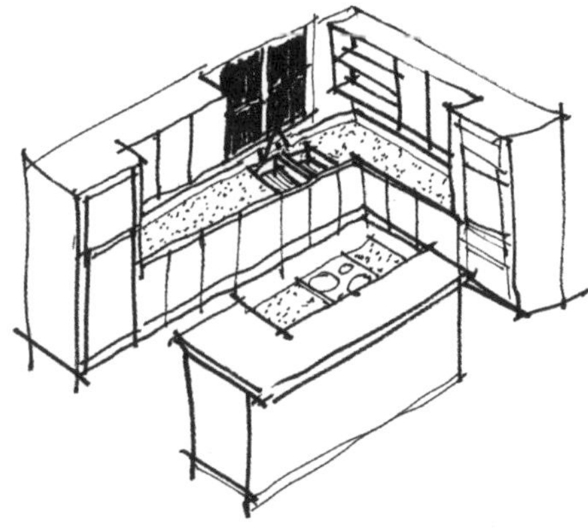

The cabin kitchen is the command center.

In our cabin kitchen, we make use of standard upper and lower cabinets as well as a versatile island (you can see it holds the microwave) and a pine hutch we bought at an estate sale.

Because the dining table is generally placed in the middle of the dining area, adequate walking space around it is necessary, giving access to the chairs and benches surrounding the table and also, ideally, allowing the traffic to move easily to the living area and porch.

On the other hand, the seating area in the living room is best designed as a dead end or cul-de-sac, with the traffic moving in and out but not through–like a bedroom. Living rooms should be oriented to the window view or to the fireplace, so be sure to include the living room window (or windows) and hearth in your drawing. A woodstove is less likely to be the center of the living area than an important feature of the kitchen or dining space. But wherever it goes, be sure to include it in your drawings, too. It can be expensive to add a fireplace or wood-burning stove as an afterthought.

Dining and living areas ideally coexist within the same space. As the drawing explains and the photograph depicts, these two spaces are natural companions along with the kitchen. However, while the kitchen and dining areas are designed to accommodate traffic flow around and through, the living area works best as a cul-de-sac, in which people can sit and talk.

BEDROOMS IN THE CORNERS

If the kitchen is at the heart of most cabins, then the bedrooms are on the periphery, or on the cabin's corners, where peace, quiet, and privacy are usually easier to come by. The sounds of late-night card players at the dining table shouldn't keep sleepyheads from getting their rest.

Although your inclination may be to group the bedrooms near a bath, you may want to locate any additional bedrooms on the other side of the cabin or above or below on another level. Or you can situate one or all of the beds in a separate building–in a bunkhouse or on a second floor above the garage or boathouse.

SEPARATE THE NOISY FROM THE DOZING

If your cabin is one level high, your options are more limited. Still, placing bedrooms away from the hub of noise and activity helps keep things flexible. Those who want to stay up can, and those who want to sleep or sit and read can do that, too. And if those staying up happen to be keeping you up, try foam rubber earplugs. I know people who never travel without earplugs and a sleep mask–they let you take a dark, quiet privacy with you wherever you go.

Separating and spreading out bedrooms is a good way to accommodate a variety of guests, from night owls to early risers. For that matter, you may appreciate a choice of bedrooms yourself–sleeping in the airy north-facing upstairs room during the summer and the smaller, cozier, downstairs corner when it's cold outside.

If you'll spend any serious amount of time at the cabin, a laundry comes in really handy, especially if kids are involved. The owners of this cabin had room for a full-size washer and dryer set, but smaller, stackable washer/dryers are a good option for smaller cabins. I've seen them set into a closet-size space, which was then covered by a curtain.

THE USEFUL UTILITY ROOM

Washing and drying clothes and sheets and terry-cloth towels is a never-ending part of life–even carefree cabin life. Remember when you got your first apartment and had to haul your clothes and towels to the laundromat and how great it was when got your own washer and dryer? They're not glamorous (at least they didn't used to be), but laundry rooms sure are good to have. So be sure to make the

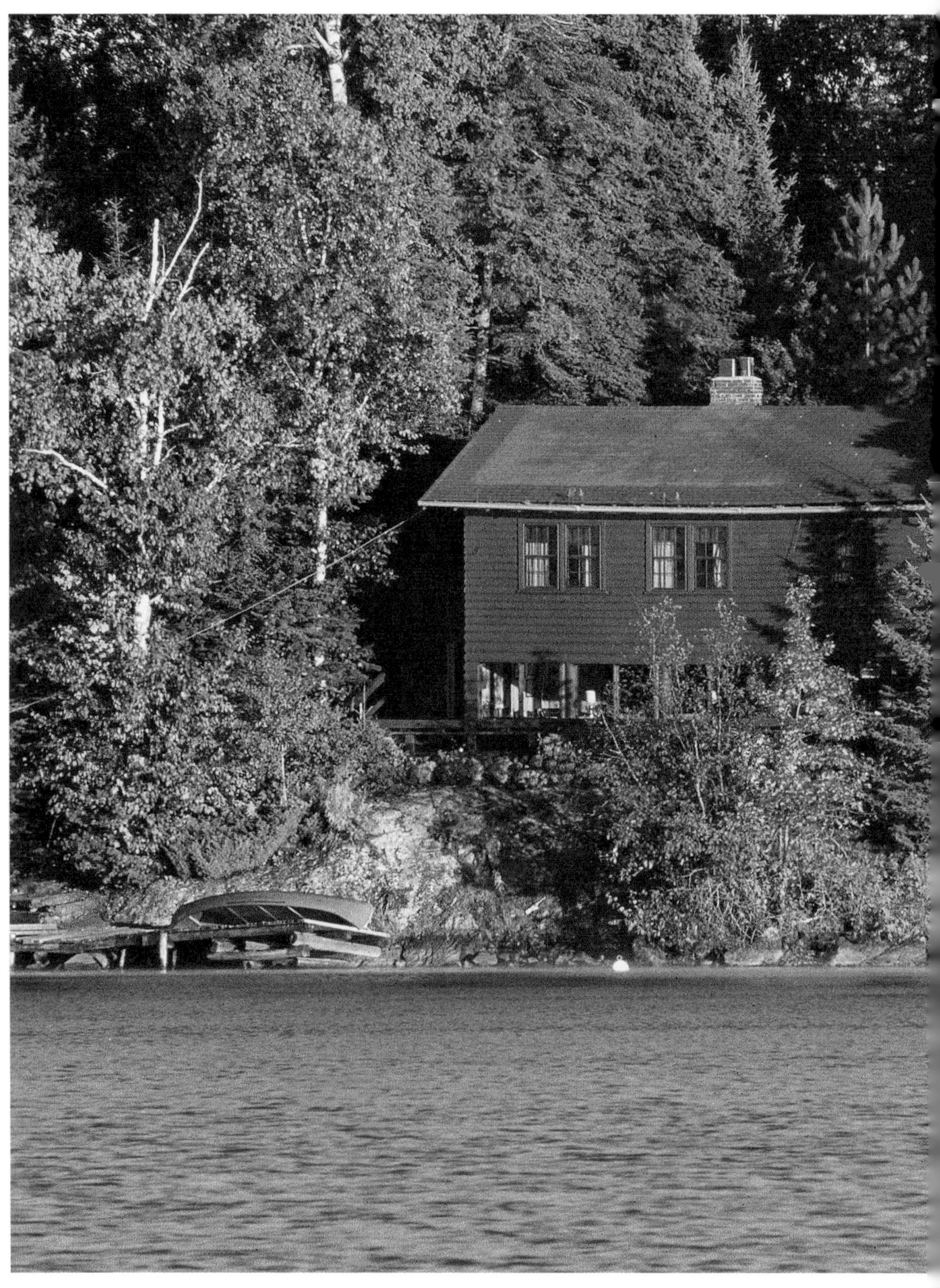

"I REMEMBER A HUNDRED LOVELY LAKES, *and recall the fragrant breath of pine and fir and cedar and poplar trees. The trail has strung upon it, as upon a thread of silk, opalescent dawns and saffron sunsets. It has given me blessed release from care and worry and the troubled thinking of our modern day. It has been a return to the primitive and the peaceful. Whenever the pressure of our complex city life thins my blood and benumbs my brain, I seek relief in the trail; and when I hear the coyote wailing to the yellow dawn, my cares fall from me–I am happy."*

– Hamlin Garland, *McClure's Magazine*, February 1899

laundry room, or laundry space, an important part of your plan.

If it makes you feel better, you can label it the *utility room* and use it for other, more pleasant things, such as storing sports or outdoor gear. This also can be the place where you put the mechanicals–furnace, water heater, and electrical panel. By any name and whatever its uses, the utility room should be convenient to bedrooms and an outside door.

Of course, you can always split the functions, putting the washer and dryer close to the bedrooms and the storage/mechanical components somewhere else–even on different levels. Just be sure to include the space in your plan. As with roofs and foundations, last-minute additions of wet spaces (like kitchens, baths, and laundry rooms) can cost you. That goes for stairs as well.

TAKE THE STAIRS

If your cabin has more than one floor, the stairway will, for obvious reasons, be crucial to your plan. Stairs, after all, connect place to place and also have a strong visual and physical presence on each level.

Stairs are best positioned near the center of the cabin, reducing the need for hallways, which can be wasted space. Architects and real estate brokers talk a lot about the "center hall plan" because the phrase refers to a

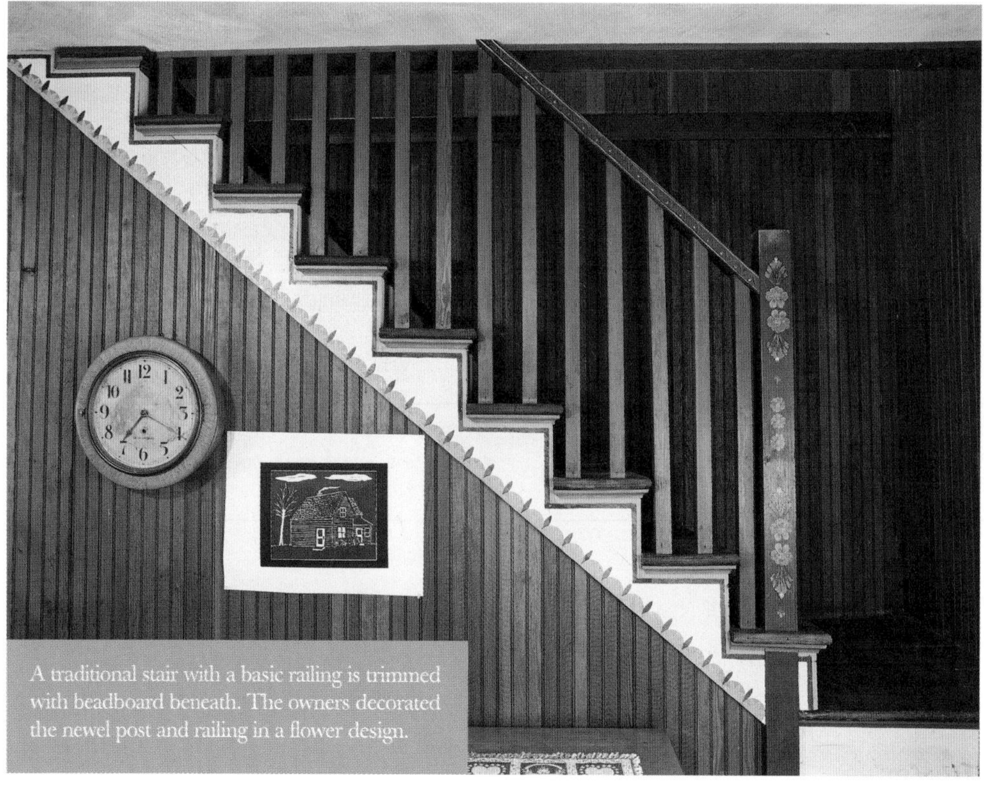

A traditional stair with a basic railing is trimmed with beadboard beneath. The owners decorated the newel post and railing in a flower design.

A "wall" of horizontal slats serves both to delineate space between the stair and living area and to allow light to pass through, brightening the entire area.

common and historically important feature of American home design—and because keeping the stairs at the center of the layout is an efficient use of space.

In a cabin, the stairs are best placed near the main-floor entry. When your guests arrive with their suitcases and backpacks, they can move on to their rooms. And, because this is a cabin, we're not talking about the kind of grand staircase your daughter wants to pose on for her prom photo but something utilitarian and informal. You not only go up and come down the stairs, but you also plop down on the second stair tread when you take off your wet boots and use the steps for seating when you have an especially large crowd for dinner.

TYPES OF STAIRS

Stairs can be a straight run up and down. Or stairs can include a landing and a turn. A stairway with a 90-degree turn is called an "L-stair," which can have a landing or be built in the old-fashioned "winder style" with pie-shaped treads at the turn. Stairs with a 180-degree switchback is called a "return stair."

Changing direction on a stair may be the best way to position the bottom of the stair near the front door and the top of it close to the bedrooms. Circular stairs let you move straight up or down from one level to the next, saving space, but they're difficult to negotiate when lugging a pair of suitcases or a bag of dirty clothes, never mind a box spring and dresser. Like other types of stairs, spiral stairs can be little jewel-like works of art made of cast iron or wood or they can be blandly utilitarian.

Of the noncircular variety, ordinary straight stairs take up the least space, but that space savings might be offset by the hallway you'll need to connect the top of the stairs to the bedrooms, unless, of course, the upper story is a simple loft.

UNDER ONE ROOF

Once you've finished drawing, doodling, and diagramming your cabin's basic functions and spaces and their relationships with each other, it's time to decide on the form, the package, the look.

You can, of course, wrap your plan in straight lines, but that will probably result in too much perimeter, too many interior walls, and a complicated roof shape—all of which will add significantly to the cost of construction. Wall and roof decisions need to be based as much on the type of construction as they do

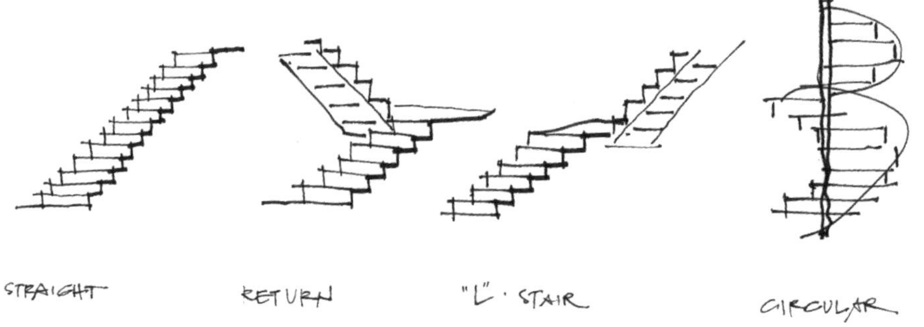

on your needs diagram. Something I hope you get from this book is a basic understanding of construction so that, every step of the way, you can make decisions that best fit your wants, needs, and budget. These decisions start with exploring the shape of the roof. Remember that design is an exploration of possibilities.

FIRST, THINK ROOF

So why are we talking about the roof before settling on a floor plan? Because it's easier to fit an effective floor plan under a good roof shape than to tack a good roof shape on top of an effective floor plan.

You've probably driven by housing developments and seen a jumble of awkwardly shaped roofs. That's typically the result of a premature commitment to a floor plan that then relegates the roof design to an afterthought. Computers have probably shaped those roofs at the expense of cost-effective simplicity and eye-pleasing structural harmony. And let me tell you, these complex roofs with their many angles, heights, and intersections are much more prone to leaking than a more basic roof shape. And when it gets time to reroof, they're also much costlier.

Most of the cabins I work on have two stories, with the second floor typically being about half as large as the first. This usually works well for a roof design when the second floor is in the roof with a mixture of gable end windows, dormer windows, and skylights. Many of my clients like cozy sleeping spaces beneath sloped ceilings as long as they don't risk banging their head when they're moving around. A 4-ft.- or 5-ft.-high knee wall with a bed and night table tucked under the eaves usually eliminates that problem.

CABIN MATTERS

GOING UP

Most cabins are built on one or two levels. However, site constraints–or a desire to have some fun–may inspire you to greater heights.

At Ludlow's Island Resort in northern Minnesota, I designed a four-level cabin, with exceptional views from the top two floors. We placed a single bedroom on the first, second, and fourth floors, while clustering the kitchen, dining area, and living space on the third. A rooftop balcony offers a beautiful view of an eagle's flight and the aurora borealis in the late-night sky. This tower cabin is a great design for families with older children or for couples who want to steal away for the weekend.

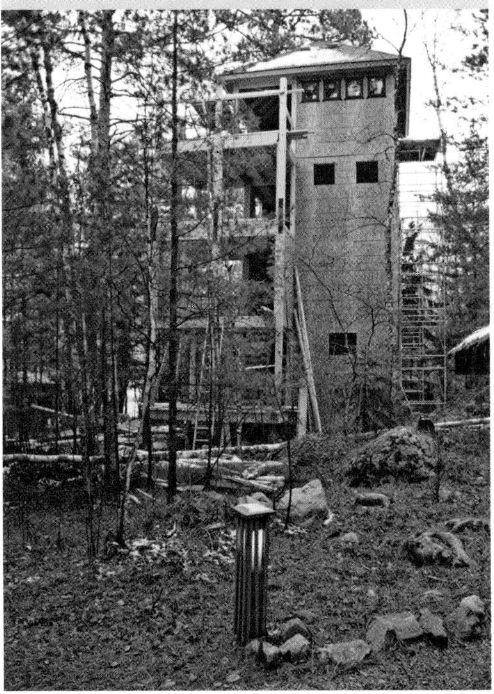

ROOF CHOICES

Cabin designs don't need complex roofs. When you take a good look at the vintage cabins that still charm us today, you notice that their simple details and textures are at least as pleasing as the turrets, roof eyebrows, and varied gable dormers that grace old homes in the city. A steep gable and a few shed dormers should be all that's necessary to protect your cabin from the elements, and such a roof is both easy and economical to build.

The A-frame is another classic cabin roof shape. During the 1950s and '60s, A-frames seemed to be everywhere–in the mountains or wherever else you'd find heavy snow as well as at the beach. Just the way the capital letter itself looks, the A-frame roof comes all the way down to the main-floor plane, taking the place of exterior walls on two sides of the cabin. On the inside, the A-frame is particularly conducive to a loft set high inside the gable ridge.

Roof shapes don't have to be gables. Hip roofs work well on single-story cabins or when used to cap a square tower. Hip roofs sit on walls that are all the same height, allowing walls to be easily framed and economically sheathed. Forest ranger stations with hip roofs atop windowed walls on all four sides have inspired countless cabins around the country.

Mono pitch or shed roofs are also effective, opening up a single façade to views and sunlight while effectively shedding rain and snow. If you're a do-it-yourselfer, this is an easy roof to build. It's a form that's most appropriate with long, narrow floor plans and with cabins only one room deep. Clerestory windows high in the tall wall allow sunlight deep inside.

Flat roofs are another economical option, and they are the easiest to fit atop complex floor plans. Flat roofs are normally associated with adobe or modern designs. Unlike the large, flat roofs you see on big commercial buildings with internal drains, flat roofs on cabins need a gentle slope for drainage and can be fitted with parapets on only three sides. It goes without saying that in northern regions flat roofs have to be strong enough to bear a season's load of ice and snow.

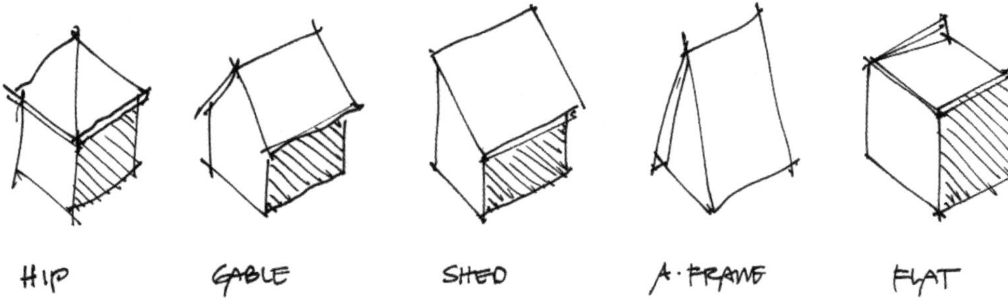

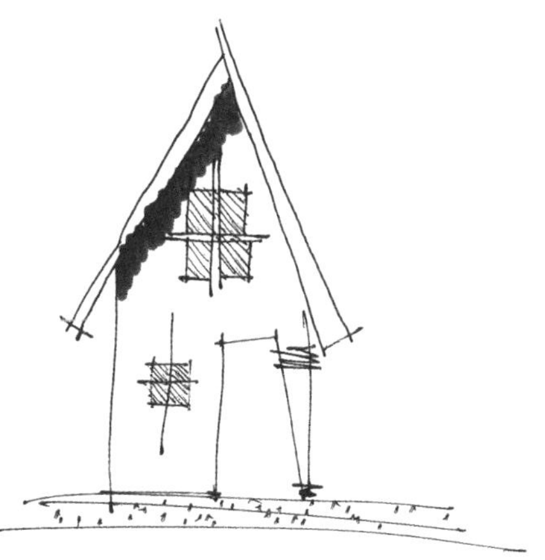

ANNA'S GATE

ABOVE: Not all cabins have to be built of logs, though many are, more out of tradition and sentiment than practicality. Logs do offer benefits because of their mass. Log walls are heavy, so they help hold in heat in the winter and coolness in warm weather. And they come in a variety of types and profiles, as do the way their corners are detailed.

LEFT: Let the child inside you have a hand at your first rough cabin drawings.

THE LAKESIDE JOHNS

My grandfather, John the first, came to Connecticut from Sicily around 1920 and eventually made friends with a man in New Haven who happened to have the same name. The other John Cavallaro was an entertainer, and in 1933 he opened a lakeside restaurant and bar with cottages and a beach area that he called the Casino.

My dad, John the second, played clarinet in a dance band that performed at the Casino. After my parents were married, this is where they went on weekends in the summer. And as far back as I can remember, I have been going up to this lake in the summertime.

Once I, John the third, reached my teens, John of the Casino offered me a job. From early spring to late fall, all through high school and early college, the Casino on the lake is where I spent my time.

Around 1965, as I was about to go into the Army, my parents bought an acre near the lake from John of the Casino, and my dad, with help from a friend, built our little cabin. In 1966, the total cost for land, cabin, and everything in it came to around $9,000. For a barber, which was my father's trade, that was a lot of haircuts.

So through the years, my first marriage, children being born, homes built, this is where we went in the summer. My oldest son, now 36, took his first steps on the painted plywood floor there. All three of my children, and now my four grandchildren, have spent their time in the lake, swimming, fishing, canoeing, and carousing in and around this cabin.

Although the little cabin has served all generations well, no matter how good a barber my father was, his hair-cutting skill didn't always translate into good carpentry. So about 10 years ago, after my father's death and years of on-and-off neglect, I started a rebuilding project. First came wide board pine over the painted plywood. Then a new double window in the back bedroom. The old paneling got a coat of white paint. Then out with the old maple family furniture, in with wicker and futons. New lights, a display board beside the kitchen to show off old photos taken at the house, a tile backsplash instead of wallpaper.

Although the little cabin has served all generations well, no matter how good a barber my father was, his hair-cutting skill didn't always translate into good carpentry.

After the third roof let go, my wife and I installed a metal barn roof. And instead of a drywall ceiling in the bedroom, we used barn siding for a warm and cozy paneling effect. Next came the large outdoor shower with no wall facing the woods. Let the critters laugh, but it's

A painting of John the second's cabin.

been five years and I've never used the indoor shower no matter what the weather. Because of limited space under the cabin, which has no basement, we built a good-sized garden shed with a sliding barn door. In 2006, we rebuilt the 40-ft. front deck. And we just started a bathroom renovation.

Of course, after 40 years, all of this work is a labor of love. It has marked the passages of my life, and now when the whole family comes to play, I get a broad view of the continuity of this place. From John the first all the way down to the grandbabies. Of course, I'm still trying to answer the question of how I got this old so fast.

But the next challenge for our little cottage is how it will continue in our family with the next generation after me. But endure I know it will.

–John Cavallaro is Assistant Production Manager, Marketing, at The Taunton Press.

WALL IT UP

With the shape of the roof in mind and a rough floor plan on the table, you can start thinking about the walls. Once again, you have an important decision to make–choosing the type of wall system that makes most sense for you, such as log, frame, timber, structural insulated panels (SIPs), or masonry.

Log walls will have different parameters than frame walls, mainly because log walls get their strength from their overlapping corners. And the length of a log wall is limited by the type of tree the logs come from and, just as importantly, by the length of the truck that hauls the logs to your site.

Pouring concrete might seem a good way to create a curved wall, but concrete walls are constrained by the specifics of their framework, or forms, which are also made of wood. The same is true of the stone walls that often serve as veneers because they have to conform to the structure's internal construction material, such as concrete blocks and stud frames, which until recently were also made of wood. Today concrete walls can be formed by hollow Styrofoam® blocks known as insulated concrete forms (ICFs).

Stud walls and concrete block walls are most cost-effective when their lengths are evenly divisible by 4 ft., which is the basic unit of construction in this country (next time you're in a home center, notice the dimensions of framing material: plywood is 4 ft. by 8 ft., studs are 8 ft., etc.).

THE SUM OF THE PARTS

I begin planning the outside walls by adding up the rough dimensions of all the parts within. Say I want the couple's bedroom to be at least 10 ft. wide, the living room 16 ft. across, the main-floor bathroom 6 ft. deep, and so on. I add up the number of feet from front to back and side to side and then tack on a few extra feet to allow for the thickness of the walls. The results give me a rough estimate of the cabin's dimensions.

Planning parameters

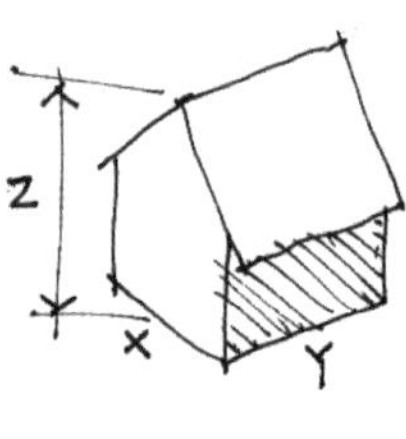

XYZ = BASICS

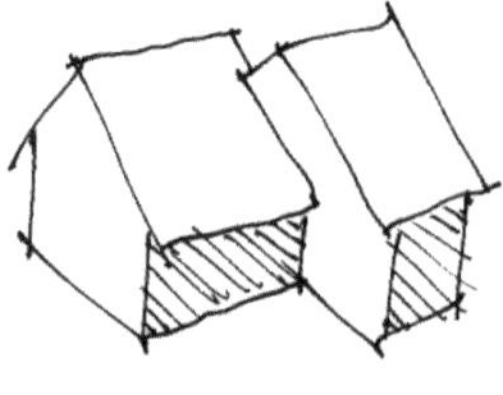

T = PHASING

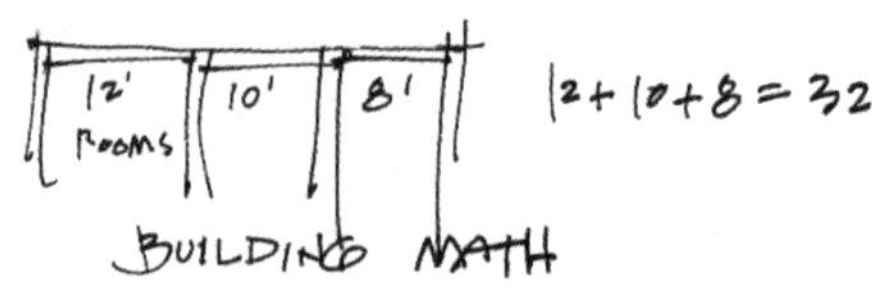

BUILDING MATH

Next, I grab a sheet of graph paper, a ruler, and a mechanical pencil and lay out the plan to a scale of 1/8 in. to 1 ft. The small scale of the first draft lets me see the big picture before deciding on the more specific sizes of windows, appliances, tub, fireplace, and the like. Think of this like a Google or MapQuest® map that lets you zoom out for a big-picture view and zoom in to get the detail. At this point, we're zoomed out.

Look closely at the plans of the older cabins you admire–there's usually a fundamental order to the walls. Aligning walls near the center of a plan often sets the bearing direction of the floor and roof. Nowadays you may want an open floor plan, which you can get by replacing walls with beams. Deciding on the beam locations with an occasional bearing post will be a helpful addition to the structural plan and can be downright fun in the design of the interior space.

SEE IT BEFORE YOU BUILD IT

You may have the ability and the imagination to completely visualize three-dimensional objects in your head, but for most of us, we need to actually see the object to really understand it. So to better visualize your cabin–roof, walls, and shape–try making a rough cardboard model of it based on your plan. A small model is much less expensive and more effective than finding out as you're building your cabin that the plan doesn't work or that you don't really like it that much.

A model is your vision in three dimensions, a visual and tactile form only suggested by a two-dimensional drawing. The model

CABIN MATTERS

ADDING TO A LOG WALL

Adding to a log structure presents an array of unique issues. In my experience, this is often best accomplished using non-log materials such as stick framing or timber-framed construction with SIP infill that fits between the timber posts. The shrinkage and movement in new logs (expansion and contraction of new wood connected to old, dry, cured wood) can cause gaps between new and old. In one log addition project, we stripped away earlier, poorly constructed additions and, using house jacks and cribbing (crisscrossed heavy timbers), supported the log cabin temporarily in place so we could pour a new foundation. Then we added a two-level companion addition to create more space for expanded family needs.

Three small-scale models give a quick view of the major design elements. Larger and more detailed cabin models with removable roofs and interior walls are shown on pages 142 and 143.

lets you see around corners and appreciate the fact that, for instance, the gable face you envisioned on the lake side may serve as a more interesting entry canopy on the opposite side or that a view of the driveway isn't that compelling when you're looking out the window over the sink.

The model can "inform" the plan and lead to a more harmonious cabin. It can allow your aesthetic sensibility rather than your logical brain to find pleasing solutions to design challenges. If you're building the cabin with a partner, a model will make your discussions more specific and concrete, reducing the chance of misunderstanding later.

I often create my models at a scale of 1/16 in. to 1 ft. Because the models are so small, we make them out of stiff paper or thin cardboard. A cereal box is ideal model material because it's both stiff and thin enough to be cut with scissors. We use tape, not glue, to hold the sides together. The result isn't necessarily pretty, but it doesn't have to be. The idea is to try different forms and shapes and see how they stand up–literally–against the plan you've transferred from your mind's eye to rough crayon sketch to a serious plan on paper.

If you like the cabin you've made, you can enlarge your model to a scale of 1/8 in. to 1 ft. and include more detail both inside and out. I usually make the larger, more detailed models out of a stiffer cardboard that requires more accurate cutting. This scale is more time-consuming and exacting, but it's an excellent way to work out your cabin design and develop a truly representative plan for the building contractor you'll eventually hire to build the cabin or to remodel the old one.

CABIN MATTERS

THE MODEL CABIN

Model making can be an art form or just a fun and messy endeavor that produces a three-dimensional facsimile of your cabin. I suggest you use thin cardboard, such as from a cereal box or a laundered shirt, which can easily be cut using scissors or a matte knife. Use transparent tape, a glue gun, or plain white glue to bond it together. I commonly produce my models at the scales of 1/16 in. equals 1 ft. (1:200m), 1/8 in. equals 1 ft. (1:100m), or 1/4 in. equals 1 ft. (1:50m). The smaller the scale, the less detailed the model will be.

A small model need only be a roof and the walls, whereas a large model can have windows, interior walls, and a removable roof.

You can fit your cabin into a contour model where each topographic contour is cut from an additional layer of cardboard. This will inform you as to how the cabin design works with the lay of the land and how many steps it may take to reach the front door. Add a few dry weeds and you'll sense your cabin's scale to the surrounding landscape.

Models can be taken with you to the site so you can perceive the views out of each face of the building. And you can test them for solar angles and shading by varying the model's angle to the sun to represent various seasons for which you intend to use your cabin.

After your cabin is complete, the models are fun to exhibit to show your friends where it all began.

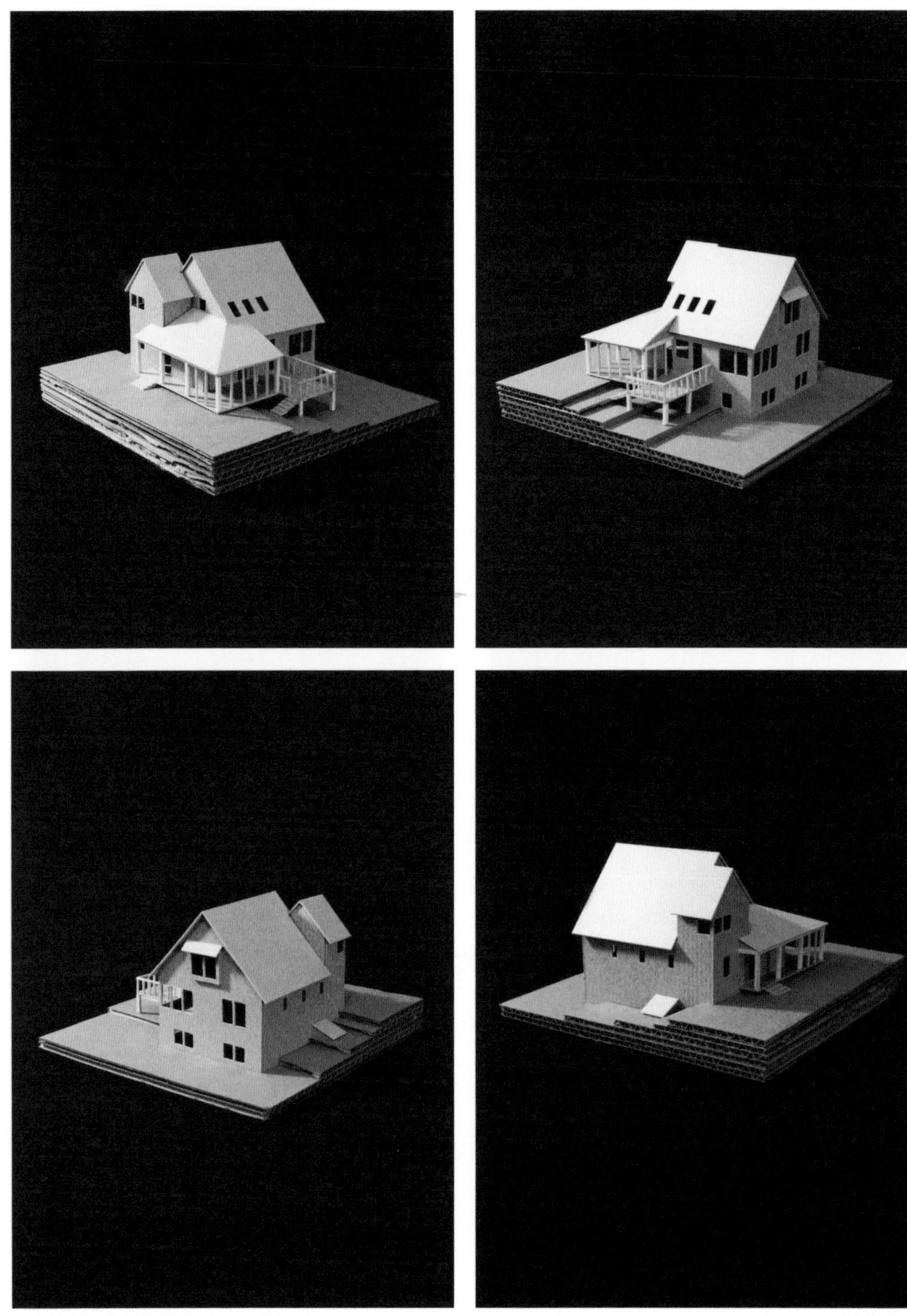

LETTING IN LIGHT AND FINDING SPACE

As your plans become firm, you'll start to explore (choose) the kind of windows you want and decide where you want them to be. You may want to have a window catalog in hand at this point, or you might be content to go with a shape and size that simply feels right. The placement of windows in a façade or within a room can be artful and playful or logical and practical. I seek a balance of both but always try to find a place for an unexpected little "Dale" window to be found.

A modest window in a big, solid wall is often referred to as a "punched opening" where the view from the inside is reading like a picture frame worthy of finely decorated framing. Similar windows set together in a group is referred to as "ganging." And a whole wall of glass is referred to as a "glass curtain wall."

Windows are not the only means to let in light, as we can use glass doors, skylights, and the latest invention, solar tubes. Each has its place and appropriateness, such as glass doors to walk through to the deck, a skylight over your bed to see the moon, or a solar tube to light a dark closet.

You'll need to decide if the windows should be centered on the roof shape (such as in the ridge of a gable) or be coordinated with the dimensions of a given room. In a bedroom, window placement may be determined by the size and location of the beds (a queen-size bed may require a different size and shape of window than a single or a bunk bed in the same space). Kitchen-window positioning requires some idea of where you're going to place the cabinets, sink, and refrigerator.

I've yet to have a client walk into a finished cabin and tell me that there are too many windows or that the windows are too tall. Everybody loves natural light, and in most cabin settings privacy isn't as important as it is in the city. Windows, however, are expensive and can quickly eat up a large chunk of your budget, so striking a balance between light and cost is important.

At about this stage in your planning, you'll want to start thinking about different openings in your wall: closets, cabinets, and mechanical chases (the hollows in the walls, floors, and ceilings where your ductwork runs).

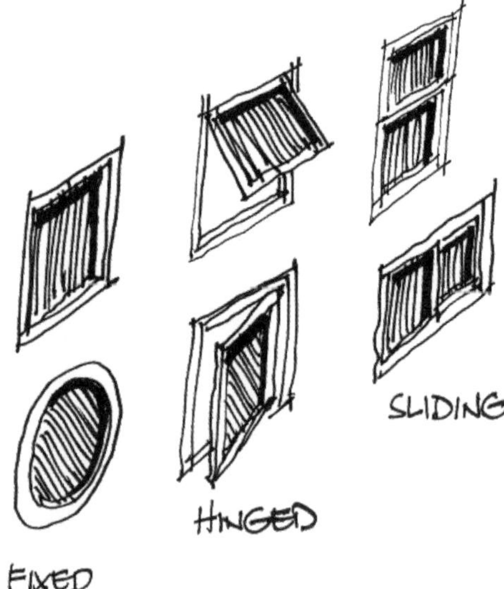

Three interesting "cabinesque" window types.

If you're building up north, you'll need to consider stacking the plumbing, with bathrooms positioned back to back or on top of each other, close to the kitchen and laundry room. By stacking the plumbing pipes, you'll have a much easier and more effective way to drain down in the fall. For that matter, it's not a bad idea to have the mechanical room close to the bathroom to ensure the shortest possible wait for hot water when you're showering.

GOING PRO

You're at the point now where logic and practicality are especially important because you'll want your cabin to function as handsomely as it looks. If you've reached a point where your plans have become overly complicated and confusing, you may decide you need the help of an architect. I won't try to talk you out of it. Architects charming, talented people.

An architect is trained by education and experience to help you create a design that makes the most of your space, squeezes the most out of your budget, and gives you something that comes as close as possible to the cabin you have in your mind (or one as close to it as your budget and other practical concerns allow).

If you can't find an architect you like and who fits into your budget, you can turn to a

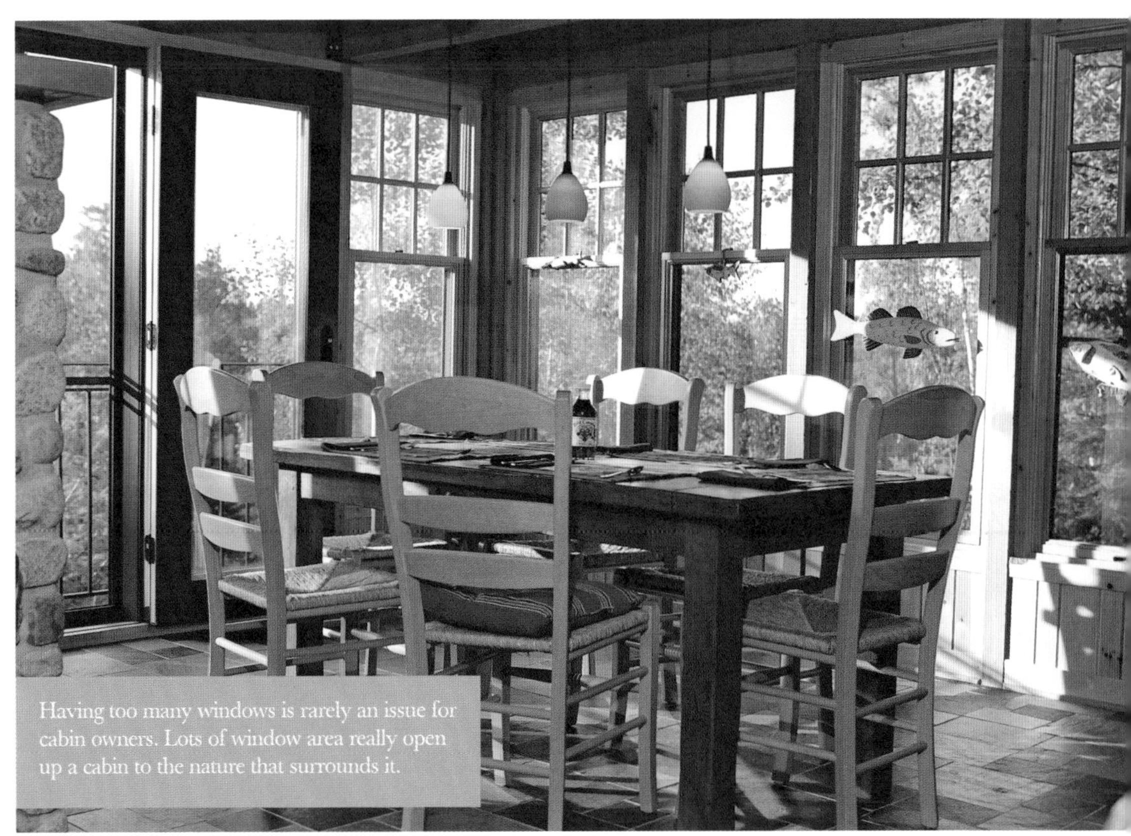

Having too many windows is rarely an issue for cabin owners. Lots of window area really open up a cabin to the nature that surrounds it.

CABIN MATTERS

WHAT AN ARCHITECT SEES

I've been studying cabins for decades and have documented structures put together by do-it-yourselfers, crafted by carpenters, and designed by architects. What's most apparent when looking at the last of these is the architect's reliance on cross-sectional drawings.

Like a doctor using magnetic resonance imaging, a good architect in his or her drawings will see "inside" an object, slicing open a cabin's structure to reveal the space under the roof or stairway so every square inch can be used to the owner's advantage.

Reading maps, site plans, floor plans, and plans of all kinds is a learned skill that most adults have attained by using atlases, looking at realtor listings, and reading magazines. By comparison, cross sections are not a common type of drawing for most people. It takes several years for students of architecture, industrial design, and engineering to get used to the value of cross-sectional drawing. This little drawing illustrates the architect's ability to use x-ray vision to truly understand how a building should work.

local draftsman. So what's the difference? A good architect looks for inventive solutions, while a good draftsman is more likely to opt for conventional solutions using materials available at the local lumberyard and construction processes familiar to area builders.

Your decision boils down to the complexity of your design–whether it's for a new cabin or remodeling an existing one. If your plans aren't particularly fancy, a draftsman might work just fine. However, if you want something quite special, if your cabin will incorporate a more sophisticated level of design, I suggest you use an architect.

Whether it's an architect, a draftsman, or your builder who helps you with your plans, you're definitely going to need somebody with technical knowledge and experience to help you with structural framing and building procedures, not to mention code requirements and other critical matters. Your final plan will require, for example, precise dimensions for window openings and the depth of roof rafters for both structural and insulation purposes. All of that can make the job especially tricky and complex–particularly if you have no background or experience in construction.

BUILDING IN PHASES

If you plan to use your cabin as a second home or retirement home, you'll approach the construction as an incremental investment–that is, more in terms of cash outlays than of mortgage payments. That's because, in most cases, planning and building a retirement home isn't done in a rush; it's done over time.

That decision will also affect the type of cabin you end up with. If remodeling, you're likely taking a cabin that was meant for use in only a couple of seasons and turning it into what eventually will be a year-round residence. And you're probably adding space and storage and lots of upgrades. If it's a new cabin, you're more or less simply building a smaller version of a house, which likely happens to be in a quieter and more beautiful place than where your current house resides.

If the cabin will eventually be a full-time home, you can pay as you go–or, more accurately, go as you pay. As the money becomes available, you add or finish another room or outbuilding, maybe with the cost-saving help of a couple of weekend warriors willing to swap sweat equity for a few weeks at the lake. Some folks put off the largest addition or improvement until last, when their children's college educations have been paid or the equity in their house can be applied to the cabin.

Ideally, building in phases is not a process of simply adding on as the opportunity arises but something you plan for from the beginning. Phasing should be thought out with an eye on practical matters. Maybe you build the bunkhouse or guest cabin first and use it until you complete the main building so you have a place to stay while you're working on the cabin. If that's the case, however, how large should you make the kitchen in the guest cabin? And is the compact galley that will eventually serve your friends going to be large enough for your family in the meantime?

FROM OUTSIDE IN

Another go-as-you-pay strategy is to construct the shell and finish the various parts of the interior as you can. If that's the plan, you'll be well advised to hire a professional contractor to build the shell, to make sure it will keep out the rain and snow, then ask Uncle Bob, the retired plumber, to rough in the essential wet zones (bathrooms, kitchen, laundry) in exchange for some time at the site.

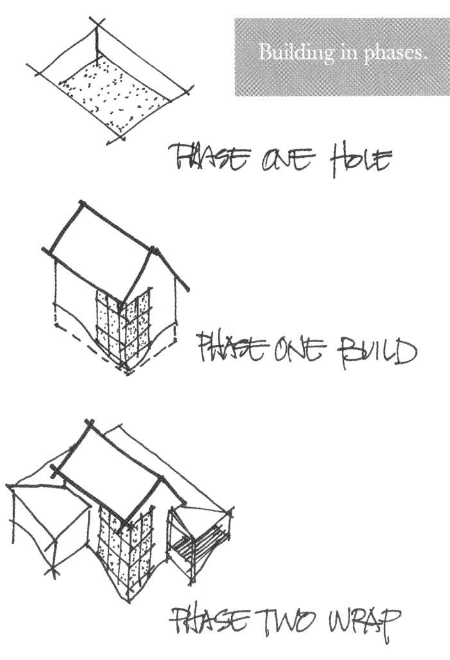

Building in phases.

Meanwhile, there are at least three major caveats to keep in mind when thinking about a phased approach to building or remodeling your cabin.

1. The local building inspector may say your building permit expires in a year and, at any rate, he needs to see the licenses of all the installers at the time he issues it.

2. Your mortgage lender may consider your project only from the perspective of its eventual resale value and won't be excited about the prospect of putting a half-done building on the market, if it came to that.

3. Your family may quickly tire of weekends in unfinished space and, as far as that goes, wouldn't be happy about spending their days at the lake with hammers and saws instead of rods and reels.

ADDING ON, REMODELING, TRANSFORMING

A lot of what I've talked about pertains to planning, designing, and constructing a new cabin, but a significant portion of the information can relate equally to remodeling. As I mentioned, the reality is that more people will buy a cabin and fix it up than will build a new one.

So odds are good that you may already own a handsome structure (or even a plain-Jane one) on a beautiful site but want to remodel and add on for more room and, frankly, a nicer cabin.

Maybe you've inherited a seasonal getaway from your wife's folks and decide you want to use it all year. Maybe you want to reconfigure a cabin you bought, both for the sake of looks as well as livability. Or maybe you've come across an old train caboose, a little red schoolhouse, even an abandoned chicken coop, and want to convert it into a cabin. Each of those possibilities will require a different plan and approach in which budget, site realities, and zoning regulations are important considerations.

GETTING HELP

When remodeling, you are not starting with a blank sheet of paper. You are starting with something that already exists, something that has rooms and a roof and a personality. If you are starting with an average cabin, which has three rooms, you are likely talking about dividing up those rooms at the very least. And in this age of open floor plans, it is logical to imagine that the functions that were built into those three rooms don't represent the way you live today. If that is the case, now is the time to free your mind for exploring alternatives.

When you're planning a new cabin, most of what you deal with at this stage is two-dimensional–plans on paper. When remodeling, you deal with three-dimensional objects.

There is a front to back and a left to right

CABIN MATTERS

MORE REASONS FOR CAREFUL PLANS

The choices you make about mechanical and electrical functions are critical to the planning process because they often affect how the rest of the building comes together.

For instance, you don't want your heating contractor to run a duct through a beam, and you'll need enough space in the wall next to the door for a light switch. The in-floor heat may come from a hydronic system in a concrete slab or from an electrical mat system buried in 8 in. of sand below the slab.

Careful planning will save you costly decisions during construction. Also, you may be required to provide an electrical plan before you're granted a building permit.

Timber frame structures make charming cabins with large volume open space akin to a converted barn. The open loft area could eventually be enclosed to form a private bedroom suite or guest rooms.

This photograph looks from the addition to the old cabin through the doorway. The original log cabin (exterior walls left visible) was built years before, and the owners used it while planning the addition.

and an up and down. So the roof becomes a critical component in your planning. One way to approach it is to build a little model of your existing cabin, which can help you understand what you might want to do with the roof. Do you extend one of the pitches to take in another room? Do you raise the roof to take in a second floor?

A builder or architect can help. He may even have tried-and-true ideas for making the changes and improvements you have in mind. Or he may say that the best plan would be to tear it down and start over. The key, as always, is to consider all the possibilities and to make the best choice for you given your circumstances.

Say you want to upgrade the cabin's conveniences, add a couple of windows, and open up the walls–in other words, you want to remodel. You may be well served by professionals who can advise you on critical concerns such as load-bearing walls and access to plumbing, not to mention more aesthetic issues such as character and style.

Adding on to a cabin may raise important regulatory issues involving zoning and construction. Many older cabins exist outside modern zoning limits, so your addition may require a variance, which means a hearing before the zoning commission. The cabin's original foundation and electrical system may not meet current building codes, and serious upgrading may be needed throughout. You can get a pretty good idea of what's going to be required by comparing the existing structure with your ideal needs diagram, but a consultation with a pro will probably be necessary before you're comfortable deciding what to do.

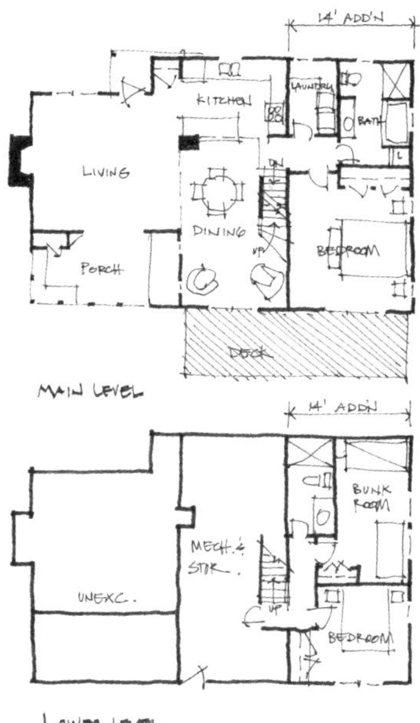

Your drawings don't have to be professional or even scaled to the actual dimensions, but they should show all rooms, walls, and important features such as fireplaces, staircases, hallways, doors, and windows. Once you've drawn out the plans, you can begin to imagine additions, remove walls, shift halls, and rearrange rooms to suit your needs.

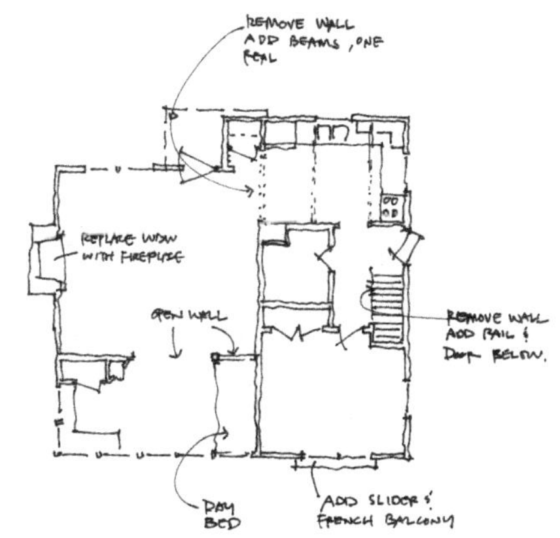

When imagining your remodel or addition, consider the original structure, with its unique personality, quirks, and charms.

GOING UP OR OUT?

You know what you want and what you need out of your cabin, but you're not sure how to go about getting it. Should you move a wall or add a wall or make do with what you have? Or should you add on?

If you add on, should you add on vertically or horizontally–go up or out? The answer depends on your needs and the amount of available space you have to work with. Additional living space is usually what folks want on the main floor, while more bedrooms typically call for a second floor.

If you do decide to go up, you'll want to get a pro to help figure out structural requirements for the addition, such as whether the existing frame and foundation can support another floor. Whether you go up or go out, you'll have to know what your zoning code allows. And you may have to expand your septic field if you're adding bedrooms (though, strangely, not if you're adding only a bathroom).

TRANSFORMATIONAL

When additions and remodeling create a whole new look (say, turning a ranch into a bungalow, for instance), architects call the process and result a "transformation." In any transformation, there has to be a pretty good reason to hold onto portions of the existing building. That reason may involve zoning, budget, tradition, sentiment, or nostalgia.

I've seen (or heard about) grain silos, lighthouses, and boats transformed into cabins. And when they're done right, the character, charm, and history of the original are preserved and sometimes enhanced, even though the original is serving an entirely new and different function.

CABIN MATTERS

A GROWING INVESTMENT

An incremental investment project I designed began with a two-and-a-half-story, 16-ft. by 24-ft. structure with no plumbing. Built a half level into the earth (helping amortize the foundation's cost), the cabin features only a bedroom and a bathroom with a chemical toilet on the bottom level, a living space with a dry kitchen on the main floor, and a sleeping room in a loft above. All things considered, there are 960 sq. ft. of space built at minimal cost. A well, septic system, and plumbing can all be added on a go-as-you-pay basis.

Eventually, the cabin may have a 10-ft. wrap around three-quarters of the main floor, enclosing an entryway, kitchen, couple's bedroom, bathroom, library, and screened porch. This final–and extensive–addition will be ready when the owners finish their teaching careers, sell their primary home, and relocate to the country. The wrap will add another 850 sq. ft. of living space that will transform the original getaway into a home that feels as big as the Ritz.

In any case, to embark on serious changes you need to be just as careful and clear thinking as you'd be if you were starting with an empty lot. You'll need a set of plans for the existing structure, with photographs of the place inside and out. The plans have to be accurately drawn, with wall thickness accounted for and the new structural system realistically imagined.

An experienced professional can help you figure out which walls are the bearing walls. But in a lot of cases with old cabins, you won't

What was originally open and unfinished space above the bedrooms will become an interesting loft space with catwalk spanning the living area.

know for sure until you open the walls, ceilings, and floors. This can be an adventure in its own right. You might be shocked by the incompetence of the "handyman" who slapped your cabin together using materials he apparently hauled in from the town dump. Then again, you may be pleasantly surprised by the finesse of a long-forgotten craftsman and amazed by the quality of the materials he used.

WHAT'S NEXT

Before you pull a permit, let alone dig, demolish, pour, wire, plumb, or frame, you'll want to have a master plan in place, whether it's for a new cabin or a remodel. Without a plan, you would have a hard time attracting builders to your project. With a plan, you and your builder can begin to develop a list of materials and specifications for the cabin. You will select the tile for the bathroom and decide whether it will be wainscot height or not, then the builder will estimate quantities and installation costs. You will select the interior pine walls in random 4-in. to 6-in. vertical boards, and the builder will know the supplier and the cost of the wood. A detailed construction plan, specifications list, and purchasing schedule are what your contractor will need for a sworn construction bid, as well as what you will need to proceed to your mortgage lender or wealthy grandparents.

Your plan and model will proclaim the scope and scale of your dream, but the specifics discussed in chapters 5 and 6 will yield the detail and richness to make your cabin special. You can leave these decisions to a builder, or you can jump in and direct the decisions to your values and desires–and then your builder, the subcontractor, and the local lumber dealer will bring you back to earth.

This is a similar-sized cabin plan with two variations, one with a broader face enfronting the lake view.

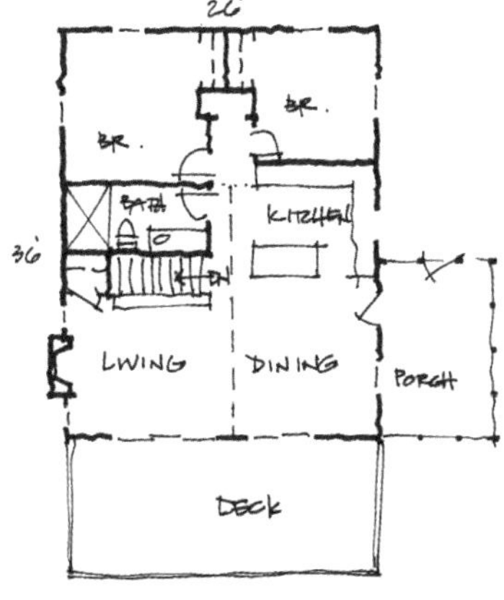

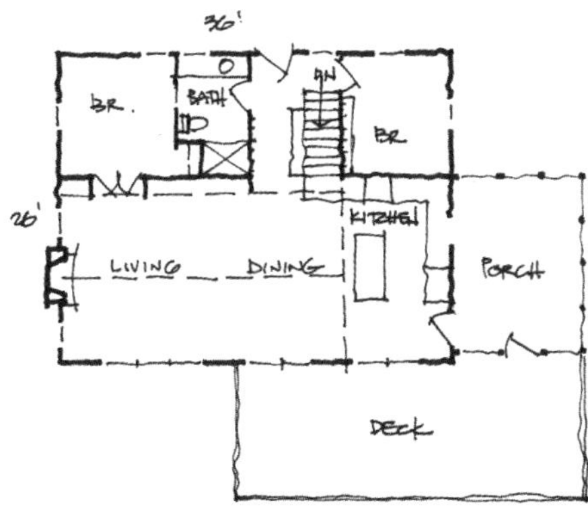

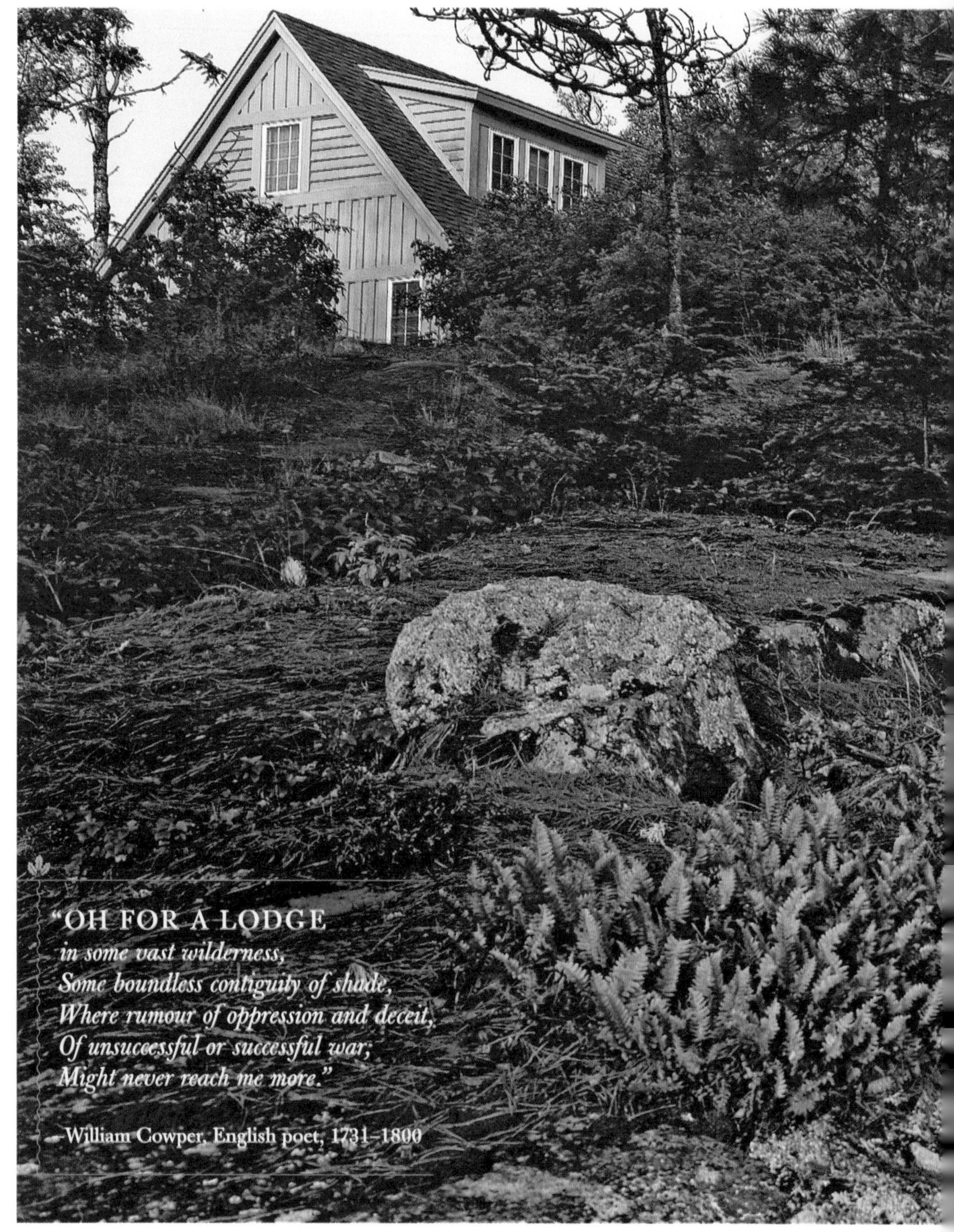

"OH FOR A LODGE
in some vast wilderness,
Some boundless contiguity of shade,
Where rumour of oppression and deceit,
Of unsuccessful or successful war;
Might never reach me more."

–William Cowper, English poet, 1731–1800

ASSEMBLY REQUIRED

CHAPTER FIVE

LET ME TAKE YOU BACK. It's a late fall day. You're 10 years old. A cold rain has you stuck inside. Scattered across the living room rug are the full contents of a cardboard canister of Lincoln Logs. As the world outside dissolves into rain, you invest the entire afternoon exploring the frontier of your imagination.

A drawing of a log fort (probably deep in Indian country) decorates the Lincoln Logs canister. It's not a fort you're setting out to build, but a cabin all your own. Brown logs, red gables, green roof, red chimney. Windows you can look through. Doors that open. A shelter for your dream. A plastic army man or two brings it alive.

Forward to your current world of job, routine, traffic. It's time to break out the Lincoln Logs again. You have a chunk of land or a cabin in need of some work. You have a plan, some drawings, maybe even a cardboard model. And you have the time and at least enough money to get things up and moving.

Let's go. It's time to develop what architects call the bill of materials

"AFTER YOUR CABIN PLANS ARE COMPLETE, *build a miniature cabin. If you are unfamiliar with reading blue prints, the miniature cabin will prove most helpful. More than this, it will serve as a perfect guide, save errors and also expense."*

–Conrad Meinecke, *Your Cabin in the Woods,*
Foster & Stewart Publishing Corporation, 1945

(a list of all the parts and pieces needed to get the project under way–like the instructions that came with the Lincoln Logs). It's time to put the pieces together.

Whether you played with Lincoln Logs, Tinkertoys®, or Legos® as a kid, we're about to turn that cabin in your mind into a three-dimensional reality.

BASIC MATERIALS

So what does the cabin in your mind look like? Is it folksy and rustic, sleek and modern, something in between? How are you putting the pieces together? And what are the pieces?

Your combinations of choices are infinite–roofing and siding, floors and ceilings, doors and windows, flooring, lighting, plumbing, appliances, kitchen fixtures. Not to mention color. The fireplace. Furniture. The list goes on and on. The good news is that whatever decisions you don't make, your builder will make for you. The bad news is that whatever decisions you don't make, your builder will make for you. If you're as particular as most cabin owners I know, you'll want the choices to be yours.

Just as your cabin can be built in any number of ways, depending on the character you have in mind, your budget, and other considerations that may or may not be unique to your situation, the same range of possibilities holds true for the materials that go into your cabin.

For a distinctly local look and feel, choose as many locally grown or manufactured

✦ CABIN MATTERS ✦

JUST THE SPECS

Specification forms used by builders generally list materials in the following categories:

- ✦ Site preparation
- ✦ Foundation and basement
- ✦ Framing material
- ✦ Doors and windows
- ✦ Exterior siding
- ✦ Roofing
- ✦ Interior surfaces and trim
- ✦ Cabinets and countertops
- ✦ Plumbing rough-in and fixtures
- ✦ Electrical rough-in and fixtures
- ✦ Heating and air-conditioning
- ✦ Hardware and supplements

BELOW: Imagine your cabin with the rooms and details you want in the real thing.

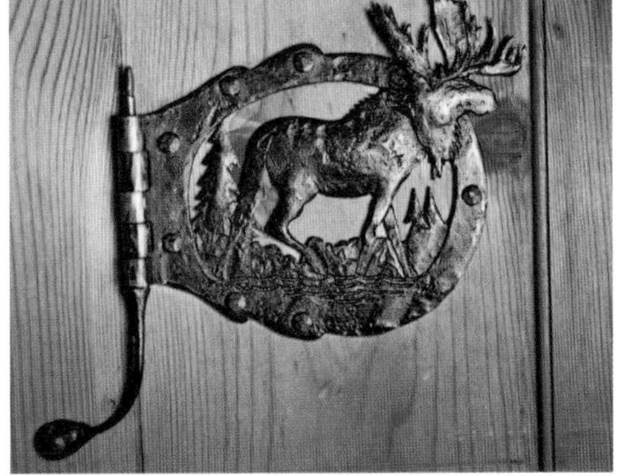

TOP: A nicely designed stair has lots of wood texture and, as a hint at your favorite pastime, a canoe paddle resting in the corner.

BOTTOM: A custom door hinge adds a touch of character and handmade craft to a cabin door.

products as you can find and afford. Or import–usually with additional transportation cost–the bulk of your materials and end up with a cabin that looks like its neighbors but that may generate hard feelings from local merchants and other town folk who naturally believe in the "shop at home" philosophy. Or buy a prefab structure "off the shelf" and have it delivered to your site, in whatever form, size, and style you desire.

KEEPING IT LOCAL

If you buy your materials from local sources–which, by the way, I enthusiastically recommend–one of your first stops, if you haven't been there already, is the local lumberyard. You'll find that local lumberyards and hardware stores are at the center of things when it comes to building. You'll discover which materials are readily available and what they're going to cost. The lumber dealer will also be able to provide a list of local builders and possibly even referrals and recommendations.

A visit to other cabin construction sites in the area can give you a lot of information about local material preferences, practices, and tradespeople. What works best in your neck of the woods? Who can you count on? Who to avoid? The best way to get answers to those questions is to ask your new neighbors.

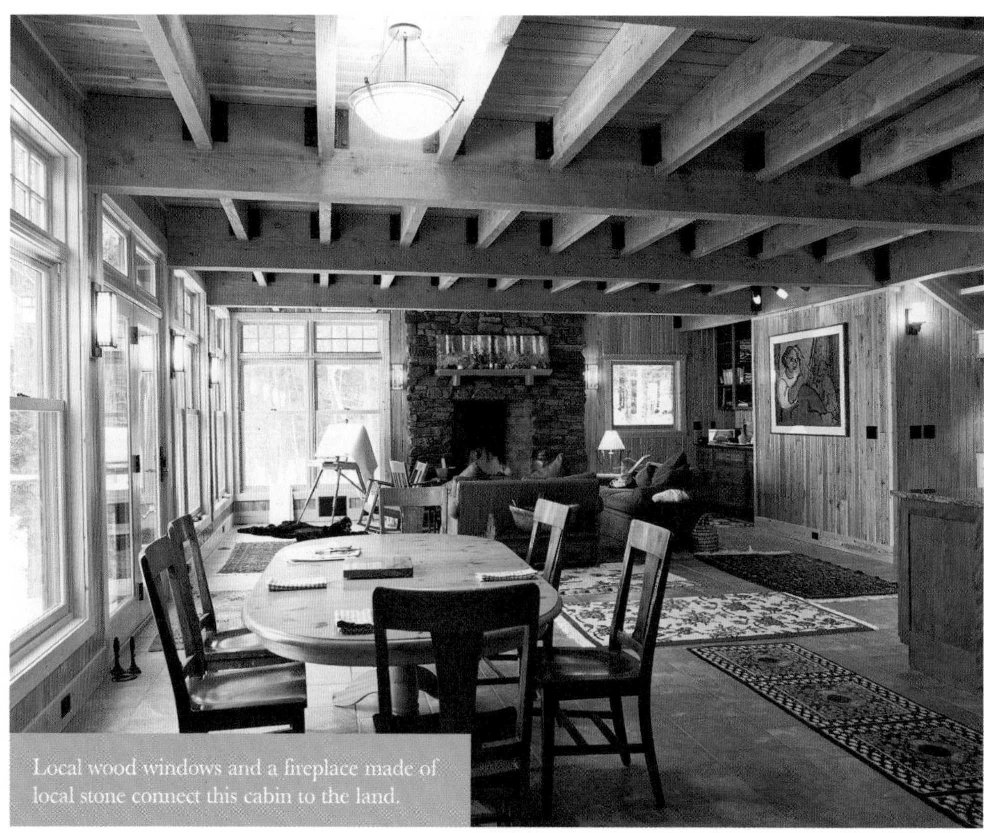

Local wood windows and a fireplace made of local stone connect this cabin to the land.

You probably already know the materials you'll likely want because you've seen them in the city, but there will be subtleties you need to be aware of. I'm keen on the use of a local wood, especially for sheathing a cabin's interior walls. Tamarack, spruce, and poplar are a few of the trees I'm partial to when designing cabins in my part of the country. As much as I love Douglas fir, it mostly grows out west, so for that reason it's not a wood I'd likely use around here.

I feel the same way about local rocks, which have either been deposited in the area by glaciers or harvested from local quarries or farm fields. However they got there, you're likely to find one or more types that are visually unique to the area.

Minnesota's taconite mines (the modern source of iron for steel making) are a great source of construction-quality stone. Including all the nearby caches of granite, limestone, Kasota stone, and sandstone, there is a large diversity of the hard stuff from which to choose in my part of the country. Whatever the source, you can use rock ranging from pebbles to boulders, in round or split-faced form, for everything from foundation to fireplace.

The materials you select will either depend on or determine the way your cabin is finally put together. The three most common framing techniques, for instance, are log, timber frame, and stick frame (what builders call two-by lumber, e.g., 2x4s, 2x6s, etc.). Each requires special know-how, although stick frame is familiar to most builders and can be most easily adapted to sites and situations. Meanwhile, new panelization methods are available wherever lifting equipment can be used.

CABIN MATTERS

THE GOSPEL ACCORDING TO PHELPS

Many helpful books have been published on the subject, but the log builder's bible is Hermann Phelps's *The Craft of Log Building* (reprinted by HarperCollins, 1989), translated from *Der Blockbau*. In it, Phelps enumerates, among other things, the many log-shaping and cornering techniques common to European wood construction.

Casement windows, barn-red logs, and lots of interesting texture create the rustic appeal of this historic cabin in Wisconsin.

LOG CONSTRUCTION

Building with logs is another way to stay local, although nowadays many log homes are prefabricated in plants many states away. Yet despite a few drawbacks, log construction is both a nostalgic favorite (remember those Lincoln Logs and, for that matter, the original Abe Lincoln boyhood cabin) and still an effective way to build a sturdy cabin. Log cabins are typically constructed by local builders who specialize in the technique. Many kinds of trees can be used for a log cabin, so long as they grow tall and straight. Cedar, fir, pine, spruce, hemlock, and balsam are commonly used, although Western red cedar is probably the choice more often than the others.

Hand-squared logs with heavy chinking is a time-honored form of log construction. This cabin also includes reclaimed timber-frame elements in the joists and posts.

While there are a slew of ways to assemble the logs, the most popular process features notched overlapping corners with protruding ends. Our ancestors, including my own great-grandfather, favored dovetail corners for their log houses, but they require especially high-quality timber, which is not so readily available anymore, at least not at prices most of us are willing to pay. Dovetail corners also demand a level of construction skill and finesse that similarly jacks up the cost.

In any event, the logs are usually delivered to the builder's yard when they're still green and can be easily peeled and sawed. The logs are cut to fit, then preassembled in a simple, rectangular shape, at which point the openings for doors and windows are cut into them (ideally toward the middle of the logs because log cabins derive their strength from the linked corners). Roof beams, rafters, and purlins (horizontal pieces that support the rafters) are added. The components are numbered, and the structure is dismantled and shipped off to your site.

Because log cabins tend to settle a lot during the first few years following construction, careful builders include contraction sleeves for the doors and windows and jacks for the posts. They also make sure that roofs overhang the buildings far enough to protect the logs from excessive rainfall, although the extended eaves make the cabin darker inside than you'd get from the roof on an ordinary frame cabin. On the brighter side, the finished surfaces both inside and out are the same beautiful material.

Like a high-maintenance lover, log cabins are not for everyone. But those who love them put up with a little extra maintenance to enjoy the nostalgic beauty. Structural movement, insect infestation, and weathering are all negatives that require attention. Inside, the built-ins will have to be scribed to fit (individually trimmed), and you will need to be precise about where electrical outlets go before the final log assembly.

Log walls can be made with a variety of log profiles from rustic hand-scribed logs, square logs, or milled smooth logs. They can be laid up with insulation and chinking at their joints. Chinking is the white grout you have seen between logs inside and out, but it is utilized only with certain forms of log assembly.

If you find an old log cabin and want to move it, it's possible to dismantle it, replace rotted logs, and reassemble it wherever you want. In the Midwest, we occasionally find log walls buried inside clapboard-sided homes, and these, too, can be recycled for your new cabin.

Many old log cabins remain charming on the inside yet worn and weathered on the outside, so reusing them might require a new exterior siding. Your guests may be warmly surprised to enter your wood-shingle cabin and find a log cabin inside.

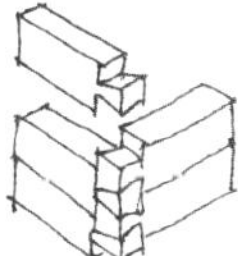

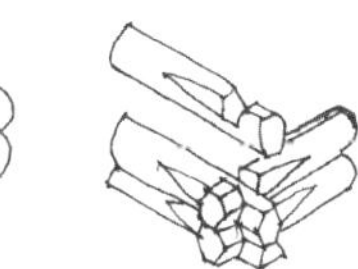

Traditional log corner details.

ABOVE: Saddle-notched round logs overlap at the corners of this log cabin and provide the nostalgic Lincoln Log look that's become the traditional detail of log cabins in many people's imagination.

BELOW: These logs are squared off at the end and cut into half-lap corner joints.

CABIN STORIES

PARADISE LOST

In 1971, when my parents were still happily married and years away from having kids or getting divorced, they bought a cabin in rural upstate New York. Thirty-five years later, the cabin is still standing–and almost the same as it ever was.

When we were very young, after my parents separated, Dad would pick up me and my brother from our house in the urban jungle of New York City to spend the weekend with him in the woods. This is why I have no fear of wild animals or insects and why I'm the only one of my friends who can catch a frog or climb a tree with total confidence. The cabin, in weekend doses, completely shaped who I am.

The house has no television, but I didn't notice this until I was nearly a teenager and started watching *Saturday Night Live*. There was simply too much to do in the endlessly entertaining woods around the cabin to even think about television.

One of our favorite pastimes was to play in the fireplace, when Dad gave us the illusion of being left alone. The only time we got scolded was when we almost burned the house down playing how-big-can-we-make-the-fire. The varnish is still melted off the wall above the fireplace.

After that incident, our favorite game became "Paradise Lost." Paradise Lost involved building a tiny "community" on top of a discarded ceiling tile and then watching it burn. The tiles had fallen from the ceiling in my brother's room and were made of compressed cardboard. This was ideal because, as we learned, if we built the city on paper, it would burn too quickly. Conversely, if we built it on plywood, it would burn too slowly. The ceiling tiles gave us a perfect burn time, thus adding to the tragedy and fun.

My brother and I would build houses out of twigs and leaves. "This is the school," one of us would say as we poked sticks into the top. There would be a town hall and a town square and sometimes we'd add a pool because it would boil before disintegrating. The people were wooden matches and had the most gruesome demise of all. After building for a while, one of us would say, "Ready for Paradise Lost?" and we'd nod solemnly. Then we'd place our little town in the fire and cheer as it burned. This was far more entertaining than television.

There was simply too much to do in the endlessly entertaining woods around the cabin to even think about television.

Now my brother and I are grown, and the cabin remains one of the few things that has been a constant throughout my life. My father lives in the cabin full time during the summers, and when we go up, it's very much the same, except my brother and I drink wine now.

And every now and then, we'll settle in for a good, long game of Paradise Lost and muse about what bizarre children we were.

–Carrie Gravenson lives and works in New York City where she has mastered the delicate balance between following her dreams and paying rent.

TIMBER-FRAME CONSTRUCTION

Over the past two or three decades, there's been a resurgence of the ancient construction method known as timber framing. Few types of construction are so visible and potentially dramatic and handsome as a beautifully designed and carefully crafted timber frame. But when fabricated the old way with precise mortise-and-tenon joints, timber framing demands considerable knowledge of advanced techniques and some specialized equipment.

Essentially, a good timber frame is as painstakingly cut and fitted as a fine piece of custom furniture, though it has the added responsibility of actually holding up your cabin. Your builder can reduce both the complications and the costs if he bolts the joints together using metal brackets and plates, a derivative framing technique known as post and beam. Or if you have the money and access to a first-rate timber framer–and they're out there–you can have it joined the old way.

To get the rich look of a timber frame where it does the most good visually, I'm partial to a hybrid construction technique: I mix several different timber elements in my cabin designs, such as floor joists and roof trusses, with normal interior and exterior frame walls that bear the weight. This lowers costs while maintaining the structural wood character. If you use recycled wood or wood that has been properly dried, you can reduce the checking and twisting frame movement common with new timber and get a look that's hard to reproduce with new timber.

Timber-frame construction requires a thermal skin for the cabin's exterior, which nowadays is often provided by structural insulated panels

TOP: True timber-frame joinery is composed of hand-cut mortise-and-tenon joinery secured by wood pegs for great strength. The timber frame is visible inside the structure, showing off both its ability to hold up the cabin and the beauty of the natural wood.

BOTTOM: A timber frame is built in "bents," which are the individual sections shown in this drawing. A crane is lifting sections of the exterior wall, with window cutouts, made of structural insulated panels (SIPs).

RIGHT: Few types of construction so clearly express strength and character of structure than timber framing.

(SIPs). SIPs form the exterior shell and are cut out to contain doors and windows. They provide the exterior weathering surface, such as clapboards, shingles, or even half-timber veneer, which creates the appearance of a log home. Interior SIP surfaces contain wiring channels that must be coordinated with the electrical plan before they're set in place. Also, because a boom truck is probably needed to install the timber frames and panels, you'll need a large enough access road to accommodate it and good clearance all around the site.

STICK-FRAME CONSTRUCTION

Stick-frame construction is still the easiest, most common, and most adaptable way to build a cabin. That's because most cabins are comparatively small and the span lengths (the distance a joist or beam can go between supports) for the lumber used to build them are generally short. Builders who construct seasonal cabins often don't even bother to sheath the walls inside. Instead, they leave studs exposed on the interior, resulting in a familiar, casual look (you've seen this look inside old garages).

STICK WALLS

Walls of stick construction require either 2x4 or 2x6 wall studs, depending on insulation needs (the deeper the stud, the more insulation the wall cavities hold). The walls are then sheathed outside with 4-ft. by 8-ft. sheets of plywood or oriented strand board (OSB), either of which provides ample lateral stability and wind resistance. On top of that, the finish siding goes up. Inside, drywall is typically installed.

STICK FLOORS

The floors of stick-frame cabins usually consist of either 2x8 or 2x10 dimensional lumber, wood I-joists (an engineered product), or floor trusses. Like the exterior walls, the floors, too, are sheathed in plywood or OSB, and the final flooring material is placed on top of that.

If you want to kill two birds with one stone and get both a floor and a ceiling, an

TIP **THINK AHEAD**

If you plan to apply structural flooring directly over ceiling joists, give careful thought to your electrical needs.

In the dining room of our cabin, we routed a channel through the top of the ceiling beam and then drilled a hole to drop electric lights through the beam. Needless to say, we were careful to avoid the electrical wire when nailing the decking.

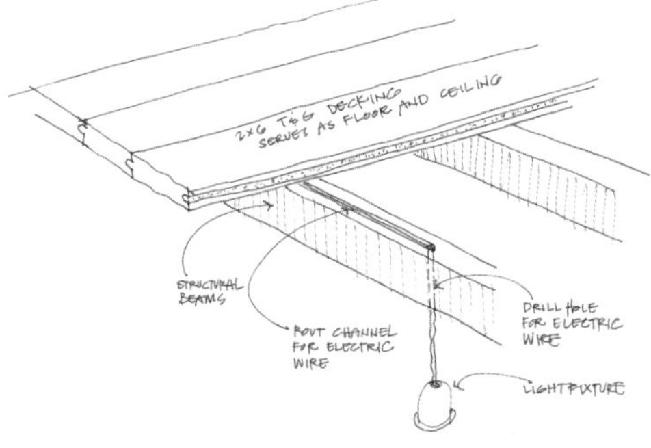

A narrow channel cut into the floor joist allows hidden electrical wiring to reach the light fixture below.

✦ CABIN MATTERS ✦

FORM FOLLOWS STRUCTURE

New methods of building are occurring every day and in every part of the country. I just accepted a revision of a standard stick-frame design into insulated concrete form (ICF) construction. Insulated concrete forms provide great strength, thermal mass, and sound insulation, as well as high energy efficiency. In this case, building with ICFs was the preferred building system for this backcountry builder. Fortunately, the plan could accommodate the extra 3 in. of wall thickness, which was simply added to the outside to avoid taking up living space inside.

ABOVE: Built for warm-weather use, this stick-framed cabin shows off its construction with open stud bays. The boards showing between the studs are both the interior finish and the outside sheathing to which the siding is attached.

BELOW: An A-frame can receive a dormer to let light in and give headroom over a bed.

ABOVE: Boards that form the ceiling also form the floor upstairs. Although this type of construction can be noisy, carpets and rugs upstairs can help hold down the noise of foot traffic overhead.

upper-story floor can be covered with a higher-quality and thicker flooring (normal flooring is 3/4 in. thick), which is finished on both sides. Often, a V-groove or beadboard profile is milled on the side that shows below. The drawback is sound transmission because every step on the floor above is a step on the ceiling below. There's also no space for mechanical and electrical systems for this ceiling/flooring.

Needless to say, you'll want a qualified professional to review the sizes, spans, and spacing of whatever floor system you use to make sure your water bed won't fall through onto the dining table below. Locally milled lumber is not graded for structural capability, so you may want to field-test it for strength. However, the building inspector may require that you use so-called "graded" lumber for all load-bearing walls and other elements such as floors and rafters. You can tell graded from ungraded by the stamp the lumber carries.

STICK ROOFS

The roofs of stick-framed cabins are also hand-framed using deeper lumber (such as 2x10s and 2x12s) or I-joists. The depth of the joists depends on how much snow (snow loads) you're likely to get in your part of the country and the amount of insulation you'll need. If

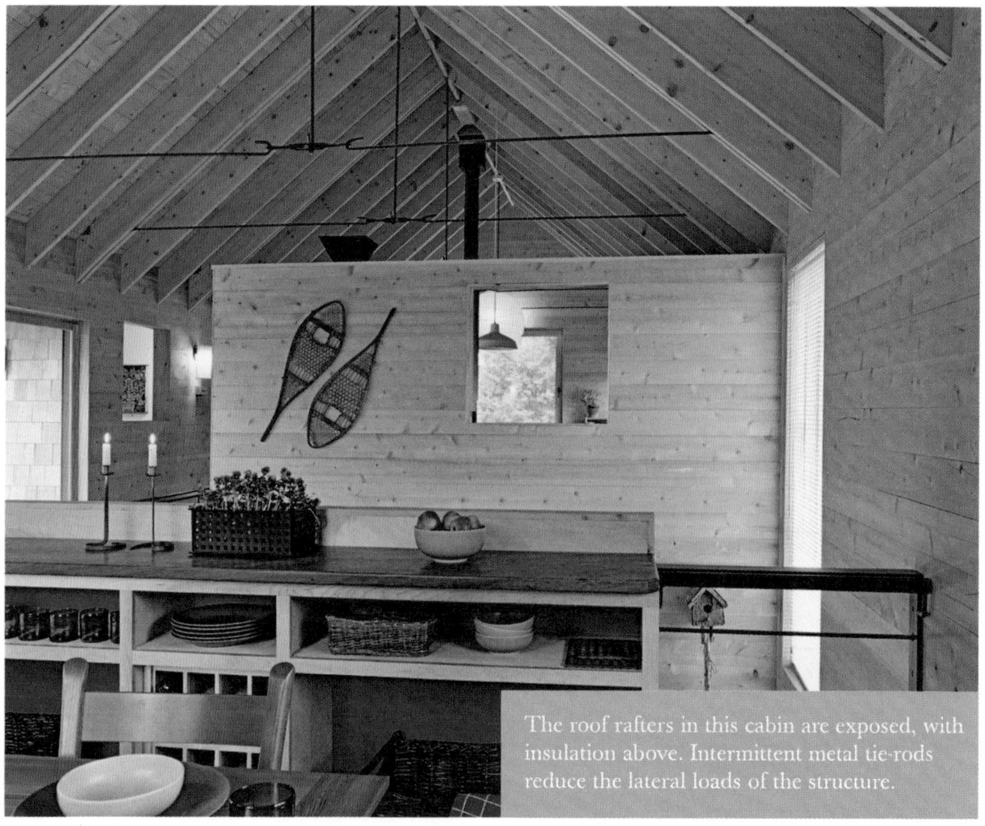

The roof rafters in this cabin are exposed, with insulation above. Intermittent metal tie-rods reduce the lateral loads of the structure.

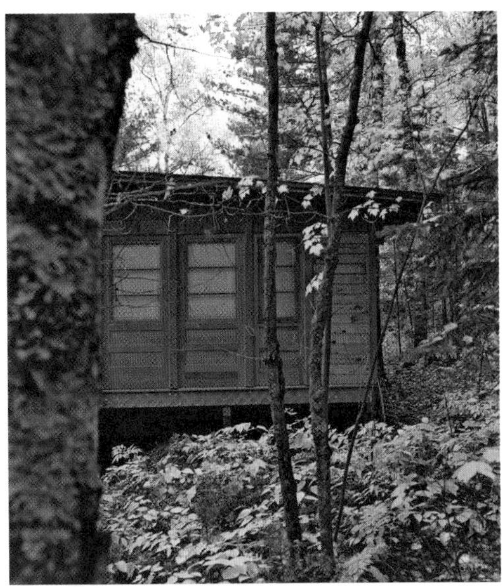

ABOVE AND RIGHT: These cabin walls are made of exterior storm doors fitted between 3x4 bearing posts. In an era when doors were cheap and cabins were just used in summer, this was an economical means of creating walls.

CABIN MATTERS

CABIN PRESSURE

One rainy night, my wife and I attended a political fundraiser at a cabin. Because of the stormy weather, the large crowd was confined inside, where we stood literally shoulder to shoulder from wall to wall. After hastily calculating the floor load, I decided it was time the two of us exited the party, with a pledge to vote for the fundraising candidate and with a renewed interest in structural calculations.

For the record, wall-to-wall people probably exceed 50 pounds per square foot (psf), while live-load criteria for residential construction is typically 40 psf.

you're building dormers or cupolas on top of the roof, the roof structure itself might require a deeper ridge rafter or girder supports.

You can also buy manufactured roof trusses that are tailored to your specifications and that conform to local codes and snow-load or high-wind requirements. Prefab trusses generally utilize several 2x4s joined with large metal plates, or gussets, to provide plenty of strength. You can buy attic trusses with space built into them to accommodate bedrooms, lofts, and storage areas.

Outside, roof frames and trusses are sheathed in plywood or OSB that accommodates the usual roofing materials (asphalt, fiberglass, metal, or wood shingles) and stands firm against the wind.

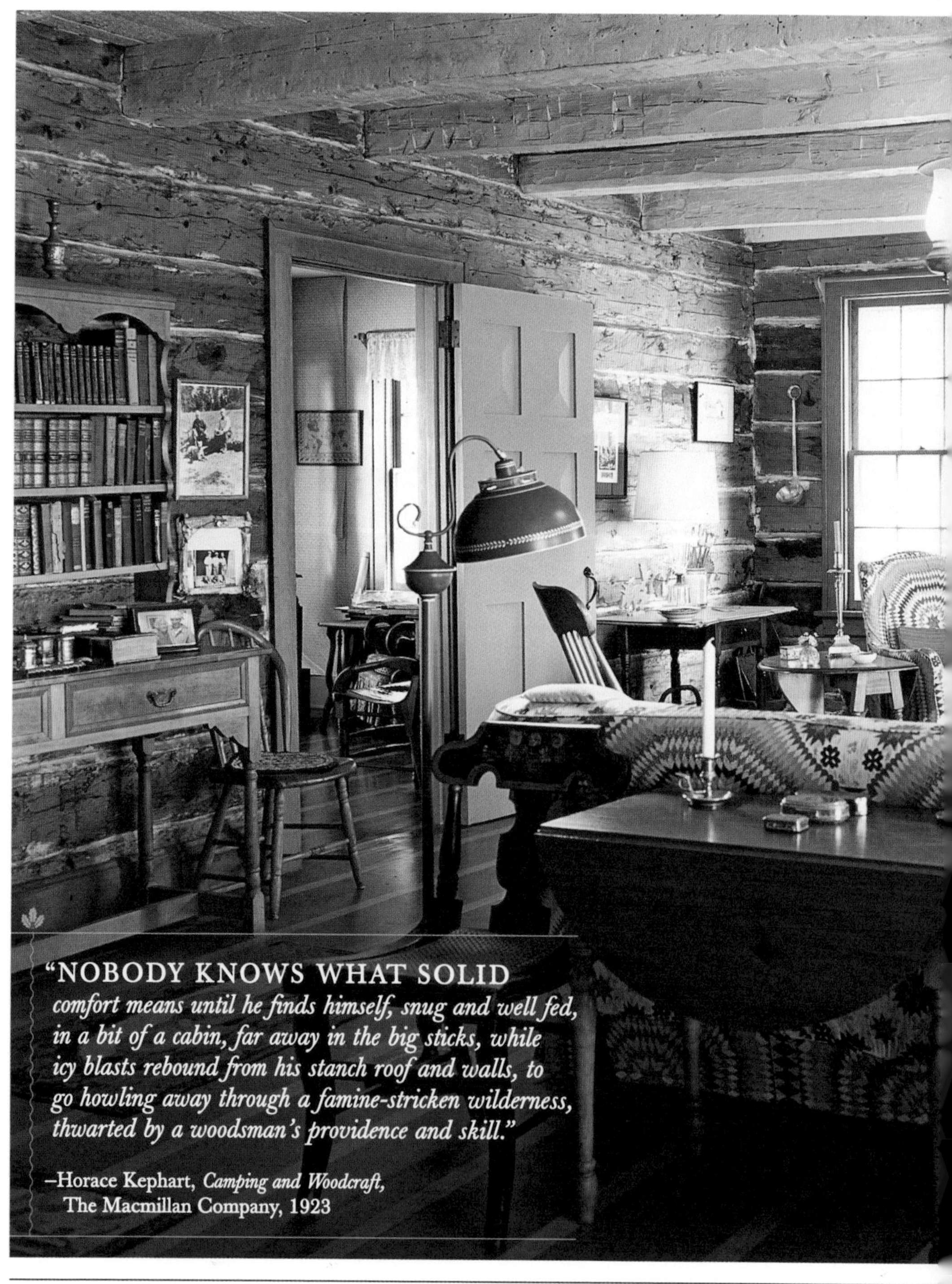

"NOBODY KNOWS WHAT SOLID *comfort means until he finds himself, snug and well fed, in a bit of a cabin, far away in the big sticks, while icy blasts rebound from his stanch roof and walls, to go howling away through a famine-stricken wilderness, thwarted by a woodsman's providence and skill."*

–Horace Kephart, *Camping and Woodcraft*, The Macmillan Company, 1923

PANELIZED CONSTRUCTION

Panelized construction refers to the pre-fabricated sections of a house, which are built in a shop to specific design specifications (say, for your cabin), that interlock at the site to form big chunks of the house. Whole houses can be built using panelization, including floors, walls, and roofs.

Panelized walls are put together in various ways. In fact, a builder can panelize any design in a shop and truck large sections of the structure to the site, where, if the sections aren't too big, they can be lifted into place by workers or hoisted into position with a small crane. The panels are typically made of composite wood sheets sandwiched around rigid insulation. Your roof can be made the same way.

TIP GOING WITH THE GRAIN

Many cabin sites are located in or near major forests, where wood is often harvested by local and occasionally mobile sawmills. Millwrights in your area should be able to provide you with inexpensive local wood for various uses in your cabin.

The upside of panelized construction is usually greater productivity with less waste because the panels are built in a shop environment where they're protected from weather and moisture and then swiftly erected at your cabin site. The down side is the cost of transporting the panels and the need for large equipment to lift them into place.

SURFACES INSIDE AND OUT

Whatever construction method you use, you're going to have to choose surfaces for both inside and out. This sounds pretty obvious, I'm sure, but the surfaces–the coverings on the walls, floors, ceilings, and stars–comprise a big part of the finished "look" your cabin has.

Most of my clients prefer some sort of wood for both exterior siding and the interior finish, despite the fact that exterior wood requires maintenance and that installing wood boards inside can get to be pretty expensive given the amount of area it has to cover. The availability of wood and its renewability makes it special to North Americans, and nowhere is wood used more extensively nowadays than in North American cabins. And it is far and away the material of convenience and choice for do-it-yourselfers.

For cabin exteriors, the wood of choice is usually some form of cedar or redwood, not because of price (it's often not the least expensive option), but on account of the natural resins it contains, which aid in weathering. Cedar and redwood come in a variety of clapboard or shingle forms and even as a form of exterior plywood. You can orient the boards vertically in board-and-batten patterns or horizontally in standard lap or shiplap arrangements. Just remember that your cabin's exterior surface must serve as a rain screen and that the appropriate flashing is necessary around all the openings.

THE WALLS INSIDE

Inside, the wood sheathing is typically made up of boards arranged either vertically or horizontally. The frame's vertical studs make the horizontal arrangement the easier choice,

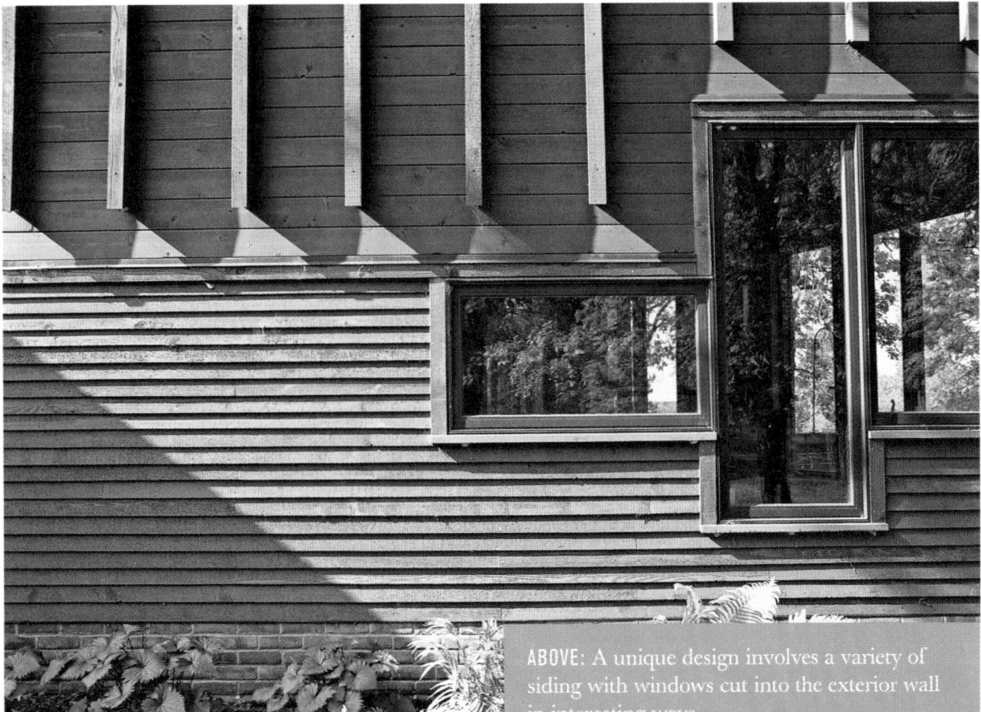

ABOVE: A unique design involves a variety of siding with windows cut into the exterior wall in interesting ways.

BELOW: Color, texture, and materials combine here, using copper accents that highlight the contrast between the window and wall.

whereas vertical finish boards require 2x4s between the framing pieces. A third possibility is a diagonal pattern (especially appealing to fans of the 1970s), which can be attractive on walls that intersect sloped ceilings and when the boards run parallel to the ceiling slope. I've found that the use of diagonal boards is best used sparingly.

If you use local woods, dressing the inside of your cabin promises all kinds of interesting possibilities. The trees you have to fell to make room for your getaway can be milled, for instance, into interior paneling–so long as you allow for ample drying time. In northern Minnesota and Wisconsin, we have access to more than 20 varieties of homegrown wood, offering everything from the heavy grain of black ash

Interior walls finished with local wood, installed vertically (below) or horizontally (above), add warmth and character.

to the more refined white face of poplar (which where I live goes by the name of popple).

I've designed cabins in which the interior wood varies from room to room and, in fact, gives each room its descriptive name: Aspen, Tamarack, Birch, etc. Sometimes I use birch- or fir-faced plywood on cabin interiors, including on sloped ceilings, which imbues a room with the warmth of wood at a lower installation cost than possible using individual boards.

Drywall is another economical possibility, although if you leave your cabin unheated in the winter, the drywall may show stress cracks at the joints. I like it finished in warm, rich colors that complement wood doors, window frames, and trim.

Speaking of color, many of the lighter woods, such as widely available pine, look great in colored stains or dyes. You can rub in blues, greens, and reds for a rich patina, with the wood's grainy variegations showing beneath the stain.

THE WALLS OUTSIDE

Many older, outdated cabins that were designed and built for use only in warm weather are now in need of remodeling. New owners are revitalizing them to make them useful throughout the year. I repeatedly have clients ask me how best to insulate their cabin's old walls.

Usually, insulating an uninsulated cabin means giving up either a charming interior surface or a charming exterior surface to allow insulation to be inserted into the wall cavities from inside or outside.

For this you have several choices. If the siding comes off, you can have foam insulation sprayed into the wall cavities. This can be pricier than standard fiberglass batts, but it provides superior insulation, prevents cold spots, and also serves as an impermeable vapor barrier (which keeps moisture out of your walls).

Preventing interior water vapor (which comes from laundry, bathing, dishwashing, and simply breathing) from getting into the walls is extremely important, both for health concerns and for the structure of your cabin. Without a vapor barrier, moisture gets into the walls, where in winter it can freeze inside the insulation. When fiberglass becomes wet, it sags and compresses, leaving cold, uninsulated areas at the top of the walls, where heat can escape. The moisture also can lead to mildew and mold in the walls, which leads to mildew and mold inside the cabin, a distinct health risk.

Another option, and one that you can perform yourself, is to blow in dense-packed cellulose insulation. Many home-center chains sell bags of compressed cellulose insulation (made from recycled newspaper treated with boric acid to prevent insects and vermin infestation) and will rent you the blower. If your cabin has wood clapboard siding, you can use a reciprocating saw to cut the nails holding the clapboards near the top of the wall and, using a hole saw, cut the appropriate sized holes in the sheathing (if there is any) to accommodate the hose. Once you've done that, you blow in the cellulose under pressure to pack the walls full. Densely packed cellulose also performs as an air and vapor barrier, keeping moisture out of the walls.

The last option, and my least preferable method, is to install fiberglass batts in the walls, once the siding has been removed. This is an itchy, dirty job, but it's another insulating method you can perform yourself if you're particularly handy.

ABOVE: Painted V-groove boards fastened vertically provide strength and beauty as an alternative to drywall or wood paneling.

BELOW: Fiberglass insulation, properly installed, is a good option for keeping your cabin warm during cold weather.

CABIN STORIES

GRAMP'S CABIN

We call it "Gramp's Cabin." Begun in 1941 and not yet finished, it has provided four generations (66-plus years of use) with Puget Sound low-bank beach life on Apple Tree Cove. I often wonder, what percentage of women in the world know how to row? Or how to sail? What percentage of families dig clams and set crab traps? How many kids know the complete luxury of a summer on the beach? How many are so connected to the tides, the rhythms of nature?

What a gift my mother Beda and father Harry gave us.

It was in the war year of 1941 when my schoolteacher father and homemaker mother decided an $800 investment at $20 a month, with no interest if paid on time, was scary but the thing to do. With the summers free to start clearing and building, my dad, uncles, and sometimes my brother Neal and I grew to respect the value of a tree: Cut it down with a two-man crosscut saw, dig out the stump, burn the small limbs and leaves, split the rest for firewood–a year's worth of work. After all that, one appreciates the energy in a tree.

We would take the ferry across Puget Sound from the town of Edmonds, 17 miles north of Seattle, to get to *our* beach. How it came to be ours is a history of Indian land stolen, homestead collapse, and lumber mill intrigue. If it rained, we stayed in the historic Kingston Hotel instead of tenting it.

This was and still is an unpretentious little cabin. In the early years, we took turns fetching water in the white bucket using the dipper with the red rim (always admonished: "Don't drink out of the dipper!") from Dad's hand-dug, 10-ft.-deep well. I still use it.

There was a wood-fired range and then the oil-fired one with heat coils so we could have hot water. I painted the outhouse a fashionable pink with lavender trim. Much later, we added a bathroom, and a $5 recycled toilet from the demolition of World War II Navy housing replaced the outhouse. My brother thought this was gross. It was he who wrote a note above the sink stating, "Hot water slightly delayed–2 to 3 years." To this day there are no light switches, but electricity has replaced kerosene lamps and there is hot water. And Dad's unique latches still secure our doors.

Our dad built the cabin with no experience, just a book, a hammer, and a handsaw. Period. The open-wall construction meant there were plenty of shelves between the wall studs for rock and shell collections. A blanket gave us kids some privacy when in our bunk beds, while the radio played Mom's favorite "Sons of the Pioneers" and Dad's "B. Battlin' Buck Ritchey."

We shooed our winter mouse tenants on Memorial Day and locked things up on Labor Day (I now live here year-round). The summers, filled with beach parties, church-group picnics, and poker nights, were a time to share our great fortune for living on the beach.

–Marilyn Liden Bode is the inheritor and protector of the cabin in Kingston, Washington. She lives a simple, artful life as a grandmother, printmaker, and peace and antiracism activist.

MARRIED COUPES PICNIC - 1945

5TH GRADE
Beach Party - 1948 - Pig pill

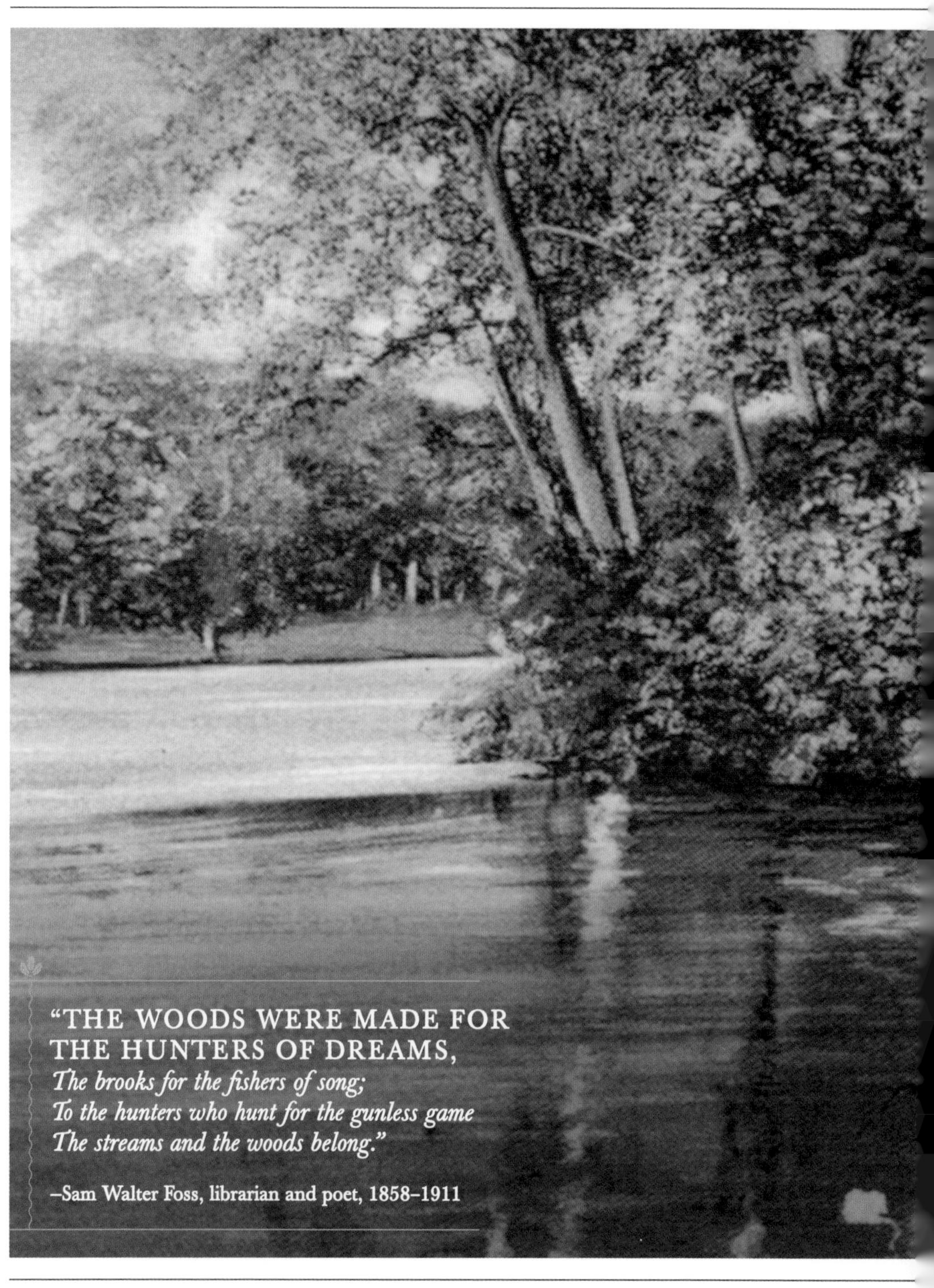

"THE WOODS WERE MADE FOR THE HUNTERS OF DREAMS,
The brooks for the fishers of song;
To the hunters who hunt for the gunless game
The streams and the woods belong."

–Sam Walter Foss, librarian and poet, 1858–1911

PUTTING A LID ON IT

For the roof over your cabin, the choices mainly consist of asphalt or fiberglass shingles, wood shingles, and metal roofing. Each option has its own variations that offer both advantages–such as longevity and reduced maintenance–and increased complications and costs.

Regardless of the type of roofing you choose, the simpler your roof shape, the easier it will be to install the roofing and keep down the labor costs. Nowadays, it's not uncommon to drive by a new housing development and see the most extravagantly complicated roofs. For your cabin, the simpler the better.

I've seen cabins roofed in clay tile, slate, even sod. But if one of those options appeals to you, be aware that each needs a particular substrata material and should be installed only by experienced professionals.

ASPHALT ROOFS

Asphalt shingles are probably the most common shingle in North America. They're versatile, relatively inexpensive, easy to install, and come in a variety of densities and textures.

Depending on your druthers and budget, the kind of asphalt shingle you choose could last anywhere from 20 to 40 years (some types even give you a longer warranty). Asphalt shingles are available in several colors that replicate the weathered wood of wooden shingles, the red of clay tiles, or the deep green of the surrounding trees, among other choices.

METAL ROOFS

If you're heating your cabin with a wood-burning stove or furnace or building in an area where forest fires are common (such as out west), choosing wood shingles may affect your insurance costs, which might make a metal roof the better idea. Depending on where you live, wood shingles may even be prohibited by your local building code.

Most metal roofs, for instance, are fabricated in long sheets, so complex valleys and other variations in roof shape result in wasted material and complicated flashing. There are other complications as well. The roof of my cabin, to use a familiar example, includes a valley that we have to clear religiously of pine needles; otherwise, the needles form a dam that causes water to migrate under the shingles in wet weather and becomes a fire hazard during dry times.

Metal roofs can likewise add color to your cabin if you don't go for a galvanized steel or copper appearance. Some brands of metal roofing come with a baked-on color finish that protects the steel or aluminum from oxidation for many years. Metal roofing is available in flat or ribbed sheets, with either capped or standing-seam joints. Most metal-roofing systems come with specialty parts for ridge caps, drip caps, and rake edging.

WOOD ROOFS

If you've got the inclination–and the money–few types of roofing go better with a woodland cabin than a wood roof. Several types of wood roofing are available, including Western red cedar, white cedar, and pressure-treated Southern yellow pine shingles.

The most durable and, for my money, the best material for a wood roof is Western red cedar (although I have absolutely no experience with treated yellow pine). Few types of roofing match the texture and color of red cedar, which is tight grained and slowly changes color from

ABOVE: A pyramidal roof caps the tower of this cabin like the head of a mushroom, joining the two gable-roof wings. A lightly pitched gabled roof covers the sheltered entryway.

BELOW: A standard gable roof tops off this cabin, which is surrounded by a porch with a shed roof. The combination is particularly pleasing with the addition of the small windows that peek out above the porch roof.

Like a Japanese lantern, the box of clerestory windows set into the roof of this cabin infuse the interior with light throughout the day.

Wood floors are great, and most cabin owners I know want wood floors in their cabins. However, other good flooring materials are available and appropriate, including engineered flooring (especially good for radiant floor heat), tile (for sloppy areas such as mudrooms, kitchens, and baths), and the old standby, linoleum.

its honey gold when just applied to the weathered dark gray-brown color it becomes after a few months.

Cedar shingles are smooth and come in random widths but are typically 18 in. long and overlap to leave 5 in. exposed "to the weather." Cedar shakes are rough textured because they're not milled but split along the grain to give the roof a look of great character.

The downside to wood roofing is their expense. A red cedar roof can cost many times that of an asphalt shingle roof, not just because of its material cost but also because of the labor. Each shingle has to be fitted in place one at a time.

CABIN MATTERS

THE LINE ON LINOLEUM

Linoleum, which we remember from our mother's kitchen and the church basement floor, has been making a comeback, in part because of its recent popularity as a "green" commodity. The material is a by-product of linseed production used in the manufacture of linen fabrics.

Nowadays, linoleum is available in rich, varied colors in both sheet sizes and 1-ft. squares. It's great anywhere in the cabin but particularly wet areas.

ALWAYS UNDERFOOT

Cabin owners I know love wood floors. Until recently, most folks have been especially drawn to those old, recycled pine planks, whose scratches and divots add to its cabinacious character. Nostalgia aside, wood floors are a good, utilitarian choice for a loft or second floor.

Lately, though, new heating options, such as in-floor radiant heat, have led to a rethinking of the old ways: Some people are now choosing stained concrete or inexpensive tile and slate for their cabin floors, which radiate heat upward in cold weather.

The newer materials, I'm happy to report, not only help keep a cabin warm but also look great and are easy to maintain, holding up nicely under wet, sandy feet, snowy boots, and dog claws. If you're building on a concrete slab, you can use one of a variety of stains to give both color and finish to a durable surface. Warmed with color, character, and electric or hydronic (hot water passing through tubes in the concrete) heat beneath, a concrete floor needs only a few area rugs to complete a graceful cabin setting.

Good alternatives to both wood and finished concrete surfaces are available in sheets of vinyl or linoleum. Both materials are durable, comfortable, and–if you wish–colorful. If you have small children or grandchildren, you already know that sweeping up spilled popcorn and beach sand is 10 times easier on a slick, virtually seamless vinyl surface than from the charming cracks and fissures of old wood.

One of the newest and most popular flooring materials is laminate, which goes by brand names like Pergo®, Moderna®, and M-Lock™. Laminate flooring can look like any type of wood–it can even look like stone–and generally is much easier to install than standard tongue-in-groove wood flooring. Although these laminates are less expensive than many other kinds, the jury is still out on their long-term durability.

WINDOWS

Important as they are, windows are easy to take for granted. They are not, strictly speaking, structural necessities such as the roof, walls, and floor. But building codes in most locations require that your cabin contain an area equal to 10 percent of your floor space in windows and that you are able to open half of that window area.

Not that you'd want to leave it at the minimal requirements set by the building code. Because windows are, after all, what connect you, inside your cabin, with the world outdoors that drew you here in the first place.

Windows are not mere holes in the wall. They provide several benefits: They allow in light, supply ventilation, and frame the natural beauty that lies beyond. To get the most out of this expensive investment, you need to consider all of those purposes in your cabin design.

There's much more to those windows than meets the eye. I'm struck by how many people say they want a tall window wall because they want to make the most of their lake view. "But, wait," I say. That lake view is horizontal, not vertical, and tall windows would add more sky, not lake, to the panorama. What's most important is the horizon

Double-hung windows, the kind in which one sash hangs above the other and both are set into a vertical track, are one of the most traditional window types. In this cabin, exterior shutters allow the cabin to be literally shuttered whenever the owners are away.

line, where the lake meets the sky, and the nearer shoreline, where the kids are going to play in the sand. For that view, I tell them, they want a horizontal line of lower windows. And, furthermore, those windows shouldn't look out on a deck, large pieces of outdoor furniture, or anything else that would be in the way of the view toward the lake.

Mountain sites, on the other hand, typically have few or no horizontal views. Instead, a snow-capped peak or grassy valley is the visual attraction, so here a vertical window plan is in order. Cabins set in deep woods will also benefit from tall rather than wide windows, the better to frame the surrounding forest and capture the light slanting down through the trees.

Too many people overemphasize the importance of a distant view. They often give little thought to the views that will evolve along with the cabin–friends walking up the path, children enjoying the tire swing in the yard, birds jockeying for position at the feeder. My wife and I have enhanced our cabin view with a field-corn feeder that draws deer to within a few feet of our living-room windows. And don't forget about the sound that wafts through open windows. We not only see the grandkids and the blue jays through the windows, but we hear them as well.

Then there's the need for ventilation. Sure, you can air-condition your cabin, but why would you want to do that except, perhaps, on the sultriest nights? Most cabin owners are eager not only to let in the views but also let in the lake, mountain, or forest air (and smells). Where you place your windows to make the most of the prevailing breezes will depend, of course, on your cabin's shape and its orientation on the site.

ABOVE: These sliding windows (sliders) move side to side to create a large opening for air circulation. Like double-hung windows, only 50% of the glassed area is open to fresh air.

BELOW: These windows drop down into the wall below to give a great open feeling for summer use.

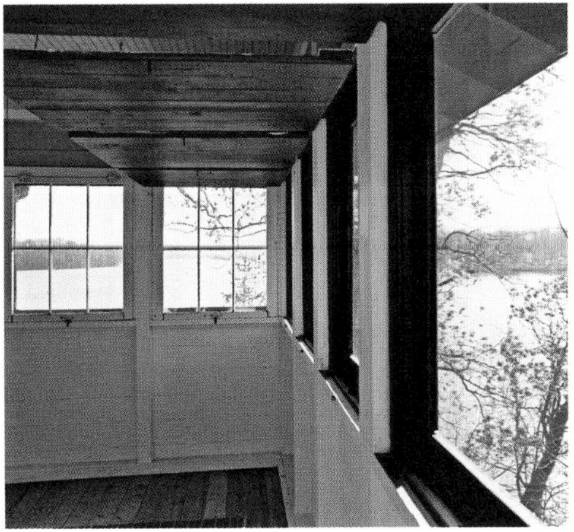

A BIT ON WINDOWOLOGY

For cabins (as well as for ordinary houses) windows come in three basic forms: those with a fixed sash, a hinged sash, or a sliding sash, the latter two then branching out into a variety of subcategories. Which type or types you choose for your cabin should depend at least in part on what you want in the way of view and ventilation. As always, your budget will be another major consideration. Windows are expensive.

Fixed-sash windows cost less than their movable counterparts and are often used, as so-called picture windows, in larger sizes and for prominent views or, in windows placed high on a wall, where it's impractical or impossible to open and close them. Also, fixed-sash windows are more readily available in unusual shapes, such as trapezoids, triangles, half-rounds, and ovals. Stock rectangles can be purchased in sizes up to 5 ft. by 6 ft. Larger sizes may require special equipment for shipping and installation. Large fixed windows can be ganged with operational (openable) windows to create window walls that pleasingly connect inner and outer worlds.

You can also use small fixed windows to highlight a piece of artwork or let outside light brighten an otherwise dark corner. In my cabin designs, I often place a small fixed window (or glass block) between the upper and lower cabinets to shed light on kitchen counters. In fact, I use the technique often enough that some have come to call the small apertures "Dale windows."

Windows that can open and close contain a sash that either swings on a hinge or slides, with a screen on one side that lets in fresh air while keeping out the bugs. Hinged windows

CABIN MATTERS

BUG OUT!

If you have a significant bug population in your area, window screens are essential. But pay attention to how and where these screens attach to your windows. An outward-swinging window with an inside screen will trap bugs after it's pulled shut. Those bugs may then lay eggs on the screen and spawn a new generation. By contrast, a screen on the outside of a sliding window will help keep your cabin pest-free the entire summer.

Depending on where you build your cabin, the bug situation can be quite perturbing in spring and summer. A screened area–porch or day room–will let you enjoy your stay without all the swatting.

commonly swing outward, so the screen is positioned on the inside, and the sash is often operated by a crank or lever. With sliding windows, the screen is on the outside, so the sash can be pushed up and down or from side to side.

Swinging windows open the entire sash for ventilation, whereas sliding windows open only halfway at most. Another difference: Hinged widows open into the wind and rain, while a sliding window is not so exposed to the elements. Both forms are now manufactured in such a way that it's easy to clean both sides from the inside, which is especially important with windows on the second or third floor. (It's bad enough having to wash windows while on vacation. It's even worse having to wash those windows while standing on a ladder.)

Swinging-sash windows are hinged at either the side, in which case they're called casement windows, or at the top, in the so-called awning

ABOVE: When open, this window latches tight to the ceiling, providing a full screened opening for ventilation.

BELOW: If the weather's hot, rainy, or if bugs grow to be too much to deal with, nothing beats a screened porch—especially one with a view.

Not all windows have to open to the outside. In this cabin, windows connect an upstairs bedroom with the family room below and with the light from that space.

ABOVE: Old-style double-hung windows like these usually included sash weights set into the window jambs. These act as a counterweight to aid in opening these heavy and sometimes hard-to-lift windows.

LEFT: So-called swinging sash windows, which can open in or out, include casement-style windows like these large sashes that open inward.

style. The latter is often used in large horizontal windows because it's less vulnerable to wind damage. Awning-style windows can be left open in a light rain since they offer some protection from the precipitation and are especially popular in the bedroom, where the soft patter of raindrops and a fresh breeze can be a pleasant accompaniment to falling asleep. Whereas casement windows are typically no bigger than 3 ft. wide by 6 ft. tall, the awning style can be ordered to widths of 6 ft. Windows that swing into the cabin—you still see them in older cabins—aren't made much anymore.

A common window type found in existing cabins is the in-swinging single-glazed casement and hopper window. I have both options in the old log cabin that came with my property. Although both types of windows have the advantage of exterior screens, neither is commonly available in standard window catalogs. Windows of old were often made locally by the carpenters who built the cabin. If you don't need the thermal comfort of new windows, then today's carpenters can indeed copy the old ones. Or if you have a tablesaw and router table, you can make one yourself.

The horizontal bar where the two sashes overlap in a double-hung window is known as the check rail. I mention it because you'll want to try to keep it out of your view line when

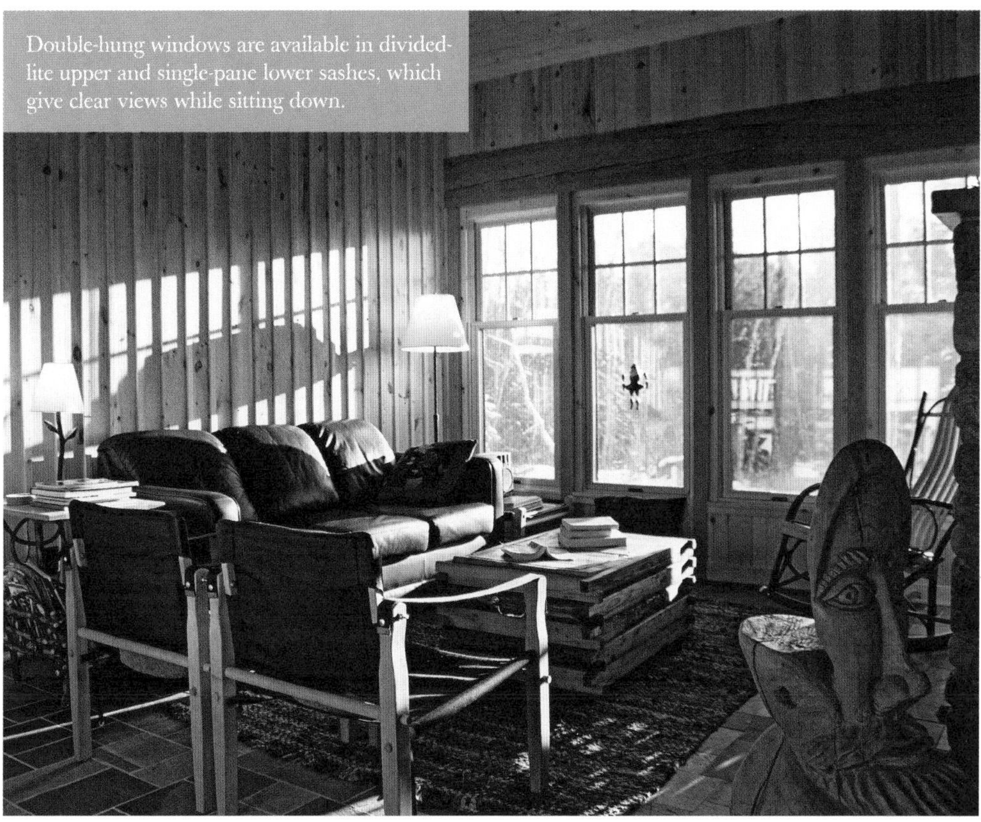
Double-hung windows are available in divided-lite upper and single-pane lower sashes, which give clear views while sitting down.

you position your windows. But your view line varies from place to place in the cabin. At the kitchen sink, you're usually standing, so the bar's obstruction will be higher than, say, in the dining area, where you're usually seated. Most manufacturers now make a special double-hung model for cabins known as, appropriately enough, a "cottage window." Its two sashes divide the window in two-fifth and three-fifth proportions, perfect for standing or sitting, respectively.

The glass used in today's windows–more good news–is often energy efficient and comes with coatings that relieve glare and reduce ultraviolet light. You should choose glass with your climatological needs in mind. In my area, with its frigid winters, I insisted on high-performance double-pane glass to help keep the heat in on cold days and nights. You'll need to use more expensive tempered glass if it's set into the wall less than 18 in. off the floor.

If your cabin has a wood interior, you'll probably want wood on the inside of your window frames. Pine and fir are the most popular options, especially on moderately priced windows, although vinyl is a practical alternative. The outside of your windows can be clad in vinyl or extruded aluminum with baked-on enamel paint in any number of colors.

OPEN THE DOORS

You can usually purchase the exterior doors you need from the people who make your windows, or you can buy them elsewhere and have them hung in prefinished door frames.

Doors, of course, are important not only for coming and going but also, like windows, for light and ventilation. But of almost equal importance is the contribution doors make to the look–the expression of personal style–that they give your cabin.

Like windows, doors come in both swing and slide varieties. Hinged doors that swing in are usually complemented by outward-swinging screens, which let in air and light. But because you'll want to keep the inside door open in nice weather, you need to think about where it stands when open wide.

You can get sliding doors in tandem sizes (four panels), with the two interior panels sliding outward. There's no mullion in the center when they're open, so you can open the doors as wide as 8 ft. If you install smaller gliders, you need to remember that the panels overlap by a few inches, so the doorway does not open a full 50 percent–an important consideration when you're carrying a tray of drinks out to the deck.

INTERIOR DOORS

Standard panel doors for interior use are available almost everywhere. More often than not, they come veneered rather than as solid wood. Only in older cabins will you see the horizontal five-panel interior door, a type that was once popular in my part of the world.

You can still have your doors–especially the old-fashioned Z variety–made by your carpenter. Although those Z-form doors are more likely to warp and shrink than panel doors, they add a definite rustic quality to your cabin. And if that Z-form bathroom door doesn't quite latch during those dry winter months, well, you can think of that as just another quirk of life at the cabin.

Pretty basic is the best way to describe the entrance door to this rustic cabin. The door is actually an old interior door, but the owner has added a latch that can be fastened with a padlock.

These beautiful panel doors are made of richly textured Douglas fir and, while utilitarian, add a touch of craftsman elegance to this bedroom.

HEATING UP AND COOLING DOWN

Few cabins are complete without a way to burn wood, whether it's a fireplace or a woodstove. For most cabin folks, the sight of a flickering flame, the crackle of burning wood, and the sweet scent of wood smoke are at least as important as the heat provided–and an absolutely essential element of the cabin experience.

Wood fireplaces and stoves come in countless types and shapes, and costs vary accordingly. The simplest, least expensive, and most effective in terms of heat production are woodstoves. You can place a woodstove in virtually any location in your cabin, the basic requirement being a metal flue that extends through the roof. The more expensive stove varieties come with cooking elements and provide heat storage with protective soapstone.

Woodstove equivalents that produce significant heat can be inserted into masonry fireboxes to simulate a traditional fireplace. In our cabin, we framed a metal insert firebox with stones I'd scavenged from an abandoned gravel pit. Besides giving it a rustic charm, the stone surround functions as a heat sink that keeps the cabin warm for hours after we turn in for the night. It's an ancient principle: The stones absorb the heat, and later after the fire is burned down, the stones radiate the heat outward, releasing their stored energy.

THE FAVORITE FIREPLACE

Nearly everyone's favorite fireplace is made up of the traditional open masonry firebox with a large masonry chimney and a prominent mantel. A fireplace like that requires a

CABIN MATTERS

THE COUNT OF RUMFORD

Benjamin Thompson, an American physicist who for many years worked in England and Germany, designed an ingenious fireplace in the 1790s. Thompson's creation thrusts the fire forward through sloped sides and back walls while drawing the smoke up the flue. Thompson was eventually designated the Count of Rumford, and his fireplace came to bear his name. Below are the three basic types of wood heat sources for your cabin. The Rumford is, of course, a version of the open firebox fireplace.

OPEN FIREBOX

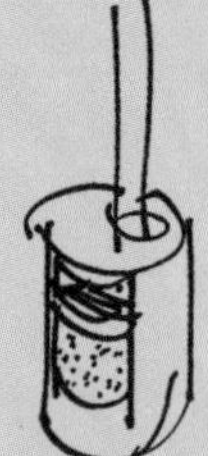

WOOD STOVE

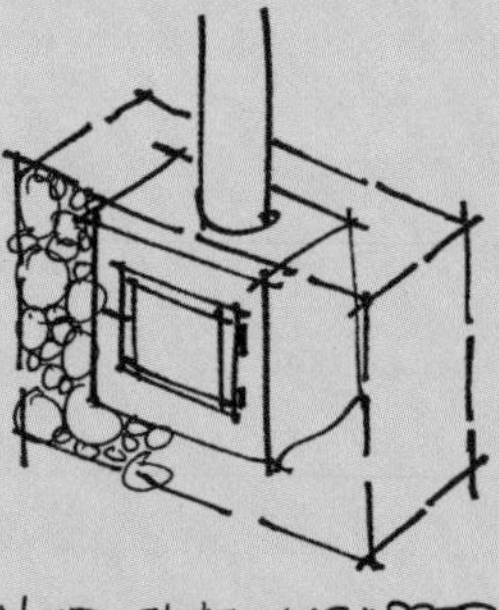

WOOD STOVE WRAPPED

substantial foundation, however, and a lot of labor, both of which can burn up a big chunk of your budget.

In its most traditional form, such a fireplace can also be a huge energy drain, sucking heat out of the cabin while you sleep. It will perform more economically if you add a fresh-air intake and glass doors. In fact, the use of a device such as a Rumford-style firebox will reduce heat loss because it yields more heat than old-fashioned fireplaces.

REALLY HEATING WITH WOOD

In any case, depending on your climate and whether you'll use your cabin in the winter, you may want to supplement your wood-burning device with a furnace, boiler, or direct electric mats to keep your cabin warm when you're not around to stoke the fire. Many folks in cold climates keep their cabins reasonably warm whether they use them year-round or only on weekends. That's because if they arrive at an unheated cabin on a freezing Friday night, it may take them until Sunday to get the inside temperature up to a comfortable level. And if you have to leave Sunday afternoon to get back for work, well, why bother?

There are two factors to consider when figuring your cabin's heating equation: energy

BELOW: Cast-iron woodstoves heat a room through radiant heat; that is, they get really hot and produce heat that radiates out through the room. The stovepipe also radiates heat. In this house, the owners cleverly installed a section of sheet metal behind the stove and pipe, which in turn reflects the heat back into the room.

ABOVE: A small opening seals off the cabin from the outside while providing fast access to the firewood.

This traditional stone fireplace is boxed in with pine to form a couple of display shelves. Its heat production is limited, but it looks, feels, and smells of warmth.

supply and heat distribution. The supply is usually provided by gas contained in a tank on the property or via electricity from the local power grid. Once in a while you'll find a cabin served by piped-in gas more common in the city. You can power your forced-air or boiler/hydronic heating system with either gas or electricity. You can also use electricity to power a heat pump in a closed-loop system in which ground temperature helps heat and cool space.

THE MECHANICALS

If you plan to cool your cabin with built-in air-conditioning, you'll need a forced-air furnace and cooling condenser. That in turn requires additional space in ceilings and lofts for air ducts and, ideally, a furnace location that cuts down on duct-run requirements. (Think about installing ceiling fans instead of air-conditioning. Ceiling fans not only cool with quiet effectiveness, but they're also much easier on the budget than AC.) If you're not using air-conditioning, your boiler can easily distribute the necessary heat through baseboard radiators, wall radiators, in-floor tubing, or a combination of those systems. The in-floor tubing, by the way, can be filled with liquids other than water to help prevent freeze-ups when not in use during cold weather.

Of course, electricity can power your baseboard or wall radiators and in-floor mats as well as ceiling panels. We heat our 1,300-sq.-ft. cabin with mats buried in the sand 8 in. below a slate-covered concrete floor along with a pair of metal-clad ceramic storage units, all of which store heat from our off-peak electrical supply. Among the benefits of that thermal mass system are low energy costs and backup in the event of brief power outages. The downside is slow response to temperature changes, which we counteract with faster-reacting electric heaters and a wood-burning fireplace that quickly takes the chill off when we arrive late at night.

Heating and cooling issues in an addition or remodeled cabin often are unique to specific circumstances, climates, and personal comfort levels. Occasionally the existing system can be maintained and a new system installed just to supplement the addition. This has the advantage of dual zoning for local room comfort and energy savings (just heat or cool the area you're using).

More often, the old system is outdated and inadequate, so a new system is installed to serve the whole structure. Review of insulation and vapor barrier conditions in the old space is paramount before choosing the optimum system for the cabin.

A variety of in-floor heating options exist, from hydronic systems in which hot water is piped through tubing in your floor to this type of electric floor warmer, here installed under tile.

CABIN STORIES

THE CABIN BOOKCASE: AN INVENTORY

Our cabin's bookcase has 14 shelves, and the books they house are of such curious variety that no standard bibliographic system is adequate to categorize them all. In no particular order, there are:

- Old books belonging to my parents that intrigue me but that I am unlikely to read.
- Books belonging to my parents that have forced me to reevaluate my adolescent prejudice that everything they read was boring.
- Classic adventure books like *King Solomon's Mines.*
- Trashy books acquired at thrift stores for "beach reading."
- A small collection of "occult" matter.
- Capital-L "Literature" (frequently lesser works by great writers).
- My dad's childhood copies of *Pinocchio* and *Wild Animals I Have Known.*
- Books I bought in Kenora.
- Theme books with titles like *At the Cottage* that I for some reason feel compelled to give as gifts to my parents.
- Genuinely useful and oft-consulted guidebooks like *Birds of North America* and, of course, *Hoyle's Book of Rules.*
- A selection of *Soap Opera Digests* whose presence shall pass without further comment.
- Impressive collections of sailing magazines (belonging to my father) and *Gourmet* magazines from the '70s (belonging to my mother), neither of which tempt me but whose presence I find reassuring.

Brian Johnson and his wife, Suzanne Waldman, reading at their cabin in Ontario.

Collectively, these books and magazines form the crust, or upper layer, of the bookcase. They are the stuff of recent, present, and possibly future reading.

Below this layer are deeper strata. If you dig a little, you'll find my teenaged years. The first thing you'll hit is a thick vein of horror: two shelves of paperbacks sporting covers with macabre scenes. Dig a little further and you'll reach the inevitable smattering of fantasy and science fiction novels. Keep digging and you'll come to the detritus of puberty: *Clan of the Cave Bear* and the sleazy thrillers of Sidney Sheldon and Lawrence Sanders. There is, of course, a modest collection of yellowed comic books that sit in a shredded heap on one of the lower shelves. Nearby, one encounters about two-thirds of *The Adventures of Tintin* (tattered and loved). Then there are the picture books that my sister and I loved: *Tawny Scrawny Lion, The Hole in the Fence,* and Angela Banner's *Ant and Bee* books.

Suddenly, we're into the muck of real childhood. For at the next level we encounter crumbling stacks of *Owl Magazine* from 1977, Canada's answer to *National Geographic's* far glossier *World Magazine*. *World* is here, too. And so are my sister's *Chickadee* magazines and an assortment of the National Wildlife Service's *Ranger Rick*–the gift of a worldly childhood friend.

All of these magazines were wonderful, but in my Canadian childhood, nature was what happened in the pages of *Owl:* those dusty-looking duo-chrome photo spreads of children collecting leaves, skating on a pond, or building walkie-talkies. The see-through illustrations of logs or snowbanks where the exterior was cut away to reveal a teeming (or hibernating) world of animal life. I can't even calculate the number of hours I spent poring over Dr. Zed's science experiments, the cozy X-ray drawings of "Animals Underground," the comic book adventures of the Mighty Mites (three kids who shrink), "Groan Time" (your bad puns), and "Hoot" (*Owl's* back page "newsletter"). Much of the content was too complicated for a five-year-old to fathom, but it was all mysterious and fascinating nonetheless. Is it any wonder that I love my mother's "Cabin Record" family diary and my father's coverless copy of Ernest Thompson Seton's *Wild Animals I Have Known* so much now? They're all *Owl* in different forms.

Over the years, the cabin bookcase has come to acquire a mythic stature in my imagination. It isn't just that it's become the gathering place of so much of my childhood reading matter; it has also become an evolving monument to my family's collective reading experiences–a microcosm of our bibliographic adventures and obsessions.

It's precious to me now because it is perhaps the only physical place where all of our reading pleasures, past and present, meet and mingle. What a marvelous thing it is to think of the shared experiences that occur at that bookcase in the wilderness when my sister or I read one of my mom's Agatha Christies, when my wife reads one of my dad's P. G. Wodehouses, when my dad picks up a science fiction book, or when my mom leafs fondly through a book she once read to me or my sister–a book she will one day read to her children's children.

Our family bookcase is one of the things that make the cabin into more than a retreat. It makes it into a wilderness home, a place where the history of a family is written. Fourteen shelves where past and present meet, where comic books rub covers with biographies and where the solitary act of reading on a sunlit deck turns out not to be so solitary after all.

–Brian Johnson is a professor of English literature at Carleton University in Ottawa, Ontario. The family cabin is in Ingolf, Ontario.

PLUMBING

Organizing your cabin's plumbing can be simple or complicated. I strongly recommend keeping it simple. Simplicity is especially important in colder regions, where you want to drain down your system to prevent the pipes from freezing in the winter. Instead of scattering the pipes around the cabin, you should stack them, keeping the system as vertical as possible and providing easy access to the drain at the bottom.

As for your plumbing accommodations, it's not a bad idea to start with the bathroom, whether there's a bath in there or not. I like bathroom sinks that come as integral countertops that we used to call "cultured marble." Those tops are available everywhere, are not expensive, and, maybe best of all, are easy to keep clean, even with a cabin full of kids.

Remember to keep it simple. Maybe you've had your eye on that sexy red sink you once saw in your Paris hotel room, but a rustic cabin is not the best place for that particular one. That's because your local plumber, while no doubt well equipped with the standard fittings for American fixtures, probably doesn't have what he'd need to repair a metric French model, much less a beret to wear while trying to fix it.

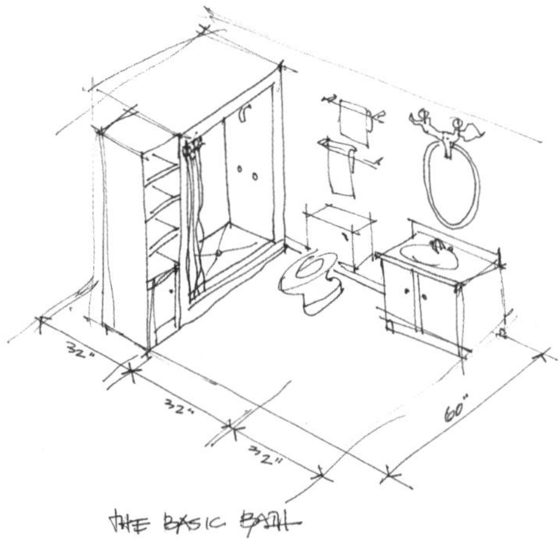

A small and compact cabin bath plan.

Toilets, meanwhile, are available in several forms. There are chemical toilets, electrical toilets, and the flush types such as you have at home. For our purposes, supposing a standard indoor plumbing system, we'll assume you're going to want a common flush toilet with a tank full of water.

Easy to overlook but something we find indispensable is the utility sink in our mechanical/laundry room. There are always dirty clothes that need soaking and other needs for that extra sink positioned close to the washer and dryer. You should also think about installing outside hose bibs for outdoor projects, such as rinsing off muddy boots, washing the car, and watering the garden.

WET 'N' WILD

You'll also find it handy to have water (you know, for brushing your teeth or taking a shower). So unless you are able to hook up to a municipal service (or a rural water system), you will need a well if you don't already have one.

WATER IN

If you simply want to produce water that meets current sanitary needs, you can use an existing hand-dug well or a sand-point well. Those old wells are adequate for modern needs; however, they just don't produce a great deal of water.

ABOVE: Built into an upstairs corner, this bathroom's walls are open to the pitched roof above.

LEFT: Just because a bathroom is in a cabin doesn't mean it has to be any less detailed or luxurious than one in a full-time residence. Earth-tone tiles and lots of wood give this bathroom the comfortable feel of a place in the woods.

Before you drill a well, you're going to consult with drillers, builders, and your neighbors. Wells are uncertain things, though. You can count on some variables. For one, the drill rig must have access to the site, so you may need to extend your driveway or remove some trees. However, there are drill rigs that run off of more modest-sized trucks. If you're drilling a new well, you never know how deep you have to go. Your neighbor's well might go down 75 ft. Yours might come in at 375 ft. And, believe me, there are costs associated with an extra 300 ft. of drilling. You can find out how deep local wells have commonly gone recently, but you don't know if the driller at your site will miss the aquifer and have to keep boring downward.

Even when the well is dug and producing enough water to meet your needs (say, 6 to 8 gallons per minute), you might get bad-tasting water that requires expensive treatment to make it palatable for drinking and so it doesn't corrode or stain everything it touches (plumbing, fixtures, clothes).

WATER OUT

If you have a well, you have to be able to deal with wastewater. At an existing cabin, you'll need to check out its existing sanitary system, which is something that a lot of people don't

For a good, hot, soaking bath, nothing beats an old-fashioned claw-foot tub, which sits more like a piece of furniture—or sculpture—than like a fixture.

know much about because they're used to municipal sewage systems. However, in most cases you need to accept the fact that it's necessary. The expense of septic systems is something else you have to accept. Depending on your site and soil conditions, you could spend tens of thousands of dollars building an acceptable system.

The size of your septic system depends on the number of bedrooms in your cabin. Your local sanitarian will also take into account the fact that you're only using your cabin for a moderate number of days during the year but that you or somebody else will eventually live there year-round. In that regard, I think many septic systems are often unnecessarily oversized.

Washing up couldn't be simpler at this rustic cabin, where a shelf holds basins for water and a kettle provides the heat.

You do have a variety of options for a septic system. The most common type of private septic system includes a holding, or septic, tank, which you have pumped out by a service every so often. This common system also includes what is variously called a gravity drain field, leachate field, or absorption field that leads off the holding tank. The design of the tank ensures that the waste in the tank separates solids from liquid. In the tank, human waste creates a bacterial action that breaks down the solids; some of that can be washed off by the liquids, which go out into the drain field. One anecdotal recommendation is that you should not have a waste disposal on your kitchen sink so that you won't be adding even more solids. If you do have a waste disposal, you probably should have a larger holding tank.

RETURN TO THE LAND

The leachate field is a minor engineering miracle. Trenches are dug, then gravel and sand are laid around an array of perforated pipe that has additional soil on top of it. The water passes through the pipe and is filtered through the gravel and sand. The gravity-feed system assumes you have soil that "percolates fluid," as septic installers call it. If you don't have the right kind of soil, you have to build a different type of septic system.

You can create your own artificial hill consisting of different layers of rock and sand. A pump forces the effluent up to the top of your artificial mound, where it filters down. That's called a mound system.

You might have a grinder, which grinds up all the solids so that they are more easily

If you're dead set against having plumbing (a well, a septic tank, a septic field, pipes, and faucets) in your cabin, you may be in the market for the Incinolet®, which is an electric incinerating toilet.

forced through the fluids. There are lots of different pieces to the grinder, pieces that are prone to maintenance concerns. And you have to have power to run the pump, so obviously you cannot use your system if the power is out, which can often happen in the wilderness.

Another system is sort of setting up your own little peat bog, in which waste is filtered through several feet of peat. In some developments, they create a system that includes a series of ponds and lagoons.

Although the above-mentioned options are the most common, every year brings refinements or new technology to the fascinating world of managing human waste.

HALF-MOON HOUSE

If you don't want or need a real septic system, you have only so many choices. It's possible that you could have an outhouse, for instance, although in many areas of the country it's not legal to install a new outhouse. Some people bring in portable toilets and simply have them emptied regularly. If you're in a location where that type of service is available to you, that may be a viable option given what a full septic system costs.

Finally, you could get an incinerating toilet for your cabin, which literally evaporates or incinerates the waste into an ash that can be disposed of in the garbage. That is assuming you have access to electricity.

POWER TO THE CABIN

Some cabin sites are located off the area's power grid and must depend on generators, solar collectors, or wind-powered devices to provide electricity for the lights, heating, and appliances.

Solar panels can be a great way to provide electricity or domestic hot water. You will need to slope your roof to optimal solar angles, and keep your roof snow free.

CABIN MATTERS

FINDING THE POWER

Excessive residential demand creates peak loads for rural power cooperatives during the heating season. To help even out the demand, many cooperatives offer reduced off-peak rates to customers with heat-storage devices.

The electricity you buy from your co-op is split into two zones–one with 24-hour full-rate service for your lights, appliances, and electrical outlets, and the other with power for off-peak heat and water-heater storage systems. The off-peak zone is controlled by the co-op, which will usually guarantee 8 hours of service per every 24 hours.

Most sites, however, have access to electrical power networks, although in some cases the cost to extend that power down a long driveway may be high. In any event, no matter how rustic your getaway, you'll need electricity to run construction equipment and a pump for your well, not to mention whatever other amenities you may be thinking about.

If you're fortunate, you might have access to off-peak power rates that will help cost-effectively operate your water heater, in-floor heat, and other systems. At our place, we operate both the heat and hot-water systems at less than half-price rates because of our heat storage and thermal mass.

Distributing the electrical power will not be much different from the way you do it at home, but the breaker panels need to be easily accessible to everybody who's going to be using your cabin. That's because you may be asking your guests to switch the breakers on and off when coming and going. (Switching the well pump off when nobody's around can spare you the worry of burst pipes in the winter.)

ALL MANNER OF COSTS

When your bill of materials is complete (all the parts and pieces you'll need to remodel or build), you or your builder can proceed to an itemized estimate of your cabin's cost. With the help of your lumberyard and the subcontractor bids, the builder will factor in all the studs, nails, brackets, and sheathing it takes plus the labor necessary to fabricate everything at your site right on through the spring rainy season.

Material costs are your initial fixed expenses in addition to the cost of your site. Heating, cooling, and electricity are sustaining costs, along with what you pay for maintenance and taxes.

Obviously, your building costs will depend on the dimensions of your cabin, the materials you choose for construction, and the people you hire to build it. Just as obviously, a modest-size structure will reduce your lumberyard bill, and a simple shape will result in less material waste and lower labor costs. As a rule of thumb, about half of your cabin's construction cost will go for materials and about half will go for on-site labor. Those costs, in turn, will be affected by the availability of materials, transportation costs, and labor wage rates. Totally beyond your control will be the effects of distant hurricanes, trucking strikes, and the international cost of copper (wiring and pipes).

Persuading your pal Ned, the high school industrial arts teacher, to help put the place together during his summer vacation will save you money. Maximizing your use of sheet goods will save you more. Plywood and OSB are great for roofs, walls, and floors, and metal sheets can be used for both siding and roofs. Sheet goods as interior finished surfaces will baby your budget in several ways. Plywood or paneling sheets on walls and ceilings cut labor costs while adding warmth and character to your rooms. A fiberglass shower surround eliminates the need for a tile setter and will add to your peace of mind if you don't heat your cabin in the winter. Plastic laminate sheets make durable countertops and look great when dressed up with a wood edge that's perfect for a cabin setting.

Sheet goods, such as plywood and OSB, are good for a number of cabin uses. In this cabin, exterior-grade plywood is used as siding to give a board-and-batten look.

Manufactured kitchen cabinets are less expensive than custom made, and cabinetry salvaged from a rehabbed or about-to-be-demolished house is typically cheaper yet. Materials purchased at recycling centers and from home-building-supply chains are, generally speaking, going to save you big time. We happily bought all of our cabinets, countertops, shower surrounds, plumbing fixtures, and slate flooring for our cabin at The Home Depot℠.

TIP **INSTANT CABIN**

Prefabricated cabins come in many shapes and "personalities." Size, however, is limited by the rules and realities of highway transportation. And your site access and driveway must be large enough to accommodate the truck that hauls it in.

It might look like a shipping container with windows and doors, but this prefabricated cabin functions just fine as both an interesting piece of architecture and as a cabin that can go anywhere you can roll in a big truck.

The old log cabin had spent years resting on or near bare earth, so to be usable it needed a new foundation. First, house movers jacked it up and set it temporarily on timber cribbing (the crisscross stacks). Later, when the new foundation was built, the old cabin was set back down to rest comfortably for any number of good years to come.

One way to stay on top of your costs is to make your estimates early and continually update them as your project evolves from concept to the real thing. Keep in mind that all of your building decisions are important, and you want them all to add up to the cabin of your dreams.

CABIN RENEWAL

Every day more and more people buy vacation cabins, many of which were built in an era when the things we find important (even indispensable) today weren't then. In the old days, it was common for families (at least the mother and kids) to take the summer off and live at the cabin (the dad would visit on weekends).

So the most common disadvantage of these old cabins is that they weren't designed for use beyond warm weather–anywhere except where skiing was prevalent, that is. When somebody buys one of these old cabins, they look at it and see that it doesn't meet their family's needs and then have some decisions to make.

THE FOUNDATION

A way to tackle the old cabin is to figure out how you can prop it up and add to it to extend the season, even make it a year-round cabin. That might involve adding a "skin" over the outside, as we considered for our old log cabin. Usually that means reviewing and renovating the foundation system. These old structures were often built on piers, wood, rocks, or concrete blocks. (It's not uncommon to find some even resting right on the ground.) Whatever the existing foundation, in many cases it wasn't built below the frost line, so years of freezing and thawing have probably moved the cabin a bit, sometimes in ways that leave it bent, twisted, or sagging here and there.

Like any kind of building that's meant to last, we start with the foundation. Ask yourself: Do I have a foundation that's worth building around or do I have to raise the cabin and build a new foundation under it? This option is pretty common. It's time-consuming and can be expensive, but it certainly is doable. You have to jack up the cabin, lift it way high in the air, support it on iron beams resting on wood "cribbing," and dig a crawl space or a full foundation under it (see the photos on the facing page).

Of course, there must be some embedded value in that thing you're lifting up. In all likelihood, that cabin's value to you is not all economic. It was your uncle's, grandfather's, or you're just crazy about the way it looks. But if you're not emotionally attached to it, is this an investment you will enjoy and find worth the time, effort, and cost?

THINK OF THE SYSTEMS

You also need to evaluate your cabin's systems. Almost certainly you will have to upgrade the electrical system. When it was built, it might have had only a 60- or 30-amp service, with a fuse box instead of a circuit breaker panel. In the old days, you would have had a refrigerator, some lighting, and a few outlets. Now you need a dishwasher, a bigger, newer refrigerator, clothes washer, television, air-conditioning, and even more if you're going to use electricity as your main heating source.

Let's say the old cabin is simply a charmer and you want to keep it as close to the way it is as possible. You want to add on and renovate the existing cabin, but how do you go about it and still maintain the look and feel that you've grown to love?

Here you have to decide which part of that charm is more important to you: whether you want to maintain the inside of the cabin as it is or the outside. Because one has to go if you are to get into the walls and add that insulation you need to use the cabin year-round. That is, unless there is an existing cavity, in which case you can blow in insulation. But then you're not going to get a vapor barrier.

If yours is a log cabin, one option is to skin over the outside of the house with a new, second outside wall, which will protect the logs and give you room between the logs and the new wall to insulate. In that way, you maintain the log character on the inside. Often when I'm asked whether to preserve the interior charm or the exterior skin, in most cases I come down on preserving the cabin's interior. Usually, it is the interior of the cabin that has the biggest impact, the part you see the most. You really see the outside only when you are coming or going.

If you feel you need to maintain the exterior character of the old cabin, you can cut holes in the exterior walls and blow in insulations. If your old cabin was built to be used in mild weather only, insulation will become a big issue in your remodel. Installing insulation isn't simply a matter of jamming fiberglass into a stud wall because there are issues of moisture control and air sealing involved. Because of those concerns, you may want a professional to handle that portion of the remodel. Yet other options will determine how you can insulate your cabin.

You probably won't find a kerosene lantern adequate for your cabin illumination needs, yet it's not a bad idea to have one handy for when (not if) the lights go out.

If you're content with a cabin that you can only use in mild weather, one like this, then open-frame walls and no insulation might do the trick. The studs and board sheathing on the outside do establish a certain character that smooth wall surfaces can't match.

GOD IS IN THE DETAILS

CHAPTER SIX

THE BEST CABINS ARE NEVER DONE, never considered finished. For most people who own a cabin, that little place in the woods is a perpetual work in progress–even if they've owned it a lifetime.

I'm not talking about major construction, continually adding on, moving walls, rearranging windows; it's not even about painting and redecorating. I'm talking about the little things, the invaluable things, the details that make it nobody else's but yours.

You know those details. The old and familiar, like the weathervane that creaked atop your grandfather's barn. The fresh and new, like the laser cutouts of birds set into the stairway handrail. As high-tech as your son's computer artwork. As down to earth as the oak fireplace mantel hand-carved by your pastor's son. As goofy as the sign by the mailbox that reads *Fishfull Thinking*.

From the plaster bust of Mark Twain you snagged at a garage sale to the pencil marks by the kitchen door that tell your family's story in quarter-inch increments, the personal accumulation of things and

"THE APPEARANCE OF THE INTERIOR OF THE *cabin depends on individual taste. Some would keep the surroundings antique and odd, others would decorate with Indian blankets and objects. Still other individuals would use the old wagon wheel and prairie atmosphere, while some would use the gay nineties style."*

–William Swanson, *Log Cabins*, The Macmillan Company, 1948

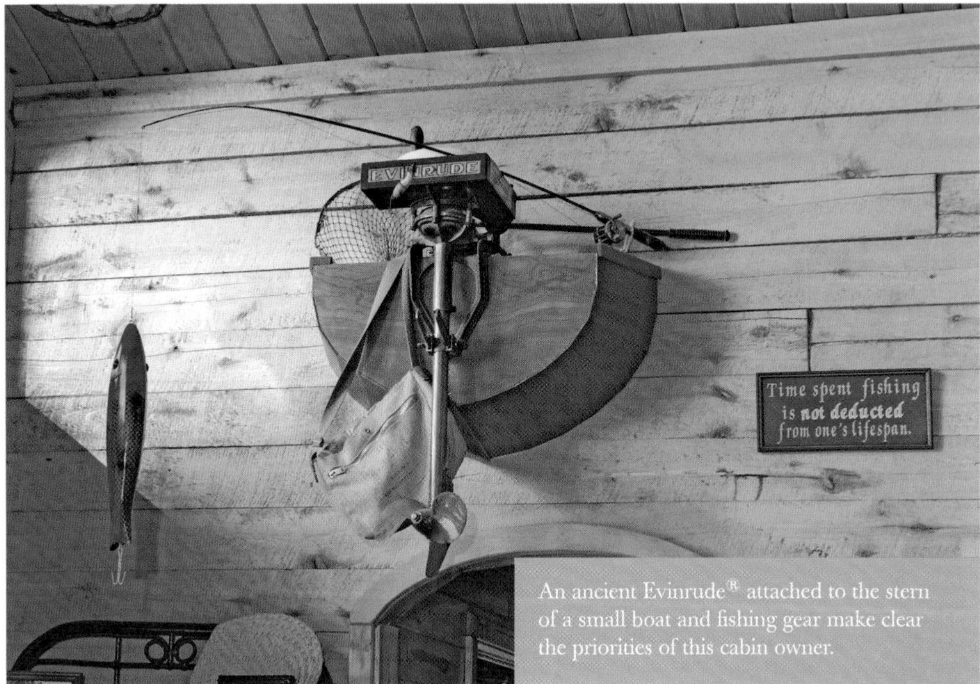

An ancient Evinrude® attached to the stern of a small boat and fishing gear make clear the priorities of this cabin owner.

This "Bug House" is shared by several families as their sunset dining room.

stains and blemishes of many hands and hard use add to the singular feeling of your cabin. And they're often the things visitors best remember years later about you and their stay at your cabin.

MAKING THE PLACE YOURS

The "little things" may not, in fact, be so little. They also may be more than just decoration. Maybe you need a place to store firewood out of the weather, plus room for axes, mauls, and all the other wood-splitting equipment that gathers like dust. So you add a modest shed to the property. Or maybe you want a sauna to round out your cabin experience, so you build one of those, too. Then it occurs to you that a screened gazebo would be a great spot for dining outdoors with guests or for grabbing an hour or two away from the kids, so you build one of those.

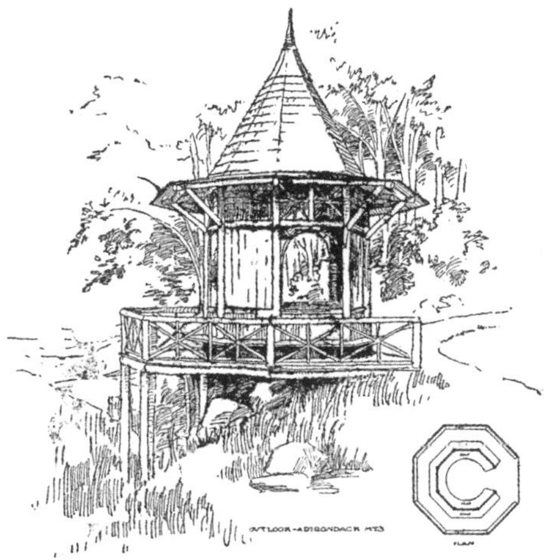

A hillside gazebo with a twig-work railing would add one-of-a-kind charm to any cabin setting.

CABIN MATTERS

RULES TO EMBELLISH BY

At the end of Christopher Alexander's excellent book, *A Pattern Language* (Oxford University Press, 1977), he talks about how to embellish a finished structure. He says that everything from a front-door bench to "things from your life" provides personal qualities that add to the personality of a structure, including a cabin. However, there are definitely "rules" to follow.

Here's Alexander's Rule #251 regarding certain furniture: "Never furnish a place with chairs that are identically the same. Choose a variety of different chairs, some big, some small, some softer than others, some rockers, some very old, some new, with arms, without arms, some wicker, some wood, some cloth."

All of those chairs would require an awfully large cabin, but you get the idea. The bottom line is this: it's your cabin, so feel free to mix it up and furnish it to reflect your tastes and your interests.

"THE BUG HOUSE"

A gazebo close by the water has provided many fond memories for the several cabin families that share it on Big Sand Lake in Minnesota.

Affectionately dubbed "The Bug House," the screened enclosure has been the site of morning coffees, shore lunches, candlelit dinners, and countless other special moments for the neighboring friends.

BIRDFEEDERS

Birdfeeders will bring many of your feathered friends into closer view and help you keep track of the progress of the migratory species in your part of the world. The feeders will also draw squirrels and chipmunks, which in turn might entice a red fox to your site.

If your cabin lies in bear country, you'll need to take special precautions with your birdfeeders, placing them at a safe distance from your heavy outdoor activity and choosing carefully what you leave for the birds.

Realtors blandly call these smaller additions "site amenities," which hardly describes the range of possibilities. Go wild because what you build is limited only by your imagination, budget, and property lines. Think volleyball court, horseshoe pit, swimming dock, putting green, skateboard ramp. A fire pit, situated at a careful, safe distance from the cabin and overhanging trees, is where you burn the deadfall. But it's also where you all toast marshmallows for the s'mores.

These little things can be as simple as a tire swing or as complex as a boathouse. It's up to you.

Obviously, the larger and more structural things–say, the woodshed or the sauna–require thought and planning. You'll want to put the shed, for instance, close to your driveway where your neighbor drops off the cordwood but close enough to your back door so the trek from shed to stove is no more than a pleasant diversion, even in nasty weather. In just the right spot, prevailing breezes dry the wood and cool the wood splitter's brow. If you really want to do it up right, connect everything–buildings, sheds, whatever–with a pleasant little path lined with local rocks and covered with gravel or wood chips.

OTHER OUTSIDE ADDITIONS

As your outpost in the natural world, the cabin is yours to make the most of, which might, for example, include having a good telescope that you'll point toward the heavens from a rooftop perch, balcony, or maybe a little platform in a clearing beyond the glow of electric lights. And because the weather plays such an important role, maybe you'll have a good outdoor thermometer or even an elaborate outdoor weather station (including a thermometer, barometer, rain gauge, etc.). Make sure the thermometer is large enough and positioned so you can easily read it from the kitchen window (or from the bedroom window so you know if you even want to slip out from under the covers).

Wind chimes won't tell you much about wind velocity or direction, but they will alert you to the arrival of a breeze that signifies a change in the weather–and few outdoor sounds are any lovelier. Just as welcome a sound, though for an entirely different reason, is the old-fashioned dinner bell that, heard even over the sound of boat motors and chainsaws, draws all to the dining table for fried fish and potato salad.

ABOVE: Dining al fresco is a distinct cabin pleasure.

BOTTOM LEFT: The perfect woodshed is close to the road, convenient to the house, and open to the air.

BOTTOM RIGHT: For a shady snooze on a summer day, few cabin pleasures surpass the hammock.

"THE VERY UPRIGHTNESS OF THE PINES *and maples asserts the ancient rectitude and vigor of nature. Our lives need the relief of such a background, where the pine flourishes and the jay still screams."*

–Henry David Thoreau (1817-1862), philosopher, author, naturalist

SPECIAL ENTRY

From the very first glance, your cabin's front door should be visually welcoming and big enough to accommodate all the human traffic and stuff it's likely to have pass through it. To comfortably pass through it with arms full of luggage or groceries, I usually recommend a 42-in. door as opposed to the standard 36-in. one. And because this is your cabin, your special place, your front door is a great spot to add some whimsy and imagination, like an antique iron knocker or a family crest carved out of pinewood (either the real thing or something you just made up).

Unless your cabin is your year-round home–or you stay there for months at a time–you probably don't need a mailbox. But a small note pad and pencil on a string permanently positioned near your front door is a great way to encourage communication between you and your neighbors–and to alert you to the fact that there's a package waiting for you in town.

Let the front door express your imagination.

THE FRUIT OF THE FOREST

We use a lot of wood in our cabins. Much of it is hidden inside the walls and roof, but that's certainly not the extent of it. Creative use of wood can be an important part of your cabin's details, large and small, inside and out.

Inside, I like to add unmilled tree parts to remind us where the grain, knots, and character of the wood come from. Deane Hillbrand, my timber-framing friend in Sturgeon Lake, Minnesota, cuts ash trees on his property, then rolls them in the wet summer grass until the bark falls off. I used three of his peeled ash trunks in our cabin–two on either side of the kitchen island to hold up the second floor and one at the entry to shore up the stoop roof. My wife painted the outside trunk red and refers to it as "our Minnesota redwood."

Some folks prefer to leave the bark on the tree trunks, and there's no question that the natural beauty of birch or red pine bark can add a lot to any cabin. My only advice would be to use that wood in less busy parts of the cabin, where oily hands are less likely to discolor the bark and a nice wool sweater is not going to snag on its gnarly hide.

CABIN MATTERS

OF ROOTS AND RAILINGS

Windstorms sometimes knock down entire trees, exposing their gnarly tangles of roots. But what might be unfortunate for the tree may provide the raw material, not to mention some inspiration, to its human owner.

Roots of cedar trees, for instance, can be a great source of curved timber for your cabin's stair railings and banisters.

SEE THE POSSIBILITY

Sometimes you'll have a bright idea for using certain tree parts–or your carpenter provides his own interpretation. Most carpenters have their personal favorites when it comes to wood. And many have a way to get what they like in the forests near their homes.

In Minnesota cabin land, the Lonesome Cottage Co. keeps a stash of trees for seemingly every purpose. If you're looking for a yoke style, something with a large burl protrusion, or something with a twisted limb attached, you can find just the trunk that will be perfect for your cabin's living room or entry. Even the misshapen trunk with the stubby limbs would make a perfect hat rack.

Architect Edwin Lundie used elaborate turned-wood columns on the exterior corners of his timber-framed cabins. He gleaned that detail from the ancient designs of *stuga* structures in Norway and viewed those corner columns as opportunities to add detail work unique to each cabin. He had some of the columns turned on

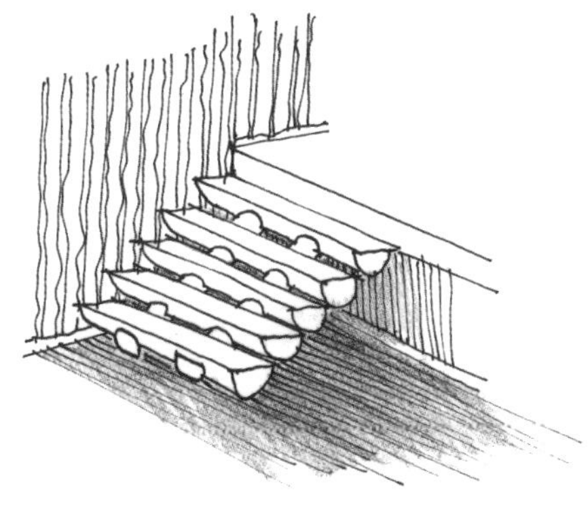

Logs halved lengthwise make great cabin stair treads.

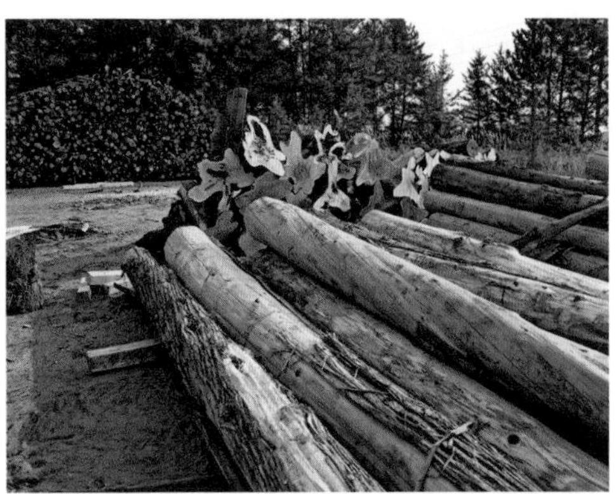

Using your imagination, you can turn logs into interesting elements—even structural ones—for your cabin.

a lathe and others sawn in a chamfered pattern. At his own cabin, he carved spoon scallops in an egg and dart pattern in his turned columns.

Brush and small tree limbs are a good source of material for railings, coat pegs, towel bars, and cabinet pulls. As far as tree species go, willow, dogwood, ironwood, poplar, hickory, and cedar are all excellent for small projects. You can also cut log slabs in half and use them as treads and stringers on stairways where there are no risers. The same kind of slabs can be used for benches and tables.

Wood that's been precut and kiln-dried is convenient to buy, easy to work with, and not as likely to check and split as much as green tree trunks. We use nominal 1-in. and 2-in. material in various species and widths for all kinds of enhancements in and around the cabins we design.

CUT IT OUT

Popular enhancements are railings for balconies, lofts, and stairs, especially where cutout patterns create silhouettes of trees, leaves, birds, flowers, or people. On one of my firm's railings, we used cutout patterns to replicate the leaves and stalks of wild rice that grow in our part of the state. The long, slender leaf pattern proved a legendary challenge to the cabin owner's father, who had committed himself to crafting it. But after directing harsh words toward the cabin's designer (me), he came through with a wild rice motif that's the highlight of the space and, to the cabin owner, worth every skinned knuckle and cuss word.

For one of our own cutout projects, my cabinmates and I gathered a collection of leaves from the woods around us. I slightly enlarged the leaves on a photocopier, then used their outlines to cut out full-scale templates from pieces of cardboard. I gave a variety of the templates to our carpenter with a pattern layout that repeats the leaf shapes but not the sequence. The leafy cutouts now fall across our railing, reminding us of the birch, aspen, and dogwood that inspired them.

A couple of caveats when it comes to cutouts: Choose a design that, when the shape is cut out, won't significantly reduce the structural continuity of the railing (by the way, vertical shapes work better than horizontal ones). And choose a motif that can be negotiated with a jigsaw and sanding paper.

WHERE ELSE?

In the kitchen, open shelves using milled lumber keep plates, cups, cooking utensils, and ingredients in plain sight, which is greatly appreciated by guests who can quickly find what they're looking for while making breakfast or setting the table. Similarly, the open

With some creativity, a design all your own becomes a one-of-a-kind stair railing.

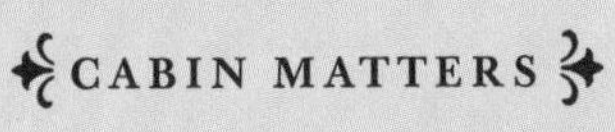

NO WATER REQUIRED

Canoe paddles, which come in varying lengths and in many kinds of wood, make excellent railings when positioned alternately up and down. One hitch: To meet building code, railing paddles have to be at least 3 ft. long, and the gap between them can't exceed 4 in. Yet once secured to the rail and floor, paddle railings offer a unique look and really cause guests to do a double-take.

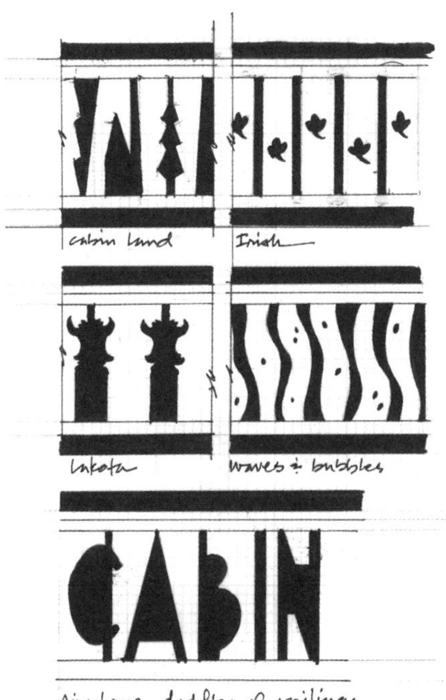

Airplane doodles of railings

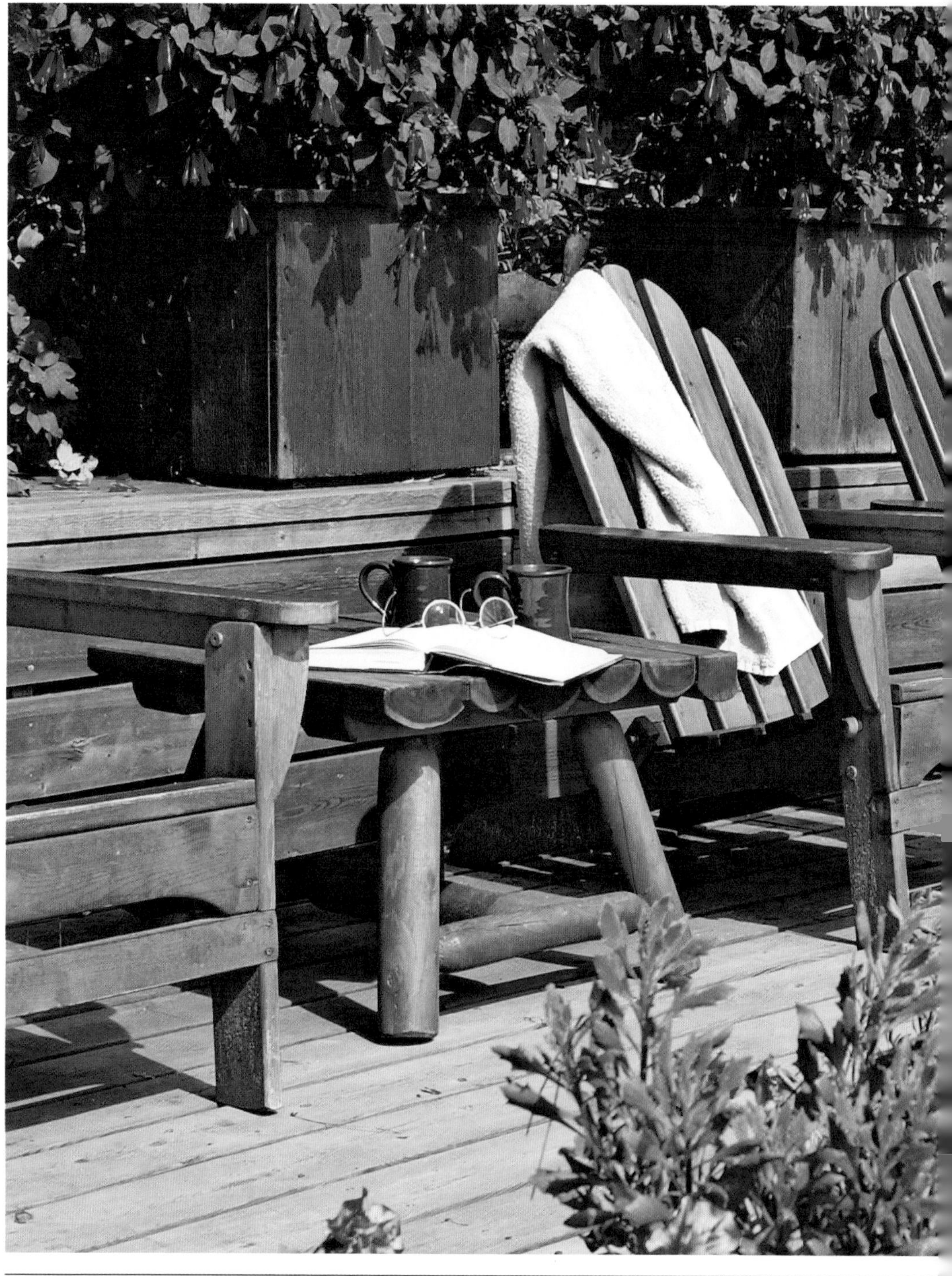

"THERE IS IN EVERY AMERICAN, *I think, something of the old Daniel Boone–who, when he could see smoke from another chimney, felt himself too crowded and moved further out into the wilderness."*

– Hubert H. Humphrey, Vice-President and U.S. senator, 1911–1978

shelving in the larder or pantry allows easy access to the soda supply, canned ham, preserves, and other good things to eat and drink.

In the living area and bedrooms, open shelves are just what you need to display your classic cabin novels, bird-watching guides, and trekking maps. In the mudroom, they're where you stick the flashlights and bug spray for easy access when you need them.

Finally, common 1-in. by 4-in. window and door trim and 1-in. by 6-in. trim for the base are readily available in pine and many other woods. Stained or left clear and finished with polyurethane, the trim will be all you need to dress up and give every cabin room a finished look.

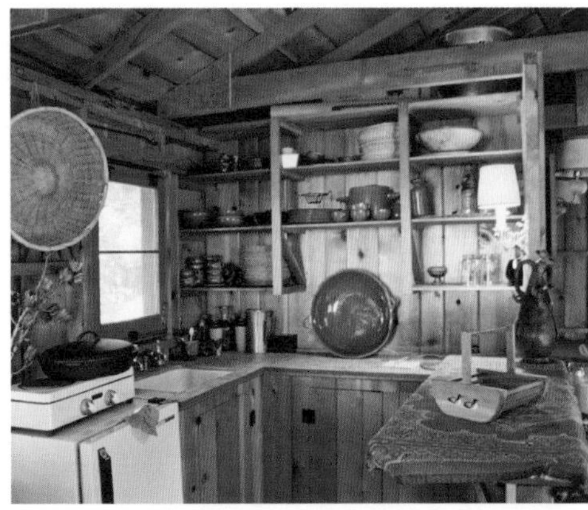

Open shelves are great storage–and design–options for kitchen or living room.

THE ESSENTIAL CABIN LIBRARY

No cabin bookshelf or night table is complete without copies of the following classics (tattered cover not required but recommended):

- *Walden* by Henry David Thoreau
- *Listening Point* and *The Singing Wilderness* by Sigurd Olson
- *Gunflint: Reflections of the Trail* by Justine Kerfoot
- *Small Is Beautiful* by E. F. Shumacher
- *Silent Spring* by Rachel Carson
- *A Sand County Almanac* by Aldo Leopold
- *The Survival of the Bark Canoe* by John McPhee

THE BEAUTIFUL BUILT-INS

Whether you're remodeling or building a brand-new cabin, it's still nothing without cabinets and doors and all the other built-in possibilities that exist.

For discussion's sake, let's say you're building a new cabin. And the woman who's doing your cabinetry is dropping by to talk about the final details for the kitchen and bathroom. She's bringing sample door styles in different woods and finishes for your contemplation. And the finish carpenter wants to show you his mock-up of interior trim, plus his layout for a window seat.

Fortunately, you've done your homework. You and yours have thought about your options and pretty much decided what your cabin will look like inside.

Elevation drawings of your cabin (whether you had somebody who knows what he's doing draw them or whether you doodled

CABIN MATTERS

CARL LARSSON'S BUILT-INS

Graphic artist Carl Larsson (1853–1919) furnished his home in Sundborn, Sweden, with several built-ins often decorated with beautiful stained wood and decorative rosemaling. The drawings in which he recorded his work have since influenced countless American craftsmen and many cabins in both Scandinavia and North America.

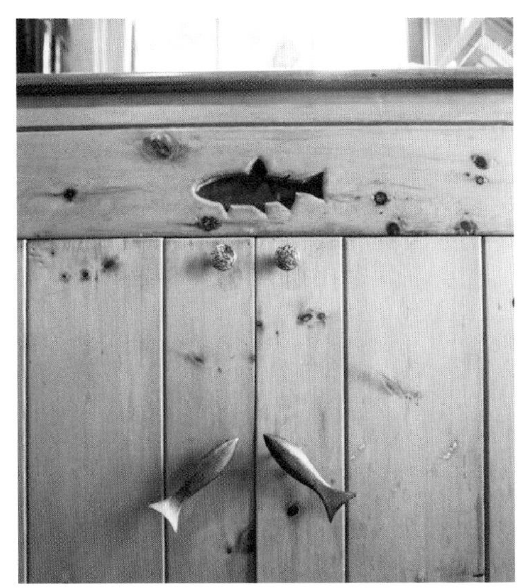

ABOVE: A simple design, like this fish, cut out of a cabinet door or into a drawer front impresses your personal style on the most ordinary objects.

BELOW: Not all storage has to be built-in. Consider an antique hutch, pie safe, or china cabinet for storage in your cabin kitchen.

them yourself) probably helped you make key decisions about the exterior. You can use the same kind of drawings to figure out everything from cabinet-door styles to the height of the window seats to the relation of the wainscot tile in the bathroom and the towel bar location. Those drawings take a little time, but they can make a big difference in the finished cabin.

The carpenters who built the cabins Edwin Lundie designed said later that all the parts went together like a fine piece of cabinetry. Lundie precisely delineated the specs for the handmade windows, kitchen cabinets, and built-in bunk beds. If it was a particularly complicated detail, he provided a full-scale template drawing that the carpenter could use as a layout pattern. He even made template drawings for simpler pieces such as the door hinges and latches.

Nowadays, new cabins usually involve assembly more than fabrication, meaning you're probably going to order a door in fir from, say, Simpson, birch kitchen cabinets

A basic bay window creates a just-right spot for a breakfast, dinner, or a good game of canasta.

from Ikea[SM], and black iron hardware from Acorn® online. What's important, obviously, is whether all these parts, when assembled and installed in your cabin, happily fit together. The less you leave to chance–or to the whims of your electrician, plumber, and carpenter–the happier you're going to be with your cabin.

PERFECTING THE KITCHEN

Often your kitchen cabinet choices are just a matter of common sense. Casual flat-slab or flat-panel styles are probably going to look better, or at least more appropriate, on your kitchen cabinets than styles featuring raised panels and fancy detailing–they're for a cabin, after all.

Overlay doors will be more cost effective than inset doors, and melamine interiors will be easier to keep clean than wood ones.

We bought the cabinets for our cabin at a big-box lumberyard where we had not only a wide range of styles and finishes to choose from but also significant differences in quality and cost. We decided to intersperse soft green-and-blue stained uppers with base cabinets of clear maple. The maple's understated grain goes well with the distinctly grained and knotty pine walls and the reddish-toned fir beams. The color stain adds a casual whimsy to the entire composition while bringing into the mix some of the colors in the Vermont slate flooring, which, by the way, we also bought at that big Minnesota lumberyard.

When it comes to kitchen countertops, there are likewise plenty of options, including concrete, butcher block, natural stone, quartz composites, and various manufactured solid surfaces.

Stainless steel–often the choice of commercial kitchens–gets more beautiful as it takes on scratches, scuffs, and a bit of hard-won patina. Plastic laminate, which was beloved by your grandmother but now dismissed by purists, is another choice, though, for sheer dollar value, I'm with Grandma. Dress it up with a wooden edge, and that laminate is perfect for a cabin kitchen.

ABOVE: Glass doors show off the contents of the upper cabinets while keeping the dust out.

RIGHT: A pine-paneled kitchen includes a combination of solid, color-stained cabinet doors and open shelving.

Rustic and basic, this kitchen keeps everything out in the open, except the sink plumbing, which gets covered by a skirt.

In our cabin, we created a niche between the mud room and the open ceiling to the living room, which is just perfect for the kids.

A WIDER WORLD OF BUILT-INS

Window seats are a great built-in. I personally like them large enough to curl up on with lots of pillows and my feet off the floor–a perfect nest for a nap or reading. Located near the dining table, a window seat can also be a bench for a guest or two. In a bedroom, depending on the window seat's size, it can sleep a child or one of your buddies up for a fishing weekend.

I have a window seat in my house that's the size of a queen-size bed, and it's where all three of our grandkids want to spend the night when they're together. You may not have space in your cabin for a window seat that big, but, as a general principle, the bigger you can make it, the better. That's partly because the area *under* that window seat makes great storage space.

The same goes for the space under the beds, incidentally. We found queen-size platform beds at an unfinished-furniture store, and that allowed for six additional big storage drawers in each of our cabin bedrooms, which means that no one has to search too far for fresh linens or extra blankets. The drawers are also great for storing out-of-season clothing.

THE OPERATIONS CENTER

Every cabin needs an operations center. That's usually not a room but simply the place where you keep the land-line phone (if you have one), the phone book, and whatever basic documents and tools may need to be easily accessed.

It's the place where you keep the plumber's cell-phone number, the name and contact information for the guy who sells firewood, and a list of the local restaurants, shops, and recreation sites you recommend to guests, not to mention such helpful data as the community band concert schedule and the movies coming to the 30-seat cinema in town.

In our cabin, the operations center is where I stash instructions for operating the powerboat, the name and number of the neighbor who happens to be an EMT, and the basic steps to take in the event of a power outage.

A small chalkboard or corkboard is a nice touch, too–just the thing for noting phone messages and posting reminders about recycling or buying light bulbs on the next trip to the store. In addition, you should allow for enough space to accommodate the crazy collection of keys you'll accumulate, a couple of flashlights (and ample fresh batteries), a few basic tools (hammer, pliers, a couple of screwdrivers, allen wrench, and saw), and a reasonably well-stocked first-aid kid including, of course, the basic remedies for sunburn, bug bites, and poison ivy.

Did I mention a fire extinguisher?

Near or even *in* your kitchen is a good place to locate your operations center, maybe in a designated and clearly marked cabinet or in a fine, old rolltop desk. The important thing is that everybody–including your guests and your guests' kids–know where it is and what they can find there in a hurry.

A good entry space for your cabin might include storage for packs and bags, a seat for removing boots, and pegs for hanging coats.

COMING AND GOING: YOUR INSTRUCTIONS

My friend Scott e-mails a five-page set of instructions to guests intending to stay at his cabin, "Norcliff," in Tofte, Minnesota.

The "Opening Up" section of his message includes directions such as flipping circuit breakers #19, 27, 32, and 34, removing chair covers, and checking for sewage-pump failure while the cabin was vacant. "Fireplace Instructions" detail opening the damper, locating the matches, and starting a fire. "General Information" includes helpful tips for grilling, snow removal, setting out birdseed, and finding the flashlights and binoculars. "Closing Down" prescribes the removal of perishables and garbage, the lowering of the thermostat setting, and replacing the chair covers.

Scott doesn't ignore the fun stuff in his instructions–e.g., where to rent cross-country skis and how to negotiate with a fishing guide–or, for that matter, a list of seven restaurants in the vicinity complete with a gourmet's critique of each!

If you have a cabin–and friends–it's most likely you'll occasionally lend it to one of them. A bit of cabin-specific information, codified into a friendly manual of instructions tailored for your visitors, will make their stay better and leave your mind easier.

CABIN STORIES

THE CABIN LIFE

I once brought a new friend to my family's cabin. We drove up the long dirt road, over the miles of bumps and rocks. We walked in silence up the little hill, carefully avoiding the big, time-smoothed roots. We stepped inside. We stood in silence for several moments.

"Wow," he said. More silence. "Wow."

I have never known a summer without the cabin. It is the single most stable thing in my life. The cabin. Small and cozy and dark. Red-and-white checked curtains. It is one room. It has a bunk bed and two simple cots made by my uncle and my brother when he was 12. It has an old pull-out couch.

There is a table, a wood-burning stove, and a salvaged sink that has lake water running through its PVC veins that flows downhill from the peeling painted tanks up the hill. One of my favorite jobs as a kid was assisting with pump duty. My dad would go down to the lake and get the old pump started. It was loud. My brother was stationed up at the tanks. My job was to run down the hill, leaping over roots, dodging trees, and galloping over fallen logs to let Dad know it was time to cut the motor.

Out on the wraparound porch are two orange canvas chair-swings hanging from the porch beams. As kids, we sat for hours reading, swinging, imagining what winter was like in the woods and fighting over who would get the swing next. Now our children do all of that.

Coming on the lake from the meandering walk through the woods is the most startling thing, the most beautiful sight I have ever seen. To this day, in my 46th year, I gasp each time I see it. It is a lovely, lovely quiet glacier lake. Some days it is still and you can see every tree and rock reflected in its surface, a dark, glassy pane; other days it is like a small sea, gray and frothy with wind-driven waves.

I love the quiet and solitude at the cabin. Even rainy days are lovely there. Without electricity, there are none of the sounds that we are used to. No music, no radio, no computers or television. Without the distraction of city sounds, I hear the wind and the birds and the mysterious creatures rustling outside. One day I sit on the porch swing and I hear the hum of a bird's wings and think, "Aha, that is why they are called hummingbirds." I see chipmunks skittering around, up and down the branches. At night I hear the slapping of bat wings overhead as they swoop over the lake to catch mosquitoes.

To this day, in my 46th year, I gasp each time I see it. It is a lovely, lovely quiet glacier lake. Some days it is still and you can see every tree and rock reflected in its surface, a dark, glassy pane; other days it is like a small sea, gray and frothy with wind-driven waves.

The path beyond the cabin leads to a field of tall ferns. Ferns, ferns, ferns. Everywhere are ferns. These ancient, simple plants are beautiful, with their repetitive shapes and veins. They are soft and lovely.

I love nighttime at the cabin. To sleep with the sound of crashing thunder and rain hard on the roof overhead or to wake to see the full moon shining on the lake. On moonless nights, you cannot see your hand in front of your face it is so dark. It is sublime.

–Kate Binzen is a housewife and teacher of the deaf who is training to be a sign language interpreter. She lives in Decatur, Georgia, with her husband, two children, a cat, and two pet rats.

If your interior walls are bare wood, whether logs or boards, you can choose a stain that fits your vision.

SPLASH ON THE COLOR

Whether your walls and ceilings are finished with wood or drywall, you're also going to decide on some form of finish. At the very least, you'll want to protect the wood with varnish or polyurethane and the drywall with paint. So what do you say to a little color? Or a lot of color?

You can stain the wood with color and choose from an almost infinite spectrum for the drywall. Of course, in many settings you'll be looking for a pleasing combination of colors, knowing, for instance, that stained wood trim looks better against rich or warm colors than with stark white walls.

Staining wood is a major commitment because you have only one shot to get it right. That's why it's a good idea to test your color choices on pieces of scrap lumber before you do anything in earnest. Take the time to get it right. Some of my clients have stained up to 30 pieces of scrap before they found the color that they liked the best. Many stain manufacturers helpfully provide small samples to make that kind of experimentation easier and less expensive.

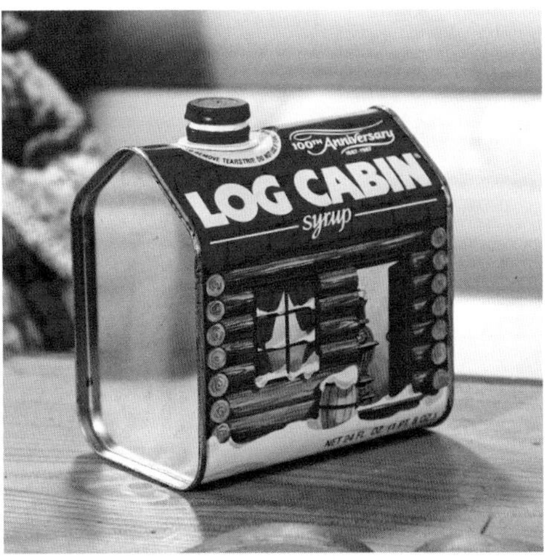

Just a touch of whimsy: a can of classic Log Cabin® syrup was the inspiration for the room to the left.

Wood can also be whitewashed. I rubbed the dregs of some white interior paint into the pinewood paneling in both of our bathrooms, then put a polyurethane coat on top of that for a squeaky clean look and feel.

Painting drywall is a lot easier than staining wood. If you don't like the shade of green you used in the bedroom, paint over it with another shade of green that you like better—or paint it blue or orange or make it silver leaf if you want. A professional may not work that way, but assuming what's at stake here is your own sweat equity, you're free to keep trying until you find exactly the right look. Two or five or ten years later, you can freshen things up with a different shade or a whole new palette.

If you're feeling especially creative, maybe you'll choose to stencil the walls with your own designs. You're surrounded, remember, with naturally beautiful and intriguing forms—oak and maple leaves, cattails, pussy willows, pinecones, four-leaf clover—that inspire lovely stencil shapes.

Maybe, especially if there's Swedish or Norwegian blood in your veins, you'll want to enliven the walls of your place with the ancient art of rosemaling. Maybe you want to turn a wall or an entire room over to the kids or grandkids and see what visual memories they can create.

THE HARDWARE

When people ask me for help choosing cabin hardware, I always offer the same advice: "Buy it black or paint it black."

This includes everything from the metal brackets used with the exposed structural timbers to door handles and hinges to cabinet knobs and handrails. Aesthetically, black works with just about any color scheme and wood treatment and can help unify a variety of materials that were pulled together even on a modest budget.

Practically, you're never going to have trouble finding black hardware at your local hardware store. And when you have so many aesthetic and practical decisions to make when putting your cabin together, not to mention so many choices in front of you at the store, you'll be happy to have gone black.

A local metalsmith or sculptor can help you personalize some of the hardware in and around your cabin. When I design cabins in northern Minnesota, I often draw on the talents of Tom Christiansen at Last Chance Fabricating in Lutsen. For one of my clients, Tom created a brass floor plaque that highlights the cabin's location on the lake. He has also fashioned balcony and stair railings for cabins in his neck of the woods. For our own cabin, Tom designed and crafted a one-of-a-kind weathervane using a metal walleyed pike instead of the familiar rooster.

Tom is one-of-a-kind himself, but I'm betting you have someone like him in your area who can add special touches to your cabin as well. Remember, it doesn't all have to be one way or the other because you can mix in the special custom hardware with the store bought.

CABIN MATTERS

IRON IDEAS

The forged-iron hardware that our grandparents bought in their local hardware stores is still available for cabin use, but it may take a little searching. In fact, a few old-style ironsmiths are forging new designs as well as producing authentic reproductions of classic pieces. Although the hardware is now typically available in cast iron, the subtleties of form and finish provided by forging offer something special.

Two contemporary sources of popular forged-iron designs such as butterfly- and fish-shaped door hinges and swordfish-shaped latches is Fagan's Forge (www.fagansforge.com) and the Old Smithy Shop (www.oldsmithyshop.com). In the meantime, no cabin stoop should be without the forged-iron boot scraper available online from Acorn Manufacturing (www.acornmfg.com).

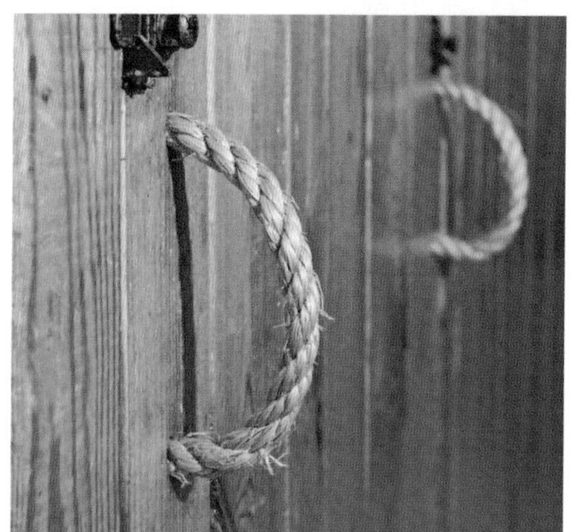

Rope cabinet door pulls express a bit of personality and are, if nothing else, practical and affordable.

LIGHTEN UP

Lighting your cabin for the nighttime demands yet more attention to detail. There are three basic types of artificial lighting: ambient, task, and decorative. You'll need fixtures for each.

Ambient lighting is what you need to find your way around your cabin once the sun goes down. Task lighting is what you need to slice the carrots. Decorative lights, a distant third in terms of importance, twinkle, blink, or otherwise call attention to themselves and the object to which they're attached, such as a decorative bower or a rack of antlers or some special thing you want everybody to notice.

The cardinal rules when selecting light fixtures are, one, fit the space and, two, meet the need. You'll need lighting to guide you and your guests safely up and down the stairs, and you'll need lighting to allow you a close, safe shave. That lighting probably doesn't call for the same sort of fixture, nor is it what you want for your bedside reading or for illuminating a hall closet.

Kitchens have their own separate requirements, such as for reading a cookbook, measuring the oregano, and setting the mood for a romantic supper of the fish you caught this afternoon.

Needless to say, the fixture is only part of your lighting challenge. Another part is where you put it. As always, use your imagination. Attaching lights under the upper cabinets in the kitchen, for instance, gives great light close to the task at hand on the counter beneath them, while taking zero precious counter space away from what you're doing.

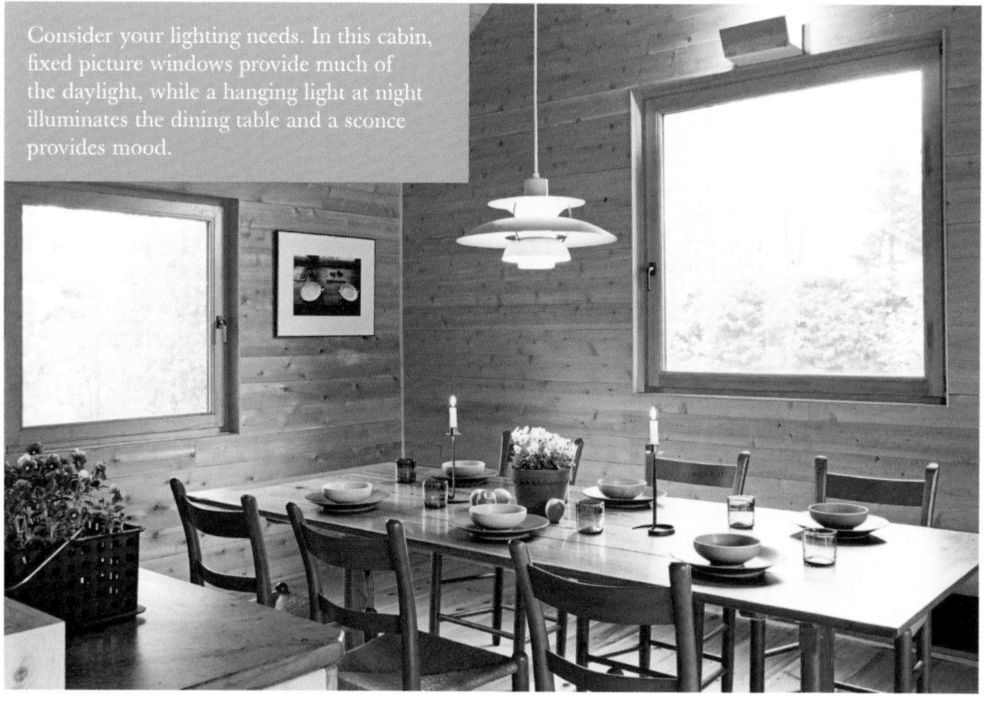

Consider your lighting needs. In this cabin, fixed picture windows provide much of the daylight, while a hanging light at night illuminates the dining table and a sconce provides mood.

ABOVE: Don't underestimate the benefit of having standby light sources such as kerosene lamps. They're cheap and reliable in case of a power outage.

BELOW: A basic bedroom should include a light for reading, a table, and a comfortable bed.

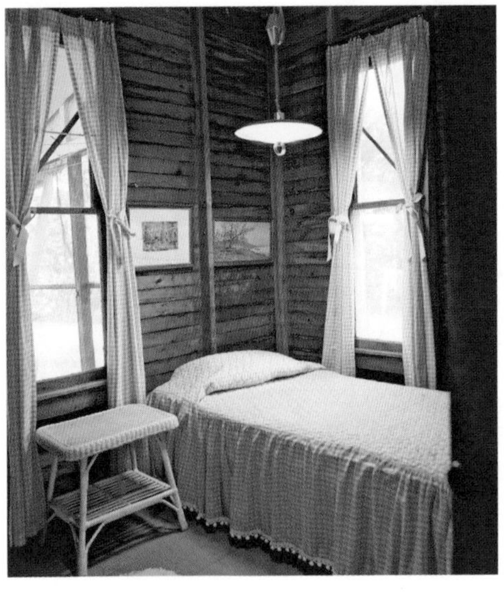

THE RIGHT LIGHT

As with most components for your cabin, selecting both fixtures and their placement often requires a tradeoff. Recessed fixtures may be slick in the finished ceiling of your living area, but you'll need several of them to do the job of a single hanging globe. Many of the cabins I've worked on have sloping ceilings that run parallel to the roof. In our chilly part of the world, the space needed for recessed lighting is simply better used for insulation.

In a bedroom, it may be tempting to connect the night-table lamp to the wall switch just inside the bedroom door, but that may not be such a good idea when you've got guests who don't know the layout of the place as well as you do.

Another rule of thumb for lighting is don't use more than you need, either inside or out. Outside, light pollution is a growing problem in many of our more heavily populated cabin areas, further reducing the naturalness of the surroundings and making it harder for us to enjoy the glories of the night, be they those magical falling stars or the magnificent Milky Way.

Outside, providing small twinkling lights at or near ground level along the path between the front door and the dock is preferable to mounting large security lamps on poles or atop the cabin roof. Inside, there are fixtures appropriate to every room, nook, and corner as well as virtually every need. Cabin bathrooms, for instance, are usually modest (to say the least), so a couple of fixtures should be all you need: one over the mirror and sink, and one in the shower, protected against breakage and bright enough for a lady to shave her legs.

Simplicity is almost always the smartest choice. Frankly, fancy brass fixtures salvaged from a suburban McMansion look silly in a rustic dining area where a 100-watt bulb in the porcelain globe that once hung in your mother's kitchen is ideal for both the place and task.

And, speaking of electrical fixtures, you may want to add a ceiling fan in some of your rooms. (Unfortunately, I find few lighting fixture-fan combinations charming and don't recommend them.) If you're like most of us, you don't want to spend summer evenings with the windows shut tight and the air-conditioning running full blast. Better (especially in bedrooms and living area) to add a quiet but surprisingly effective overhead fan.

FURNISHINGS

What you choose to sit on, lie on, eat off, and put things in at your cabin can do as much as anything to add, or detract, from the look and feel of your cabin.

We've all seen jam-packed cabins where anything goes. (Or where everything's gone.) Instead of reassigning a worn-out hide-a-bed to the basement or to the Goodwill outlet at home, folks haul it to the cabin, where it's the focal point of the living area. "Early attic" is what this particular "style" of furnishings is often called.

We've all seen cabins, on the other hand, where the rule has been, "If it cost more than $15 at a garage sale, it doesn't belong here." I happen to agree with Chilson Aldrich, author of *The Real Log Cabin*, who wrote way back in 1928, "Don't ship to your new cabin the junked contents of your attic or storeroom in town. You desire a wilderness home, a restful abode of the primitive, not an Asylum for Aged and Infirm Furniture."

I also believe–as I've said many times–in the principle of simplicity and proportion. I see too

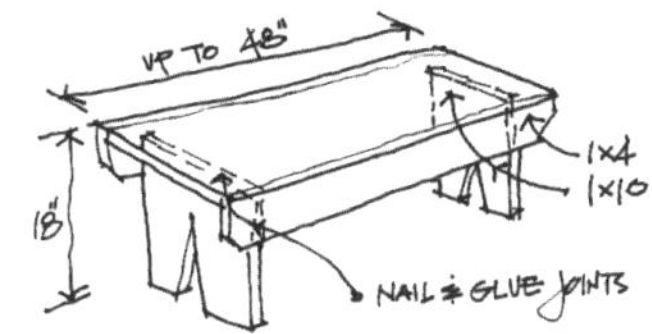

YOUR BASIC BENCH

many cabins where the furniture is hardly junk, but it's just too big and bulky for the space. A fat, overstuffed chair simply doesn't look right in a small, spare room with knotty pine walls.

I'm partial to furniture I often see in older cabins, where the chairs and tables look as though they were designed and built by local craftspeople specifically for that space. These artisans used handy template patterns and local woods, and the furnishings they created will never go out of style. The classic Adirondack chair may be the best example of a timeless pattern for a cabin setting. I've made a few pieces of furniture myself–a couple of benches and a chest–and I'm satisfied enough with the results to use them with some small pride in our cabin.

Whether a twin-bed-size window seat or bunks with integral storage, built-in sleeping facilities add to the flexibility of your cabin's use.

THE SOFTWARE

Finally, there are the finishing touches that set off the furniture, the "soft" details that include everything from pillows, quilts, and bedspreads to glassware, dishes, and artwork.

All of this can be bought in stores, of course, but, again, my tastes run to the quirky, one-of-a-kind, highly personal stuff that's as unique and individual as you and your cabin. I'm lucky to have a brother who's an excellent potter and is happy to make the wonderful fish platters and "Cabinologist" coffee mugs that add so much to our cottage. But then cabin country seems to attract potters the way it draws people who fish, so it shouldn't be difficult to find someone in your area to provide you with unusual or even one-of-a-kind tableware and decoration.

Our cabin memories are warmed by images of colorful Hudson Bay blankets and heavy Pendleton® throws with Native American designs on them. Well, many of those patterns are still available along with new designs from the likes of Laurie Jacobi's Wellspring Collection at Faribo Woolen Mills in Minnesota. But, again, you might feel even warmer snuggling under an afghan crocheted by your grandmother or with a handcrafted spread you discovered just down the road from your cabin, under a rough sign that read, "Quilts and Rag Rugs for Sale."

This is not evidence of a skiing accident but a display of a personal passion for the winter sport of cross-country skiing.

THE ART PART

Then there's cabin art. What's often so great about it is the fact that no one seems to worry about "how it's going to look" the way they do in their homes in the city. Where city art is often restricted by the "rules" of taste and status, cabin art is simply what it is, meaning kitschy, funky, and often laden with lore (although no one may remember the details).

It's Aunt Hattie's watercolor of Niagara Falls, the oversize sepia portrait of Pancho Villa you brought home from a long-ago holiday in Puerto Vallarta, or the "Home Sweet Home" sampler made from corn kernels that you'd never dream of putting up back home but looks just right over the cabin's kitchen table. You could also have Elvis in velvet or dogs playing poker–it's your cabin and it's where you can express a part of your personality that you normally keep hidden.

I'll admit it–I'm a big fan of chainsaw art. In fact, I'm trying to collect as much as I can before the Museum of Modern Art or some

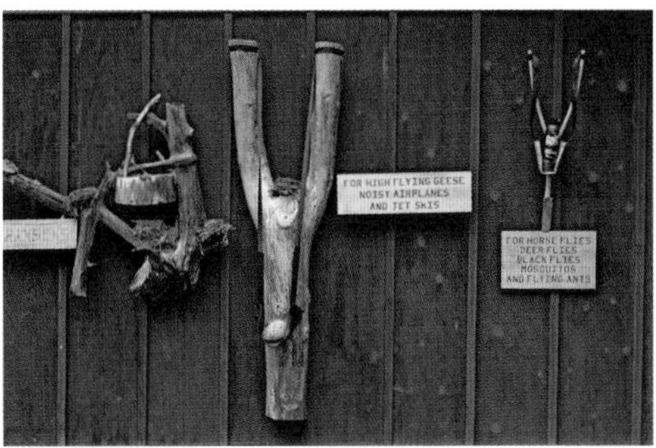

Arts, crafts, or any combination of the beautiful and merely decorative, accumulated over time and displayed on the walls and shelves of your cabin, are a personal statement as unique as your signature.

other temple of high culture discovers it and drives up the prices. I'm especially partial to the chainsaw art that doesn't try to look too real but is instead distorted by the natural lines of the tree trunk it's cut from. My "Yogi Bear," for example, looks like a bear that was put in a trash compactor, and "Sir Tyrone Throne" (actually, a chair) sports a long, flowing beard that was part of the tree's root system.

I also own a chainsaw-crafted masthead named "Bruce" that looks like an old woodsman whose hair is standing on end, while the unnamed raccoon hanging in a tree looks as though he just witnessed the theft of his lunch.

Our cabin's Art Committee–chaired by my wife–has put at least a temporary kibosh on the other committee member's acquisition of more chainsaw art. Your cabin's Art Committee will have its own opinions on what's in and what's out, and that judgment will no doubt cover such familiar but sometimes controversial items as your stuffed moose head and multiple trophy bass catches. (Marital counseling, rather than an art appreciation class, may be advisable.) But we are more than happy to keep adding to the fish-themed drawings and paintings provided by our grandkids and meaningful single pieces such as the watercolor rendering of our cabin painted by a particularly treasured guest.

"Art," clearly, is how you define it, and no more so than at the cabin. And the things you use to enliven your walls can sometimes be as useful as they are fun or beautiful to look at. I'm thinking, for instance, of a large, detailed wall map of your region, with your cabin's location highlighted for your guests. (YOU ARE HERE. ENJOY YOURSELF!) Those big, wonderfully detailed United States Geological Survey maps that show off your slice of the country in all its glorious detail are available at sporting-goods stores. Old maps and charts (real or copies), especially when they relate to your region, are endlessly fascinating additions to the art hanging on your cabin's walls.

A guest book isn't exactly art (then again, it might qualify as "art" as much as that "Home

PARTING WORDS

Although not revealing anything *too* personal, the following heartfelt comments are excerpted from the guest book at the Mulfinger/Dittmar cabin in Minnesota:

"Thanks so much for a most comfortable stay! I found your place so nice that I asked Heather to marry me. She found it so nice she said yes. Memorable times indeed."

"I have a new image of paradise! The weather doesn't really change, does it??? You've also convinced me to come back for a trip to the Boundary Waters and perhaps even a little property hunting–thanks so much for your hospitality."

"It's a long journey from our home in Buenos Aires, but this shack is better than the Hilton®, and Jan's walleye cakes served in the fresh, piney air is a savory memory we'll never forget."

Sweet Home" sampler above the kitchen table, or maybe even as "literature"), but it's an essential finishing touch. It's where your guests jot their impressions and express their gratitude for the weekend you've given them among the whispering pines. It is, or will be, many of your best cabin memories collected and preserved between two covers. And you may be pleasantly surprised to discover what a poignant writer your normally tight-lipped Uncle Bob is when he waxes poetic about his sojourn on your lake. Or was that the wine talking?

WHAT'S IN A NAME?

Sometimes plenty.

There's no rule that says you have to give your cabin a moniker, but a lot of people believe that the right name for their beloved hideaway is its crowning touch. A name can sure be a neat way of summing up the cabin's role in your life at this stage or even its spiritual or symbolic meaning. "Dunworkin" graces more than one cabin I know of. "Pine Nest" makes its pretty point in simple language, and "Walkers' Retreat" carries multiple meanings.

How you present that name is yet another way to add to your cabin's charm. Some people have it engraved on a handsome plaque that's mounted at the edge of the driveway (on the mailbox, maybe), above the cabin's main entryway, or at the end of the dock.

Others like a more rustic approach, carving the name in a piece of pine they've cut into the shape of a catfish, or painting it on a slab of weathered barn siding or on a large rock. In any case, however you proclaim the name "Fawnfair" to the rest of the world, you'll be creating an important first impression.